Secret *AND*

■ ■ ■ ■ ■ ■ ■ ■ ■ Sanctioned

Secret *AND*

⬛ ⬛ ⬛ ⬛ ⬛ ⬛ ⬛ ⬛ ⬛ Sanctioned

Covert Operations
and the
American Presidency

STEPHEN F. KNOTT

New York   Oxford

OXFORD UNIVERSITY PRESS | *1996*

Oxford University Press

Oxford   New York
Athens   Auckland   Bangkok   Bombay
Calcutta   Cape Town   Dar es Salaam   Delhi
Florence   Hong Kong   Istanbul   Karachi
Kuala Lumpur   Madras   Madrid   Melbourne
Mexico City   Nairobi   Paris   Singapore
Taipei   Tokyo   Toronto

and associated companies in
Berlin   Ibadan

Published by Oxford University Press, Inc.
198 Madison Avenue, New York, NY 10016

Oxford is a registered trademark of Oxford University Press

Library of Congress Cataloging-in-Publication Data
Knott, Stephen F.
Secret and sanctioned : covert operations
and the American presidency / Stephen F. Knott.
p. cm.   Includes bibliographical references and index.
ISBN 0–19–510098–0
1. Intelligence service—United States—History.
2. Presidents—United States—History. I. Title.
JK468.I6K56   1996
327.1273'09—dc20   95–19177

The views expressed in this book are solely those of Stephen F. Knott,
and do not reflect the opinions of the United States Air Force Academy,
the United States Air Force, or the Department of Defense.

Published by arrangement with Ballantine Books, a division of Random House, Inc.

9 8 7 6 5 4 3 2 1

Printed in the United States of America
on acid-free paper

For my parents
and for Lorna

Acknowledgments

This book would not have been possible without the generous assistance of Helen McInnis, vice president and executive editor of Oxford University Press, and Owen Lock, editor in chief of Del Rey Books. Irene Pavitt, assistant managing editor at Oxford, and Elizabeth Jones, who copyedited the manuscript, provided invaluable guidance. Walter L. Pforzheimer was most generous with his time, expertise, and enthusiasm; his suggestions helped to improve this work a great deal. Additionally, I would like to thank my doctoral dissertation committee at Boston College, particularly my committee chairman, John Tierney. Professor Tierney's professional advice and friendship have been a source of strength from the day I first entered Boston College. Professor Robert Scigliano was an invaluable source of expertise on the American presidency, and his suggestions served to improve this study vastly. Professor Dennis Hale took time out from his busy schedule as chairman of the political science department at Boston College to assist my work. Arthur S. Hulnick, currently teaching at Boston University's Center for International Relations, was a helpful source of information on the literature related to American intelligence activity.

I would also like to thank Michael Joyce of the Lynde and Harry Bradley Foundation for critical financial support that enabled me to complete this book. I am especially grateful to Dr. Christopher Bruell and Dr. Robert Faulkner for the assistance they provided me. My friends Susan Collins , Diane Gamache, and Lisa Fruitt were of great help, offering encouragement and thoughtful criticism as the work progressed. Most importantly, I would like to thank my parents for their support and my wife, Lorna, for her vital editorial and computing contribution. This book would not have been completed without her help. I would like to dedicate this work to my parents and to Lorna.

Contents

Secret *AND*

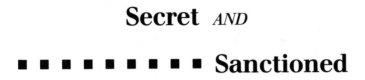 Sanctioned

Introduction

> Covert Action: "those secret governmental operations designed to influence events and affect conditions abroad without acknowledgement by or attribution to the United States."[1]

This work was begun in 1988 as an attempt to examine the short and stormy history of the relationship between the president and the intelligence committees of Congress. The topic appeared to be of particular importance as Congress, in the wake of the Iran-Contra affair, was on the verge of expanding its intelligence oversight authority.

When I began my study, I undertook a survey of the literature for the purpose of reviewing historical precedents on the early use of American clandestine activity. I was surprised by the constant repetition of one theme: that the use of covert operations by the United States was a phenomenon of the Cold War.[2] The prevailing assumption was that covert activities were grafted onto the American system in 1947. It was said that Congress, in the mid-1970s, attempted to restore a sense of balance to the American system by reining in executive discretion over clandestine operations and by restricting the use of certain covert practices considered alien to traditional standards of American conduct.

The discovery of an article by Edward F. Sayle, "The Historical Underpinnings of the U.S. Intelligence Community," in the *International Journal of Intelligence and Counterintelligence* altered the direction of my study. Sayle, a former curator of historical intelligence at the Central Intelligence Agency, outlined a picture of American clandestine operations stretching back to the American Revolution. As a result of this article, I decided to change course and begin an examination of the use of clandestine operations from Washington to Lincoln. Although I was concerned at first that there might not be enough material to form the basis of such a study, I quickly realized that my fears were unfounded. After digging through scattered secondary sources and collections of presidential and diplomatic papers, I discovered that Edward Sayle had only scratched the surface. The United States has a rich history of clandestine operations—operations conducted in times of war and peace—that range from kidnapping to covert efforts to topple foreign governments. This study should serve to end the myth of America's pre–Cold War innocence of clandestinity and place the "abuses" of America's Cold War presidents in proper historical perspective.

The end of the Cold War has raised hopes in some quarters that the United States can eliminate the use of covert operations and restrict itself to gathering intelligence. Proposals have been made to cut the CIA's budget as part of the "peace dividend" emanating from the end of the U.S.–Soviet confrontation. I believe that this attitude flies in the face of two hundred years of American history, which demonstrate the need for a covert capability as part of effective foreign-policy making. In the past twenty years, a series of highly publicized confrontations has occurred between the executive branch and Congress over the use of covert operations in American foreign policy. These confrontations generated demands in Congress for reform and led to the creation of a strengthened congressional oversight apparatus. Presidential control over covert operations has been sharply curtailed, as Congress has adopted a variety of measures designed to limit executive discretion through a system of formal and informal constraints. Contemporary observers, whether in scholarly circles or in the media, tend to see the reforms of the past twenty years as a healthy development, a return to the principles and practices of the Founders. The truth, however, is that those reforms represent nothing short of a complete rejection of almost two hundred years of deference to the executive in the realm of secret operations. What was at one time the most protected tool in the executive foreign-policy arsenal has become a focal point for executive-legislative contention, and the latter institution is winning the struggle.

This study is an attempt to restore a sense of historical perspective to the contemporary debate by examining the use of covert operations during a period—from 1776 to 1882—approximating the first century of the nation's existence, a period for the most part slighted by scholars of American intelligence history despite the fact that the foundation for executive control of covert operations was built during this time. I have used primary sources wherever possible so that the various players speak for themselves. As the reader will see, Washington, Jefferson, and their successors engaged in a number of activities that in themselves are now condemned by critics of covert operations as alien to traditional American standards of conduct. These operations, which took place in times of both war and peace, included intervention in the domestic affairs of foreign nations through bribery and support for insurgent movements, kidnapping, employing journalists and clergymen for intelligence and propaganda purposes, and using secret service funds for domestic purposes. It could be argued that this era, including the presidencies from George Washington through Abraham Lincoln, represents the pinnacle of American covert activity.

Although my study concludes with a discussion of events in the twentieth century, I do not pretend that this part of the work is as comprehensive or as original as the examination of eighteenth- and nineteenth-century American practices. The goal was to examine which types of activities were considered permissible by our early presidents and secretaries of state and to compare these early activities with those of the modern era. The time is past due to clarify the historical record, to confront those who have misrepresented America's clandestine past and have used this distorted history to assail the conduct of America's Cold War presidents and the agency that did their bidding.

The reader will note that I do not discuss the period running from 1849 to 1861, encompassing the administrations of Zachary Taylor, Millard Fillmore, Franklin Pierce, and James Buchanan. On the verge of civil war, America was looking inward and appears to have ignored foreign policy to a great extent. During a brief period, members of the Pierce administration seem to have given certain tacit signals to private adventurers interested in acquiring Cuba for the United States, but no evidence that I have seen links President Pierce directly to this episode. Additionally, the presidents on whom I have chosen to focus have for the most part been credited with leaving a lasting impact on the office of the presidency. This cannot be said of Taylor, Fillmore, Pierce, and Buchanan.

The distorted view of America's clandestine past worked its way into two reports that reshaped American attitudes toward covert activity: the Church Committee report, released in 1976, and the Iran-Contra Committee report, which appeared in 1987. The former stated that covert action was a tool of American foreign policy "for the past twenty-eight years,"[3] while the latter stated with equal certainty that "peacetime covert action became an instrument of U.S. foreign-policy in response to the expansion of Soviet political and military influence following World War II."[4] The blame for this development is generally laid at the doorstep of a series of "imperial" presidents who were seen as having run roughshod over the Constitution. This notion of an imperial presidency has captivated the American political and scholarly community, as Senator Church's comments regarding a covert operation in Chile revealed. Church noted that President Nixon peered "like Caesar into the colonies distant from Rome."[5]

This study does not seek to demonstrate that covert operations offer a magical solution to the problems confronting American policy makers. Covert operations do not always work and can aggravate a situation. Presidents may make decisions favoring the use of covert operations that in retrospect appear to be unwise. Presidents make mistakes, and the covert arena is no exception. These mistakes can be the result of a threat perception that is overblown or a desire to exploit an opening that turns out to be illusory. Covert operations are not always the right policy option, but they are one the president needs. This office is best suited to make these difficult decisions, which are unavoidable in the untidy world of international relations. These options are not cure-alls, but neither are they intrinsically unethical, immoral, or un-American.

This understanding has been replaced in some prominent quarters of American political life by a contemporary faith in ill-defined notions of international law and by an unbending devotion to process and procedures. In some quarters, adherence to international law has superseded the national interest as the standard by which to measure American conduct. For example, former Senate Majority Leader George Mitchell defended those colleagues who insisted on "the rule of law in our involvement in Central America."[6] Representative Don Edwards of California has argued against a Justice Department proposal to permit the United States to kidnap terrorists hiding in countries that provide safe haven. Edwards asked, "How can we expect other nations to respect our law if we don't respect theirs?"[7] There is a large bloc within Congress that views intervention of any sort as immoral, as a vestige of antiquated power politics. Senator Daniel Moynihan noted, "The issue is intervention. Intervention in the internal affairs of another nation is a violation of the U.N. Charter, the Charter of the Organization of American States. It is a violation of law."[8] The issue of covert intervention in Nicaragua was, for Congressman David Bonior, a matter of a Republican administration "not living up to the democratic standards that this body [Congress] represents."[9] The principle of nonintervention overrides all other considerations; as Walter LaFeber of Cornell comments, "It's not ethical to overthrow other governments no matter how corrupt the other country happens to be."[10]

Any decision made in secret is immediately suspect. For example, Senator Robert Byrd noted in a debate over covert aid to non-Communist Cambodian rebels, "[Secret policies] . . . are suspect on their merits precisely because of the methods of their origins."[11] Former president Jimmy Carter stated in 1976 that "there is no reason for our foreign policy to be concealed from the American people. There is no reason for the law to be broken or circumvented as the President makes a secret decision that the CIA can overthrow a government against the law."[12] Former New York governor Mario Cuomo found George Bush's candidacy for president questionable on the grounds of Bush's previous service in the CIA. Secrecy and corruption are synonymous in Cuomo's understanding of politics. Cuomo remarked, "You're going to have a president who's good at secrets, corruption that's not disclosed. . . . What's the CIA? I mean that's going to be the presidency. . . . He was involved with the CIA. You draw your own conclusions."[13] The chief counsel of the House committee investigating the Iran-Contra affair, John Nields, stated during the committee hearings that in "certain communist countries, the government's activities are kept secret from the people. But that's not the way we do things in America, is it?" The chief counsel noted that "a principal purpose of these hearings is to replace secrecy and deception with disclosure and truth."[14]

The Founders understood that the ability to capitalize on rapidly changing world developments required presidential secrecy and dispatch. They also understood that no nation, particularly a great nation, can conduct its foreign policy completely aboveboard at all times. Presidents will always face situations where the only options that will serve the national interest are secret. This was the rationale behind Washington's proposal for a contingency fund in his first annual message to Congress and behind that body's decision to approve such a request. Alexander Hamilton, concerned about possible hostilities with France in 1798, believed that it was "essential that the Executive should have half a million of secret service money." Expenditures from this fund should be made without congressional "incumbrance" but, if necessary, with the approval of three members of each house of Congress.[15] Hamilton's proposal is strikingly similar to the arrangement of limited congressional oversight of secret operations that existed from 1947 to 1974. This arrangement between the president and the senior members of Congress represented a significant concession to congressional interests. It was an appropriate attempt to balance the need for executive "secrecy and dispatch" with Congress's right to oversee the large bureaucratic intelligence establishment created in 1947. Yet this arrangement has been scrapped in favor of a system dominated by congressional committees that place a premium on hesitation and democratized decision making.

America's understanding of its purpose as a world power has undergone a radical change in our era. Jeffersonian notions of the United States playing a special role in the world are seen as a sign of naïveté today. Thomas Jefferson's belief that the United States represented the "last, best hope" of freedom-loving peoples allowed him to sanction operations designed to bring "uncivilized" powers into the world of democratic enlightenment. This attitude is particularly evident in Jefferson's dealings with the Indian nations (Chapter 4), in his willingness to assist a covert operation against the Barbary pirates, and in his advocacy of covert operations against Britain in the War of 1812. One senses a certain zeal for the cause of republican government among some of the earlier operatives sent abroad, operatives who sparred with the agents of the monarchical powers in the Americas and sought to enhance American interests throughout the hemisphere. By contrast, some contemporary critics of clandestine operations seem to couple their beliefs in the immorality of American intervention and the corrupting effect of secrecy with the notion of moral equivalency among nations. America's loss of faith in itself in the wake of the Vietnam War has produced a committed bloc within the Congress determined to prevent U.S. power from wreaking global havoc. As a result of this new conception of America's role in the world, the president—and those agencies that execute his policies—is seen as being in need of constraints from a legislative branch devoted to openness and accountability and possessing greater wisdom due to its diversity of opinions.

It should be said that Congress has not prohibited the use of covert operations. In fact, the Iran-Contra Committee's final report stated that "covert operations are a necessary component of our Nation's foreign policy."[16] But Congress has shifted the locus of decision making away from the executive branch, primarily through informal methods such as threatening to go public with knowledge of proposed covert operations. As a result, individual intelligence committee members can stop an operation dead in its tracks. The committees modify proposals to suit their wishes; and although the president can legally withhold information from the committees, he does so at great political risk. Commenting on the "gentlemen's agreement" between President Bush and the intelligence committees that there would be forty-eight-hour notification of all covert operations, former Senate vice chairman William Cohen warned the Bush White House that the committees "would take a dim view" of any violation of this agreement.[17]

While acknowledging them as a "necessary component" of American foreign policy, Congress has set unrealistically high standards for its approval of covert operations. The tendency is to sanction only those capable of winning public support in case of exposure. The notion of being a co-conspirator with the CIA is a scary prospect for some members of Congress, causing them to avoid high-risk operations that might disturb constituents or the media in the event of a leak. For other members, it is not so much a fear of possible electoral or media repercussions as a genuine belief that the wisdom of the people should prevail in foreign-policy decision making. Under this criterion, only those policies announced to the public should be pursued through covert means. This was the conclusion of the Iran-Contra Committee, whose final report stated that all covert activities be consistent with publicly declared policy. After revelations of the arms deal with Iran, the Reagan administration was accused of operating in secret because the American people would never have approved—an assertion that is probably true. For many congressmen, this was reason enough to demonstrate that the operation should never have gone forward.

This new approach—approving only those covert operations that promote publicly stated policies—no doubt helps the president and Congress steer clear of controversy. It also allows them to avoid making those difficult judgments expected of those holding high political office. By using the Iran-Contra Committee standard, Congress and the president can essentially conduct policy on the basis of opinion polls. Under this system, the president can buy himself "risk insurance" by going to Congress before undertaking any high-stakes initiative. It is a scenario that guarantees lethargic policy making; for instance, Henry Kissinger's covert diplomacy in the early 1970s, in contradiction to publicly stated U.S. policy opposing the Communist regime in China, would most likely have failed to win prior approval of a congressional board of overseers and the American public.[18] As the Founders understood, the president needs the flexibility to seize opportunities as they arise. He must be able to make judgments on the basis of what will benefit the national interest, not on the basis of what would withstand a national plebiscite.

Of course, judgments about the propriety of covert operations in the Cold War era depend on individual perceptions of the Soviet threat. Many of the controversial operations conducted by both Democratic and Republican administrations—whether in Iran in 1953, Guatemala in 1954, Cuba in the early 1960s, Chile in 1970, or Nicaragua in the 1980s—were the result of policies implemented to contain Soviet expansionism. The presidents who authorized these operations did so out of a belief that resistance to Communism was appropriate American policy and that options short of war, but more vigorous than diplomatic denunciations, were required to carry out that policy. As President Polk noted in 1846, in times of "impending danger," presidents need access to secret operatives capable of obtaining information or "rendering other important services."[19]

Many Third World countries have served as the battlegrounds for the overt and covert manifestations of the Cold War conflict between the United States and the Soviet Union. American covert operations in these nations may appear to some as repulsive examples of superpower bullying. However, for the presidents who conducted them, these operations were part of a larger struggle that compelled U.S. intervention on strategic and political grounds. Moreover, these contemporary operations should not be viewed in a historical vacuum, for the United States has a rich history of presidential use of covert intervention. Many of these earlier missions were conducted in situations less threatening to U.S. security interests and in a time when America was not called on to play the leading international role it accepted in the mid-twentieth century.

If America's Cold War presidents are to be condemned for abusing their right to conduct covert operations, then it is only fair to reexamine the actions of some of their revered predecessors. If this study serves to broaden our understanding of two hundred years of American reliance on covert activity, it will have achieved its purpose. The United States can no longer deny its clandestine history and must come to grips with the unpleasant necessity of covert operations as part of our nation's foreign-policy machinery. For any world power, it is not enough "to guess where events [are] leading; it [becomes] necessary, short of war, to shift events in the desired direction."[20]

I ▪

BUILDING THE FOUNDATION

The Founding Fathers and Covert Operations

1 ■

George Washington and the Founding of American Clandestine Activity

[T]here are some Secrets, on the keeping of which so, depends, oftentimes, the salvation of an Army: Secrets which
cannot, at least ought not to, be intrusted to paper; nay, which
none but the Commander in Chief at the time, should be acquainted with.

GEORGE WASHINGTON to PATRICK HENRY,
February 24, 1777[1]

■ The American clandestine tradition began under extremely
taxing wartime conditions. This tradition is derived primarily
from the efforts of one man, the commander in chief of the
American army, George Washington. Significantly, his first major expenditure after taking command of the Continental Army was the payment of
$333.33 to send someone "to go into the town of Boston to establish secret
correspondence."[2] It was Washington who exercised total discretion over
an elaborate intelligence network that penetrated major American cities
under British control; in a remarkably short time, a group of individual
networks—each controlled by the state within which it existed—was

transformed into a centralized intelligence service equal to that of Britain, the greatest power in the world.

One of the earliest steps taken in this direction was the establishment of a system of correspondence between General Washington and the committees of safey operating in secret throughout the states.[3] However, this system was crippled by delays in communication and a tendency to circulate unfounded rumors. Washington's reliance on this loose network was gradually supplanted by a system under his direct control. One of his most successful ventures involved a spy network that operated with great effectiveness in the environs of New York City. This operation and others contributed to the estimated $17,617 that Washington spent on secret intelligence operations, a sum representing 11 percent of Washington's total military expenditures.[4] These funds were provided by the Continental Congress on November 27, 1776, when it ordered "the Secret Committee [to] take proper and effectual measures to procure a quantity of hard money, not less than 20,000 dollars, to be lodged in the hands of the commander in chief, for the purpose of secret services." This was the first American appropriation of funds for intelligence purposes.[5]

George Washington was appointed commander in chief of the Continental Army on June 16, 1775, by the Second Continental Congress. The Continental Congress had come into being as relations between Britain and its American colonies had soured over a variety of grievances related to regulation and taxation of the colonies. The First Continental Congress, which convened on September 5, 1774, led to a declaration of rights and grievances that made it clear that the colonies were not and could not be represented by the British Parliament. The First Continental Congress had adjourned on October 26, 1774, with the delegates confident that the British government would respond in a peaceful manner to the colonists' demands for home rule; in return, the colonists reassured the mother country of their allegiance to the king. By the time the Second Continental Congress met in May 1775, events had ruined any chance for a peaceful settlement of the crisis. Following the bloodshed at Lexington and Concord, Massachusetts requested that the direction of its military operations be assumed by Congress. The Congress responded by naming one of its own delegates, George Washington, to assume command of the "Continental Army."[6] During the war, Washington reported to the president of the Continental Congress, though in the area of secret operations he withheld any detailed account of his actions, and his requests for funds for these operations were always stated in the most general terms.

As the war progressed, the Continental Congress created secret committees designed to conduct specialized intelligence functions, including the Secret Committee, the Committee of Secret Correspondence, and the Committee on Spies. The Secret Committee, established on September 18, 1775, was charged with clandestinely procuring arms from abroad. Its members included, among others, Benjamin Franklin, Silas Deane, John

Langdon, and Robert Morris. Two months later, on November 29, 1775, the delegates created the Committee of Correspondence (after January 30, 1776, it was known as the Committee of Secret Correspondence) "for the sole purpose of corresponding with our friends in Great Britain, Ireland, and other parts of the world." The Committee of Secret Correspondence included Benjamin Harrison, Benjamin Franklin, Thomas Johnson, John Dickinson, John Jay, and Robert Morris.[7] The Committee on Spies was created by Congress on June 5, 1776, "to consider what is proper to be done with persons giving intelligence to the enemy, or supplying them with provisions." Among its members were John Adams, Thomas Jefferson, Edward Rutledge, Robert Livingston, and James Wilson.[8] This congressional network (Chapter 2) focused primarily on activities abroad and operated in concert with Washington's activities at home. In supervising such activities, these congressional committees directed America's first foreign agents abroad and assisted in the eventual triumph of American arms. Years later, after the establishment of the American constitutional order in 1787, the new Congress would cede this authority to the executive branch, operating at the discretion of President George Washington.

Throughout the American revolution, General Washington placed great importance on learning British intentions and shielding his own army's activities. Elaborately coded communications were used by the general to communicate with his spy network through a system implemented by staff officers such as Alexander Hamilton. The degree of personal control exercised by Washington over many of these missions is striking.[9]

Although more than a century would pass before the United States began to institutionalize its intelligence operations, the practices begun in 1776 can safely be considered the birth of the American intelligence tradition. Despite the fact that some of the operations had an amateurish quality and occasionally worked at cross-purposes, American efforts in this area did produce results, especially during the climactic battle at Yorktown. In February 1776, the United States engaged in its first covert operation. That same year saw the capture of Nathan Hale and James Aitken, the first Americans executed by a foreign power for engaging in espionage and covert activity.

Washington as Intelligence Practitioner

Washington's most successful intelligence initiative was the operation of a spy network in New York City known as the Culper Ring.[10] As headquarters for the British army in the United States, New York City proved an irresistible target for American intelligence operatives. Washington noted New York's importance in a letter written in the spring of 1779:

As all great movements, and the fountain of all intelligence must originate at, and proceed from the head Quarters of the enemy's army, C—— [agent code name], had better reside at ——— New York, mix with, and put on the airs of a Tory to cover his real character and avoid suspicion.[11]

Washington's desire for accurate intelligence was hastened by the arrival of the French fleet outside New York harbor in July 1778.[12] A letter written to French admiral Comte d'Estaing at this time reveals Washington's desire to penetrate British headquarters and his frustration at not being able to do so.[13] After the disastrous experience of Nathan Hale's capture and execution while attempting to infiltrate New York City in September 1776, Washington was determined to regroup and successfully penetrate the city.[14] He selected a cavalry officer named Benjamin Tallmadge to organize the Culper Ring, or chain, as Washington called it.[15] Although Tallmadge's biographer describes him as "the manager of Washington's Secret Service during the Revolutionary War," he would more appropriately be described as a high-level case officer who ran agents for the chief of American intelligence, Washington himself.[16] Tallmadge (alias John Bolton) appears to have had the complete confidence of General Washington and was entrusted with supervising one of the most perilous operations of the war. In his memoirs, Tallmadge's description of his activities as a spymaster was relatively brief:

This year [1778] I opened a private correspondence with some persons in New York (for Gen. Washington) which lasted through the war. How beneficial it was to the Commander-in-Chief is evidenced by his continuing the same to the close of the war. I kept one or more boats continually employed in crossing the Sound on this business.[17]

Tallmadge's chief operatives were Robert Townsend (alias Culper, Jr.) and Abraham Woodhull (alias Culper, Sr.), who kept an eye on British activities on Long Island Sound and relayed Townsend's reports from the city. A merchant and part-time journalist with a knack for writing articles with a Tory slant (Tory was the name given Americans who remained loyal to the crown), Townsend was perfectly situated to gather intelligence.[18] Other members of the chain included prominent New York publisher James Rivington; a courier named Austin Roe, who carried the messages over a hundred miles on each mission; and Lieutenant Caleb Brewster, who ferried the messages across Long Island Sound to Tallmadge in Connecticut. Brewster's crew was composed of army regulars whose own commanders were unaware of the nature of their assignment. Washington had to intervene personally to keep these men from being shifted to other duties, telling subordinate generals the men were engaged in "a service of a particular nature."[19]

The Culper Ring was designed to avoid the pitfalls of the Hale mission. Tallmadge was instructed to report directly to Washington but never to bring any of the agents to meet him in person, for the preservation of their secret identities was of utmost importance. Failure to preserve this anonymity, Washington noted, could "blast the whole design."[20] Washington requested that correspondence from his agents be written in invisible ink and sent in a manner that would generate the least suspicion.[21] Messages from agents should be written

> on the leaves of a pamphlet, on the first, second, and other pages of a common pocket book, or on the blank leaves at each end of registers, almanacks, or any new publication of small value or sent in a familiar letter on domestic matters . . . interlining with the stain his secret intelligence.

The business at hand was "so critical and dangerous" that the information should be delivered by designated persons "to no one but the Commander-in-Chief."[22] In 1779, Tallmadge added to this layer of protection by developing a cipher and code that used codebooks available only to himself, Townsend, and Washington.[23]

Washington's correspondence with Tallmadge and other intelligence managers reveals his keen understanding of the importance of accurate information and the methods needed to acquire it. Washington was comfortable with ruthless methods of intelligence gathering, in one instance instructing a chaplain to convince two captured spies facing execution to reveal vital intelligence as part of their final confession to their maker. Washington wrote to the chaplain:

> Besides the humanity of affording them the benefit of your profession, it may in the conduct of a man of sense answer another valuable purpose. And while it serves to prepare them for the other world, it will naturally lead to the intelligence we want in your inquiries into the condition of their spiritual concerns. You will therefore be pleased to take charge of this matter upon yourself, and when you have collected in the course of your attendance such information as they can give, you will transmit the whole to me.[24]

As this example demonstrates, Washington had no qualms about using the death penalty for captured spies, particularly as a lever for acquiring information and other forms of assistance.[25] Washington's execution of British officer Major John André for the role he played in arranging Benedict Arnold's defection in 1780 was undertaken in the face of powerful appeals to spare the young officer. Two of his own spies in the Culper Ring had urged Washington to pardon André.[26] The earliest known letter in which Washington mentions the subject of spies shows his unsparing attitude toward captured agents. The letter was written to the governor of Virginia while Washington was a colonel and commander of Virginia forces during the French and Indian War: "Your honor has had advice of two spies, that were taken at Fort Cumberland; one of whom they quickly hung up as his just reward."[27]

Washington's letters repeatedly refer to the importance of adhering to certain procedures designed to maximize the chances of successful intelligence gathering. One important concern was sifting groundless rumors from hard intelligence data. Washington appears to have been inundated with "vague and idle stories . . . which have no foundation in fact," something he feared because "false intelligence may prove worse than none."[28] Washington instructed his agents never to trust their sources without continually checking the accuracy of their data with their own eyes and ears. He encouraged his intelligence managers to seek men of discernment and knowledge as their operatives. Men with these characteristics would make the best agents, for they would be capable of comparing and contrasting voluminous amounts of information obtained through a variety of "different channels." By using multiple sources, Washington could better sift through idle rumors and British disinformation: "By comparing their accounts, I shall be able to form a pretty good judgement."[29]

Washington constantly pressed his agents to seek precision in their intelligence estimates and not to focus simply on "great objects of information" such as troop movements but to ferret out those "many things upon a smaller scale." The information should always be communicated "not in general terms, but in detail, and with the greatest precision."[30] Intelligence should be acquired as often and delivered as fast as possible, for "the good effect of Intelligence may be lost if it is not speedily transmitted."[31] A letter to Elias Boudinot[32] in May 1779 indicates Washington's thirst for fresh information conveyed in the "most speedy, safe, and effectual manner."[33]

As previously noted, Washington often expressed his concern that the circle of those involved in espionage operations be drawn very tightly and that all agents be instructed never to confide in individuals outside this circle. Operations should be conducted with the greatest amount of secrecy, "for upon secrecy, success depends in most enterprises of the kind, and for want of it, they are generally defeated."[34] At times, the ring of secrecy was drawn so closely that Washington instructed Boudinot to make sure that his correspondence gave the appearance of private letters to prevent "any of my own family [staff] from opening it."[35]

Washington also encouraged the use of aliases or the omission of names in communications. General Scott, an intelligence manager for Washington, was urged to tell one agent "to withhold his name from his letters or else assume a false signature. But I do not see the necessity of any name so long as the writing is known by the parties."[36] In New York City, one productive source for Washington operated under the dramatic code name "Z."[37] Reasoning that they would allow an agent to operate under "the mask of friendship," Washington also began the American practice of using business establishments as a cover for intelligence operations.[38] In a letter written to Benjamin Tallmadge, Washington urged him to persuade Culper, Jr., to maintain his business while gathering intelligence:

I would imagine that with a little industry, he will be able to carry on his intelligence with greater security to himself and greater advantages to us, under cover of his usual business, than if he were to dedicate himself wholly to the giving of information. It may afford him opportunities of collecting intelligence, that he could not derive so well in any other manner.[39]

In reading Washington's correspondence with his intelligence managers, one is struck by his weariness with the whole business. In one letter, Washington bemoaned the fact that "ambiguous characters" had to be employed in the work.[40] He constantly urged his managers to proceed with caution and to be alert for the presence of spies and double agents. After all, he had been rudely introduced in the earliest days of his command to the pernicious skills of British intelligence. During the siege of Boston, Washington was stung by the discovery that his director general of hospitals, Benjamin Church, had reported "every move" of the rebel army to the British prior to his arrest. This lesson—and others—led him to admonish his intelligence managers repeatedly always to remain on guard and to make certain that their agents proved themselves worthy of trust.[41] He was particularly skeptical of those acting as double agents:

In my last I took the liberty to drop you a hint upon the subject of the danger of putting too much confidence in persons undertaking the office of double spies. The person alluded to in the present instance appears very sensible, and we should, on that account, be more than commonly guarded until he has given full proofs of his attachment.[42]

The business of controlling a broad espionage network can often tax the resources of the most able intelligence director, and Washington was no exception. He had his own problems with renegade intelligence officers who used their positions for personal enrichment and engaged in illicit and unauthorized operations. Washington discovered that two agents "employed to go on Long Island on pretence of procuring intelligence are mere plundering parties." In response, Washington created a secret team to acquire evidence against the rogue operatives and arrest them.[43]

While commanding the Continental Army in Cambridge during the siege of Boston, Washington wrote to Josiah Quincy, "There is one evil I dread, and that is, their spies."[44] Fear of that evil led him to urge his intelligence managers to balance zeal for the country's cause with a healthy dose of skepticism toward those proferring intelligence, particularly that favorable to the American cause.[45] Both sides became adept at disseminating false information designed to confuse the enemy.[46] Washington became proficient at deception and disguise, and used his espionage network to funnel disinformation into British hands. He kept the British guessing as to his real intentions, especially in and around New York City. His army procurement officers were instructed to make false purchases of supplies in locations designed to convince the British that an attack against the city was forthcoming.[47] Deceptive communications were prepared directly by Washington to fall into British hands. In one instance, during the autumn of 1777, Washington instructed three of his leading commanders (Major Generals Putnam and Dickinson and one of his intelligence managers, Major John Clark) to mislead the British that an attack on New York was imminent. Dickinson had false reports disseminated to suspected British agents, and Putnam was ordered to do likewise. At the same time, one of Major Clark's operatives delivered to British general Sir Wiliam Howe a memorandum outlining American troop strength and intended movements toward the city. In Washington's words, the effort was designed to "distract and alarm the Enemy and perhaps keep a greater force at New York than they intended."[48]

Washington's expertise at deception was further demonstrated by his ability to continually mislead the British over the size of the Continental Army, a factor contributing to British reluctance to move against his force.[49] Time and again, disguise and deception played a critical role in keeping the vastly outnumbered Continental Army intact by throwing the British army off balance for the duration of the war. The success of the American Revolution depended on the survival of Washington's forces. Absent Washington's knack for deception and skulduggery, that army and the revolution would not have prevailed.[50]

The Clandestine Spirit of 1776

A number of ambitious American intelligence operations merit attention if only for the fact that they shed some light on the Founders' view of the propriety of clandestine activities.[51] These missions demonstrate that the Revolutionary generation was not averse to utilizing surreptitious techniques condemned by many modern observers of intelligence practices. The leaders of the American war effort planned and executed secret operations involving kidnapping, psychological warfare, and mail openings; at least one covert operation directed at acquiring a "fourteenth colony" in Quebec; a special operation designed to sabotage dockyards in Great Britain; the creation of newspapers for propaganda purposes; and the use of clergy for espionage. Additionally, a "private," "off-the-shelf" navy was created and placed at the disposal of American agents operating in Europe.[52]

Washington himself authorized at least three kidnapping attempts:[53] one designed to return Benedict Arnold to stand trial, a second to seize British general Sir Henry Clinton,[54] and a third—the most daring effort—to capture King George III's son while he was visiting New York City. In March 1782, Washington approved the plan submitted by Colonel Matthias Ogden to kidnap the heir to the throne, the future King William IV. Washington wrote to Ogden, "The spirit of enterprise so conspicuous in your plan of surprising in their quarters, and bringing off the Prince William Henry and Admiral Digby, merits applause; and you have my Authority to make the attempt; in any manner, and at such a time, as your own judgment shall direct." Following the kidnapping of the prince and the admiral, Ogden was to turn his captives over to the Continental Congress.[55] However, the plot was called off when British intelligence received information about a possible attempt to seize the prince and doubled his guard. Washington's motive for approving this risky kidnapping attempt remains unclear to this day. According to one theory, Washington considered establishing William as the king of an independent United States. It seems most likely that Washington was interested in possessing a prestigious bargaining chip, perhaps looking forward to a prisoner exchange involving the hated Benedict Arnold.[56]

Covert techniques were coupled with overt military force in attempting to sway Quebec to the American cause. Throughout the war, Washington's intelligence managers maintained contact with operatives in the Canadian maritimes and in Quebec.[57] These agents provided intelligence for generals Montgomery and Arnold during their ill-fated invasion of Canada in 1775. In addition to providing data and assistance to invading American forces, the network in Canada engaged in propaganda and disinformation efforts designed to play on the fears of both British and French residents of Quebec.[58] The most ambitious effort was a congressionally approved covert operation designed to solicit the support of the Catholic majority in Quebec. This was to be achieved by funding a pro-American press in the province and dispatching an American Catholic priest to win sympathy for the rebel cause. The covert-press operation was authorized by Congress on February 26, 1776, when a "Monsr. Mesplet, Printer, [was] engaged to go to Canada, and there set up his press and carry on the printing business," where his expenses and a sum of $200 would be provided by Congress.[59] The service of Father John Carroll was enlisted after reports indicated that British intelligence had persuaded Canadian clerics to preach about the evils of the American Revolution. One proponent of the mission to Canada remarked that Carroll's work with the populace in convincing them of the benevolent intent of the Revolution "would be worth battalions to us."[60] The Carroll mission (he was part of a committee consisting of Benjamin Franklin, Samuel Chase, and Charles Carroll) ended in failure. Likewise, Mesplet's journalistic endeavor did not persuade Quebec to join the American cause, though his newspaper survives to this day as the *Montreal Gazette*.[61] One other foreign newspaper, the *Gazette de Leide* (Leyden, Holland), was penetrated by a secret American operative. Charles Dumas, a Swiss journalist and friend of Benjamin Franklin, was an American agent who cultivated the editor of this publication and planted a number of stories favorable to the Americans. One important goal of this operation was to acquire a favorable credit rating for the United States in Dutch financial markets.[62]

At various times throughout the war, the Continental Congress and several state committees of safety engaged in mail opening. For example, on July 2, 1775, members of South Carolina's Secret Committee and the Committee of Intelligence forced the postmaster in Charleston to surrender twenty-six packets of government mail, copies of which were forwarded to the Continental Congress for its review.[63] The practice quickly became subject to abuse, and Congress attempted to limit the authority given to intercept mail but did not curtail it.[64] Much of the mail consisted of letters written to and from Tories in the United States. Throughout the war, Congress published some of the intercepted material for propaganda purposes.[65]

A prominent group of Founders helped to create and implement a psychological-warfare program designed to cause desertions among Hessian soldiers hired by King George to fight in the United States. Benjamin Franklin, Thomas Jefferson, John Adams, and George Washington all participated in one way or another in writing or distributing a variety of documents (printed in German) to achieve that goal.[66] The most ambitious was a fraudulent letter penned by Franklin. The letter purportedly was from a German count to the Hessian commander in America, urging him to run up his casualties so as to increase the count's payment from the British.[67] Other documents held out the promise of large tracts of land for Hessian defectors and a guarantee of all "the rights, privileges and immunities of natives." It is estimated that between five and six thousand Hessians deserted, at least partly as a result of the psychological-warfare efforts.[68]

One of the most aggressive American efforts was the mission of James Aitken, who conducted the only known sabotage operation inside England. Aitken was dispatched by Silas Deane, an American envoy to the French government. Entering the country with a false passport supplied by the French government, he set off for London. Aitken set a series of fires that destroyed matériel at the naval shipyard in Portsmouth and torched several warehouses and private houses in Bristol before being captured and hanged.[69] Deane, Franklin, and the other American agents abroad not only assisted Aitken, but had at their disposal a clandestine navy to aid them in conducting a variety of secret activities. Operating under the direction of the Committee of Secret Correspondence, this flotilla was entirely separate from the regular navy. In addition, Benjamin Franklin directed from his base in Paris a small fleet of Irish and French privateers that preyed on British shipping.[70]

Funding and Control of Intelligence Operations

The financing and control of American intelligence operations during the Revolution were fairly loose: Washington's requests for congressional appropriations for intelligence services appear to have been routinely approved with no questions asked. In most instances, the funds were given directly to Washington to disperse as he saw fit. However, the delivery of the funds was often subject to lengthy delays, a problem that plagued the entire American war effort. For instance, in a letter written to the president of the Continental Congress in August 1778, Washington reminded him of promised funds for espionage operations.[71] The request itself appears to have been highly secretive, with Washington at first having "hinted" at the need for funds to a congressional committee. This approach was followed by a personal letter from Washington to the president of the Congress appealing for funding for secret services (noteworthy since the bulk of Washington's correspondence was written by his staff). The president in turn suggested to "two or three Members" the necessity for such funds, and the motion was accepted "without a pause."[72]

It seems from this transaction and others that the congressional circle involved in financing Revolutionary espionage activities was limited to the president of the Congress, the superintendent of finance (for a good part of the war, Robert Morris), and at various times members of the Secret Committee (Chapter 2). Washington was given complete discretion over the funds, with Congress accepting his accounting of expenditures. In at least one instance, Washington did not account for an intelligence expenditure until seven years after the fact. A payment made sometime in 1777 was explained in 1784 by Washington's writing the comptroller of the currency, "I remember to have received [the payment]; the time and circumstances of it being too remarkable ever to be forgotten by me."[73] Washington's word that the funds were to be well spent and essential to the war effort was apparently sufficient justification.[74] The funds, Washington wrote to the president of the Continental Congress, shall be expended "as the exigency of the service may require."[75]

One entry from the secret journal of the Continental Congress reveals a glimpse of the Founders' attitude toward executive control of intelligence activities. In April 1779, a proposal was made in Congress to send hard money to Washington immediately for secret services. It appears that some members, jealous of congressional prerogatives, amended the proposal to direct the president of the Congress to write "the Commander in Chief and enquire whether he is in want of specie for secret services."[76] At this point, Sam Adams and Gouverneur Morris moved to expedite the process by giving Washington the funds without inquiring whether he needed them and to "inform him that if he is in want of specie for secret services, he may draw for any sum or sums to the amount of two thousand guineas upon the treasurer, who will pay the same."[77] Although it is difficult to ascribe motives to the participants in this sparsely recorded debate, it would appear that the Adams–Morris faction sought to enhance the discretion of the commander in chief in controlling intelligence operations.

Under pressure from a system wracked by horrid delays and congres-

sional foot dragging, Washington was often forced to conduct his operations with a "scanty" supply of hard money.[78] Washington complained to
Congress in September 1778 that "for want of supplies of this sort [hard
money], we have been very deficient in intelligence."[79] The delays associated with the approval and delivery of congressionally authorized funds
forced Washington to utilize money not allocated by Congress. In one
letter, Washington directly addressed the issue of bypassing the legitimate process by which funds were to be procured for intelligence purposes:

> I have submitted to grope in the dark [due to lack of funds] without those
> certain and precise informations which every Man at the head of an Army
> ought, and the public Interest requires he should have, and this maugre [in
> spite of] the aid of my private purse and other funds which were not applica-
> ble to this essentially necessary purpose.[80]

By using private money and unilaterally transferring funds designated
by Congress for other purposes, Washington was able to sustain his "essential" intelligence operations.

A foreign country also contributed funds to keep Washington's
fledgling intelligence operation afloat when congressionally authorized
funds were hard to come by. The French provided funds for American
intelligence operations through Lieutenant General Comte de Rochambeau, commander of the French army in America. In a letter written
to Benjamin Tallmadge in September 1783, Washington revealed that
"Count de Rochambeau . . . told me that he had put money into your
hands, and would continue to furnish you with more for the purpose of
obtaining intelligence."[81] In return for providing this desperately needed
specie, the French were given direct access to much of the intelligence
data generated by the Culper Ring.[82]

The Revolutionary Crucible

Sympathetic American historians tend to overplay the contribution of
intelligence operations to the success of the Revolution, but even the most
sober assessment must acknowledge their vital importance. Various spy
rings performed their deceptive practices so well that when British forces
withdrew from American cities at the war's close, many agents' lives were
endangered by an outraged public convinced of their Tory sympathies.[83]
One chronicler of the period believes that after the Hale fiasco, Washington created with remarkable speed a system "in which information poured
into his headquarters and no lives were wasted. . . . By 1777 the Continental Army probably had the best intelligence service in the world."[84]

Unquestionably, the American victory at Yorktown was achieved in
part through Washington's deft hand at deception. Washington was able
to trap Cornwallis at Yorktown by once again convincing the British that

New York City would be attacked. Looking back on the critical events of that year, Washington wrote to Noah Webster in 1788:

[I]t was determined by me (nearly twelve months beforehand) at all hazards to give out and cause it to be believed by the highest military as well as civil Officers that New York was the destined place of attack. . . . That much trouble was taken and finesse used to misguide and bewilder Sir Henry Clinton . . . is certain.[85]

This, Washington's final ruse, was also designed to mislead his own countrymen, for he wanted the eastern and middle states to supply his army but believed that their total cooperation could not be gained unless they thought New York was the target. An effort was made to mislead his own army as well: "Nor were less pains taken to deceive our own Army; for I had always conceived, when the imposition did not completely take place at home, it could never sufficiently succeed abroad."[86] It was not until three weeks after the American army marched through Philadelphia that the British realized the troops were heading for Yorktown.[87] In the days leading up to the battle itself, agents were sent across British lines with misleading information about American capabilities. This misinformation affected British general Charles Cornwallis's planning for the battle, causing him to remain in Yorktown and ensuring his eventual entrapment.[88]

Washington emerged from the war the preeminent military leader and statesman of his country. All along the path to independence, he had engaged in practices that he undoubtedly found distasteful but that were conducted out of a desperate necessity. As commander of an outnumbered and ill-equipped army, Washington resorted to time-honored techniques of deception and intrigue so often employed by smaller forces against greater powers. One historian who has recorded Washington's role as America's first intelligence director notes:

There have been few men who lied so skillfully, so frequently and with such enthusiasm as the hero of the cherry tree. . . . I have never known an officer who could deceive the enemy so well, who took so much obvious delight in deceiving the enemy, and who had such a carefully worked out system.[89]

The legacy of executive leadership bequeathed by Washington to the American political tradition contains many of the elements of covert operations recounted in this chapter. Washington displayed few qualms about the ruthless methods he employed when confronted with forces hostile to the survival of his nation. The type of clandestine actions pursued by Washington and the willingness of congressional authorities to cede control over many of them can perhaps be excused as a unique occurrence related to the problem of founding a nation under wartime circumstances. However, Washington's intelligence correspondence reveals that he believed these activities to be an intrinsic part of the Machiavellian world of conflict and competition between nations. His actions were rooted in a belief that the security of his country required him to seek advantage over foreign adversaries with all possible means. Washington's attitude toward clandestine activities was forged during the crucible of a long and bitter war, a war in which, to borrow from Thomas Jefferson, "the laws of necessity, of self preservation, of saving our country when in danger" overrode the written law or standards of traditional conduct.[90]

Washington's position justified to him a series of actions that would be certain to generate condemnation from modern critics were they to be carried out today. Moreover, Washington's thinking appears to have been shared by the other Founders. His intimate involvement in this clandestine world was shared in part by many of the men who would go on to design and implement the new American government. Alexander Hamilton and John Jay, contributors to *The Federalist* and key advisers in the Washington administration (1789–1797), would be most influential in molding the office of the presidency and influencing the course of American foreign policy (Chapter 2). The control of overseas clandestine operations that had been conducted by various committees of Congress during the American Revolution would be absorbed by President Washington when the first American Congress convened under the Constitution of 1787. The new American government would have at its disposal the resources to conduct covert operations for peacetime as well as wartime use (Chapter 3).

Many of the clandestine activities undertaken by the Founders were no doubt lost to history, but we know enough to state that these men possessed, in Washington's words, "knowledge of innumerable things, of a more delicate and secret nature" that would remain forever "confined to the perishable remembrance of some few of the present generation."[91]

2 ∎

Hamilton and Jay

The Constitution, *The Federalist,* and "The Business of Intelligence"

It is essential the Executive should have half a million of secret service money. If the measure cannot be carried without it, The expenditure may be with the approbation of three members of each house of Congress. But twere better without this incumbrance.

ALEXANDER HAMILTON to OLIVER WOLCOTT, JR.,
June 5, 1798[1]

∎ Alexander Hamilton and John Jay made significant contributions to the development of an American intelligence capability, both in their writings and in their actions as leading statesmen of their day. Each man's experience in the war for independence gave him firsthand knowledge of the harsh world of clandestine operations and secret negotiations. These veterans of war and diplomacy incorporated their hard-won lessons into their design for the office of the presidency. In their written work, both men urged that the executive be granted discretionary power over secret initiatives. As political leaders, they were intimately involved in the clandestine arena of the American Revolution and in shaping the postwar relations of the United States with foreign nations.

As General Washington's favorite aide-de-camp, Hamilton was immersed in the world of clandestine operations. At the same time, Jay was deeply involved in counterintelligence and espionage activities in New York and as a member of the Committee of Secret Correspondence, America's first "intelligence directorate."[2] We will begin by looking at the latter's wartime activities as director of "the most vigorous counterintelligence" program of the American Revolution and an overseer of the nation's first intelligence operations abroad as a member of the Committee of Secret Correspondence.[3] Jay's small but important contribution to *The Federalist* focused on the importance of foreign policy and the need to equip a president with the tools to capitalize on the rapidly changing currents in foreign affairs. Hamilton, perhaps more than any other man, attempted to shape the office of the presidency with as many of these tools as the tenor of the times would allow.

"That Best Oracle of Wisdom, Experience"

The rise of Hamilton and Jay to political prominence took place in a time of divided loyalties, broken friendships, and an awareness that one misjudgment about trustworthiness could mean death. It was in this environment that both young men formed their political beliefs. As major figures in the struggle for independence, Hamilton and Jay developed an appreciation of the need for executive "decision, activity, secrecy, and dispatch" in directing activities designed to protect the national interest.[4]

John Jay: "I Have Adhered to Certain Fixed Principles"

John Jay was appointed by the Continental Congress as a member of the Committee of Secret Correspondence on November 29, 1775.[5] He was pleased with the assignment, describing the committee as one of "the two great secret committees" of the Congress.[6] The committee was formally charged with "corresponding with our friends in Great Britain, Ireland, and other parts of the world" but wasted little time in establishing an intelligence network.[7] The day after the committee was given its mandate by Congress, it wrote to one of its key overseas operatives, Arthur Lee, in London:

> Our institution is with design to preserve secrecy and thereby secure our friends. . . . It is considered as of the utmost consequence to the cause of Liberty, that an intercourse should be kept up, and we shall be obliged by your sentiments of the most probable and secure method of effecting it.[8]

Less than two weeks later, the committee wrote to Lee again, designating him as their secret agent in London. A letter sent from Jay, Franklin, and John Dickinson asked Lee to determine "the disposition of foreign powers towards us" and reminded him, "We need not hint that great circumspection and impenetrable secrecy are necessary."[9]

Membership on the Committee of Secret Correspondence exposed Jay to some of America's most sensitive clandestine operations of the war and revealed to him the importance of secrecy in achieving foreign-policy objectives. For instance, at the same time Jay's committee was dispatching Arthur Lee to London, it met with a French intelligence agent in Philadelphia, a meeting that marked the beginning of a clandestine relationship with a nation whose covert and overt assistance proved crucial to the American cause.[10] The committee had a number of "assets" at its disposal, including its own network of agents, the aforementioned naval force separate from the regular navy to assist in conducting secret operations, and a rudimentary courier network to handle overseas dispatches.[11]

Jay's son described his father's work on the committee as "enveloped in the most profound secrecy" and noted that it "led to important results."[12] Jay, whose brother developed the secret ink used for intelligence correspondence, appears to have been a central link in the secret communications network between the committee and its secret agents abroad.[13] It was Jay who provided Silas Deane with his supply of invisible ink prior to the latter's departure for France as an American agent in March 1776.[14] Deane was instructed by the committee to operate under the cover of a merchant seeking goods "suitable for the Indians." The committee believed that the contract for "the Indian trade" would provide "good countenance to . . . appearing in the character of a merchant . . . it being probable that the court of France may not like it should be known publicly that any agent from the colonies is in that country." The true nature of the Deane mission was an ambitious plan to acquire "clothing and arms for twenty-five thousand men, with a suitable quantity of ammunition, and one hundred field pieces."[15]

The secret communication arrangement between Jay and Silas Deane preserved the confidentiality of some important correspondence. For example, a letter from Deane addressed to Robert Morris appeared, in its undeciphered state, to have been simply a "cold insipid letter." This letter from "Timothy Jones" discussing the safe arrival of a traveler and his health condition actually contained a message to the committee regarding a shipment of military supplies and urged Congress to commission privateers to prey on Portuguese shipping, thereby winning the friendship and support of Spain.[16] Despite the great precautions taken to write in invisible ink—or in code—and to use only special agents to deliver important documents, it is estimated that more than half of America's correspondence was intercepted and deciphered by the British Foreign Office.[17] This fact would remain a constant source of frustration to Jay throughout his involvement as a member of America's fledgling diplomatic corps. In one particular instance, Jay experienced firsthand the high cost of these British intercept operations. A letter allegedly written by French agent Barbé-Marbois to the French foreign minister was intercepted and given to Jay by British agents. The translation raised serious questions in Jay's mind regarding France's fidelity to the American cause. To this day, it is unclear whether the letter was genuine or part of a British disinformation effort designed to demoralize the Americans, though recent evidence seems to favor the former interpretation.[18]

The bulk of the missions authorized by the Committee of Secret Correspondence were concerned with the acquisition of desperately needed supplies from sympathetic European states. One particular mission that Jay appears to have had a hand in launching was that of Dutch adventurer Johann Philip Merkle. Merkle was recommended to Congress by a letter of introduction written by John Jay in May 1776. He was referred to the Secret Committee, by which he subsequently was employed in an operation designed to purchase "merchandise, arms, and ammunition" in France and Holland.[19] During Jay's tenure on the committee, secret overtures to obtain arms and support were made not only to France and Holland but also to Prussia, the latter in the form of a mission undertaken by William Carmichael to the court of Frederick II ("the Great") in October 1776.[20]

Jay was a participant in another highly secretive foreign operation of the war: the creation of a front to transmit supplies from France to the United States during the early years of the war. The operation was conducted by Arthur Lee and Silas Deane, the first two agents sent abroad by the Committee of Secret Correspondence. Lee began the project by conveying reports of inflated American strength to a French secret agent in London, Pierre-Augustin Caron de Beaumarchais.[21] Beaumarchais dispatched his intelligence to the Comte de Vergennes, the French minister of foreign affairs, proposing secret French assistance to aid the colonies and designating himself as the agent to run the program.[22] Beaumarchais's lobbying effort with Vergennes and Louis XVI led to the establishment of a front operation known as Roderique Hortalez and Company to funnel supplies to the Americans.

The French government insisted on maintaining layers of "plausible deniability" to protect it from exposure; France's role was to be kept secret not only from the British but from the Americans as well. In keeping with this objective, Beaumarchais informed Arthur Lee that because of his frustration with his own government he was creating his own company to supply the Americans in return for tobacco products.[23] Beaumarchais wrote to the French king, "Your majesty knows better than anyone that secrecy is the soul of business and that in politics a project known is a project lost."[24] Beaumarchais set up a $3 million operation, $1 million of which came from a secret donation from Spain. Silas Deane became the main American contact with Beaumarchais and, on December 3, 1776, wrote to John Jay about the operation, revealing the circumspection of the French government: "If my Letters arrive safe they will give you some Idea of my situation. . . . I send 30,000 Fusils, 200 pieces of Brass Cannon, Thirty Mortars. . . . Mons. Beaumarchais has been my Minister in effect, as this Court is extreme cautious."[25]

How many other details of this operation were known to Jay is not clear; there is no record of any other correspondence between Deane and John Jay during 1776.[26] It is certain that Congress maintained silence about the whole operation, perhaps unaware of the origins of Beaumarchais's bountiful assistance but more than willing to accept it. However, by January 1779, Jay wrote to Beaumarchais on behalf of the Congress, thanking him for his efforts: "They [the Congress] lament the Inconveniences you have suffered, by the great Advances made in support of these states. Circumstances have prevented a compliance with their wishes, but they will take the most effectual measures in their power to discharge the debt due to you."[27]

The Struggle Against "Intestine Enemies"

In the midst of his work as a member of the committee overseeing America's foreign intelligence operatives, Jay became deeply involved in the internecine warfare that marked the struggle for independence in New York. New York was a hotbed of rebel and Tory agitation; and Jay, a respected jurist with a wide circle of acquaintances, initiated and directed a number of security measures often targeted against old friends who remained loyal to the Crown. By the end of 1776, the initial ad hoc efforts against enemies of the Revolution became a full-fledged counterintelligence network with at least ten agents who operated, by and large, under the direction of John Jay.[28]

In a letter written on March 21, 1776, Jay expressed his concern about subversive elements and proposed that those who are "notoriously disaffected" should be forcefully relocated out of reach of the enemy's influence.[29] A short time later, on May 27, 1776, the provincial congress in New York appointed Jay to a five-member board designed to deal with the problem of "intestine [internal] enemies."[30] Jay was immediately tapped, along with Gouverneur Morris and Philip Livingston (a prominent New York political figure and signer of the Declaration of Independence), to investigate a series of high-profile cases of treason and subversion including the pro-British activities of the mayor of New York City, the treasonous activities of two members of George Washington's personal guard, and the secret plan of New York's governor to aid British troops when they arrived in New York City.[31] Washington exhorted the board to further action in a letter written on July 13, 1776, requesting that steps be taken to relocate disaffected persons from the environs of New York City, for "the safety of the Army, the Success of every Enterprize, and the Security of all, depends so much on adopting the most Speedy and effec-

tual Steps." Washington noted, "A suspicion, that there are many Minis-
terial Agents among us, would justly alarm Soldiers of more experience
and discipline than ours. . . . In case of an Attack and Alarm, there can
be no doubt what part they will take and none can tell what influence they
might have."[32]

In September 1776, the worsening military situation in New York led
its provincial congress to grant enhanced powers to its own counterintelligence board. The result was the creation of the Committee to Detect
and Defeat Conspiracies in the State of New York. This committee of
seven members was given broad powers for "inquiring into, detecting and
defeating all conspiracies."[33] Jay often acted as chairman and appeared
throughout the committee's existence to have been the dominant force in
directing its activities. Evidence of his intimate involvement can be found
in the minutes of the committee meetings that are written in Jay's hand.
Additionally, Jay organized a team of secret agents who acquired evidence against British sympathizers and agents.[34] The committee had a
detachment of troops under its command and express riders to ensure the
security of their communications. The accumulated intelligence was used
in many of the over five hundred cases of questionable loyalty and outright subversion brought before the committee.[35]

Jay worked closely with two figures who would eventually become
almost legendary characters in the annals of American intelligence history. One of his counterintelligence agents, Enoch Crosby, appears to
have served as the model for the central character in James Fenimore
Cooper's *The Spy,* the inspiration for which Cooper allegedly took from
Jay himself.[36] Fellow committee member Nathaniel Sackett would go on
to become a key intelligence operative in General Washington's spy network in New York and New Jersey.[37] During this period, Jay's correspondence reveals the burdens of having to function in an atmosphere sur-
rounded by "plots, conspiracies, and chimeras dire."[38] Many of the steps
taken by Jay were personally painful: an old friend named Peter Van
Schaack was subjected to banishment to England partly as a result of
Jay's efforts. Writing to him years later, Jay explained his painful devotion to duty:

> I have adhered to certain fixed principles, and faithfully obeyed their dic-
> tates without regarding the consequences of such conduct to my friends, my
> family, or myself: all of whom, however dreadful the thought, I have ever
> been ready to sacrifice, if necessary, to the public objects in the contest.[39]

Jay's role on the Committee to Detect and Defeat Conspiracies ended
when the committee was disbanded on February 11, 1777, and replaced by
a similar body of which Jay was not a member.[40] During this crucial
period in his political growth, whatever doubts he may have felt toward
the cause of independence disappeared. Formed through the long and
bitter experience with the problem of committee control of wartime opera-

tions, Jay's belief in the need for executive discretion over matters of war and peace also emerged. Jay's wartime correspondence reveals frequent despair over the lack of congressional secrecy and a tendency on the part of that body toward foot-dragging in implementing initiatives designed to further diplomatic or security-related goals.

Jay's attitude evolved as he encountered the necessity of defending his home state. In a letter dated July 1, 1776, Jay wrote to Robert Livingston, "They tell me that a Resolve has passed granting certain powers to the Gen. [Washington]. God knows what they are. I think of it with Fear and Trembling." The powers to which Jay was referring included the authority "to take such measures for apprehending and securing dangerous and disaffected persons as he shall think necessary."[41] Within two months, Jay's change in attitude can be seen in his proposal to grant broad executive authority to the commander in chief:

> Whereas it is no less consonant to Reason than confirmed by the Experience of almost all Nations, that military Operations whose Success often depends on the proper Use of Critical Moments and Contingencies not [to] be foreseen, should never be encumbered delayed or perplexed by Plans drawn by or Consultations with large Assemblies of Politicians unpracticed in the Art of War.[42]

Jay's belief in the need for executive latitude in directing matters related to the nation's security interests would harden further following his service as president of the Continental Congress and diplomatic envoy abroad.

President of the Continental Congress and Envoy Abroad

John Jay, elected president of the Continental Congress on December 10, 1778, was immediately confronted with a crisis over a leak of classified information involving Beaumarchais's secret program of French assistance to the United States. The leak was a result of the factional strife that had gripped Congress for months. Accusations of foul play were traded back and forth between rival cliques supporting Arthur Lee or Silas Deane. The source of the leak turned out to be Tom Paine, secretary to the Committee for Foreign Affairs, who had revealed to a Pennsylvania newspaper the existence of the Beaumarchais network.[43] The French minister to the United States demanded that Paine be disciplined for his "indiscreet assertions," for he had violated an oath of secrecy he had taken upon assuming his position. Congress, after two weeks of delay, dismissed Paine and demanded the return of all papers in his possession. Congress also issued a statement intended to repair the diplomatic damage wrought by Paine's disclosures by denying the existence of the secret aid network: "His Most Christian Majesty, the great and generous ally of the United

States, did not preface his alliance with any supplies whatever sent to America." Jay led the inquiry into the affair and became the target of vituperative attacks by Paine, the latter believing that Jay carried the inquiry and the punishment beyond what most members of Congress desired. Jay wrote to the French minister that the matter affected the "dignity of Congress, the Honor of their great Ally" and that "the explicit disavowal and high disapprobation of Congress" would settle the issue.[44]

The Paine incident marked the beginning of a series of events that reaffirmed Jay's belief in the inherent weakness of legislative bodies to direct national affairs with the necessary attributes of secrecy and dispatch. For instance, Washington had written a letter to Jay in April 1779, wondering why the frigates of the American navy were spending an excessive amount of time in port.[45] Jay's response reflected his dismay over congressional indecisiveness and the inability of that body to keep secrets:

> While the maritime affairs of the continent continue under the direction of a committee they will be exposed to all the consequences of want of system, attention, and knowledge. . . . It [the committee] fluctuates, new members coming in and old ones going out . . . few members understand even the state of our naval affairs, or have time or inclination to attend to them.[46]

Jay went on to describe the difficulties in maintaining secrecy in Congress:

> There is as much intrigue in this state-house as in the Vatican, but as little secrecy as in a boarding school. It mortifies me on this occasion to reflect that the rules of Congress on the subject of secrecy, which are far too general and perhaps for that reason more frequently violated, restrain me from saying twenty things to you which have ceased to be private.[47]

In his capacity as president of the Continental Congress, Jay was an important link in maintaining the flow of specie to Washington's intelligence operatives. Ironically, one of the first requests that Jay received from Washington was for secret service funds designed to assist the intelligence activities of Jay's old New York acquaintance General Alexander McDougall. McDougall ran a productive intelligence network covering the area from Morristown, New Jersey, to Manhattan.[48] By this time, in comparison with other presidents of the Congress, Jay's three years' experience as an intelligence and counterintelligence manager seems to have led him to a greater involvement in these matters. This included personal recommendations made to General Washington to engage the services of secret agents with whom Jay was familiar—for example, Elijah Hunter, one of his former spy catchers. Hunter became part of General McDougall's operation and, acting as a double agent, appears to have penetrated the upper echelons of the British command in New York City. While he was president of the Continental Congress, Jay was briefed about the agent's activities by Hunter himself, who appears to have been

Jay's favorite operative (General Washington was less than impressed with his services).[49]

Another example of Jay's familiarity with American intelligence operations can be found in his authorization to Washington to draw on the treasury for 2,000 guineas for secret service activities on May 4, 1779. In a letter drafted by Hamilton, Washington thanked Jay for his assistance and expressed regret that "ambiguous characters" often must be employed in obtaining intelligence. In return for conducting these missions, many of these "characters" were allowed to run black-market operations and were therefore often arrested by unwitting state and local authorities. Washington appeared to be asking Jay for help in getting the states to cease the prosecutions. Jay no doubt found the situation disturbing but lacked the authority to rectify it.[50] He had no qualms about allowing Washington to conduct his intelligence operations as he saw fit, telling him in one instance that "if he [the agent] still perseveres, I do not wish to be informed of any other Particulars."[51]

The correspondence between Jay and Washington reveals their deep mutual respect, though there is one instance of a difference of opinion on an issue related to secrecy and intelligence matters. Washington sought the release of intelligence material that he believed would improve the morale of the citizenry. The release of the information, in an "authentic and pointed manner," would give "a certain spring to our affairs in general."[52] Jay responded, "The opinion that greater advantage results from communicating important Events to the People, in an authentic manner; than by unauthorized Reports, is certainly just, tho often neglected. The Intelligence alluded to, is unfortunately of such a Nature, or rather so circumstanced, as to render Secrecy necessary."[53]

Jay's term as president ended on September 28, 1779, when he accepted the appointment as minister to Spain. As he left for Europe, his experience with the Paine incident weighed heavily on him, as did the constant sniping over Washington's conduct of the war. Jay had inherited a Continental Congress crippled by factional strife from within and subject to a variety of unseemly influences from without. In matters of secrecy and intelligence, Jay's attitude could perhaps best be summed up by his own comment in a note to his friend Alexander McDougall, whom he chided for sloppiness in communicating confidential material: "The fewer Parties [involved] the better."[54]

Jay's diplomatic career reinforced his belief that large bodies of decision makers impeded the smooth and steady implementation of policy. The goals of American foreign policy were undermined continually by a congressional-committee system characterized by unsteady administration. Jay experienced additional humiliation while serving as America's envoy to Spain. His every move was carefully monitored by the long arm of British intelligence, an organization that knew as much about the operations of Jay's compatriots in Europe as he did. Mail openings, coun-

terfeiting, disinformation, and the "turning" of agents were common occurrences in the diplomatic world of eighteenth-century Europe. Jay's
letters at this time plead for remedial action on the part of Congress to
ensure the success of America's secret diplomatic initiatives.

The problem of congressional policy vacillation was coupled with difficulties in obtaining "prompt information," rendering competent decision
making problematic.[55] Jay's concern for the secure and speedy dispatch of
diplomatic information can be seen in numerous letters written during his
service in Spain. "We must do like other nations—manage our correspondence in important cases by couriers, and not by the post."[56] In one letter,
Jay emphasized the need to protect secret dispatches and took the
congressional-committee system to task for its deficiencies:

> It is true that I might write to Congress very often. . . . They [the letters]
> would all be inspected, and many suppressed. . . . One good private corre-
> spondent would be worth twenty standing committees, made of the wisest
> heads in America, for the purpose of intelligence. . . . I now get more intel-
> ligence of your [congressional] affairs from the French ambassador than
> from all the members of Congress put together.[57]

Jay's plea for congressional action to secure the privacy of American
communications came up for debate in March 1781. The resolution stated
that "there is great reason to believe that the communications of Congress
to their minister at the court of Madrid . . . are interrupted by the
machinations of the instruments of the court of Great Britain." In a move
that would not have surprised Jay in the least, consideration of the motion was postponed.[58]

Jay's frustration with congressional inaction did not abate during the
four-year period he spent abroad as a diplomatic envoy. A letter to his old
friend Robert Livingston captures Jay's view of Congress and the absence
in that body of the qualities necessary for dealing with foreign nations:

> I am not at liberty to mention the manner in which this paper [secret docu-
> ment] came to my hands. To me it appears of importance that it should for
> the present be kept a profound secret, though I do not see how that is to be
> done if communicated to the Congress at large, among whom there always
> have been, and always will be, some unguarded members.

In closing the letter, Jay noted the successful ingredients in conducting
foreign policy: "You will see how necessary prudence and entire circumspection will be . . . and if possible secrecy."[59]

John Jay's commitment to executive control over the tools of American
foreign policy grew under the duress of fighting a long war and forging a
peace to bring that war to a close. Throughout these years, Jay was a
prominent member of a group within Congress that rejected the idea of
executive government through congressional committees. Jay and the
other members (Washington, Robert Morris, Franklin, Livingston) believed that large amounts of discretionary authority should be granted to

Washington as commander in chief and to Franklin as head of the foreign legation in Paris. As diplomatic historian Francis Wharton has noted, it is through Jay's "resolute" stand against "the management of foreign as well as domestic affairs by congressional committees that the gradual growth of the executive department system is to be largely traced."[60]

The fruits of Jay's bitter experience as an intelligence and counterintelligence manager, president of Congress, and foreign envoy can be seen in a number of significant documents and institutions of the young American republic. The New York State constitution, with its strong executive vested with "the supreme power and authority of the state" and commander in chief of the armed forces, was primarily Jay's creation.[61] Jay contributed five pieces to *The Federalist,* the most important of which, No. 64, was primarily concerned with the importance of secrecy and dispatch in conducting foreign affairs and the need for presidential control of the "business of intelligence." In 1789, after becoming president under the newly adopted Constitution of the United States, Washington asked Jay to discuss with him the state of American foreign affairs. One of the first proposals to come out of these meetings was the plan to reorganize and absorb the Office for Foreign Affairs into the Department of State, placing the control of foreign policy in the president's hands.[62]

The hard lessons learned by Jay over the years were shared by his fellow *Federalist* author Alexander Hamilton. We turn now to Hamilton's wartime experience and its effect on the development of executive control of secret operations.

Alexander Hamilton: "Experience Is the Parent of Wisdom."

Many of the views Alexander Hamilton would subsequently express in *The Federalist* stemmed from his role as aide-de-camp to General Washington from 1777 to 1781.[63] This position placed him in a unique vantage point from which to observe the conduct of military operations. Hamilton lived in "personal as well as official intimacy with the Commander in Chief" and emerged as the preeminent member of Washington's command staff.[64] Strictly military, his wartime experience differed from Jay's, and yet both men dealt in a variety of secret operations. One of his biographers states that Hamilton was "at the nerve center of the war, where came all intelligence and whence issued all major orders and correspondence with public authorities."[65]

Hamilton appears to have more than fulfilled Washington's criteria for aides-de-camp, "in whom entire confidence must be placed" and who had to possess the ability "to execute duties with propriety and dispatch."[66] Hamilton's stature with General Washington is reflected in his decision to allow Hamilton, more than any other aide-de-camp, access to the details of American intelligence operations. Historian John Bakeless notes that

Alexander Hamilton was the only officer on Washington's staff known to have handled intelligence reports.[67] He goes on to suggest that Hamilton was probably unaware of the identities of Washington's secret agents, though that assertion is certainly disputable. One dramatic incident that would seem to challenge it occurred during July 1780. In Washington's absence, acting on the basis of intelligence reports received from the Culper Ring in New York City, Hamilton took steps to prevent an attack on the French fleet moored in Newport harbor. Bakeless believes this warning was the most important intelligence coup provided by the Culper Ring, information that saved the French fleet from a potentially disastrous situation. Hamilton's speedy response and the relay of information to Lafayette in Rhode Island were of critical importance. They would not have happened if Hamilton had lacked confidence in the sources of the information or if he had been unable to develop the "secret stain" utilized by the spy ring.[68]

Washington's confidence in Hamilton's abilities as an intelligence officer was further demonstrated by his reliance on his young adjutant to conduct an investigation of an American operative suspected of serving as a double agent for the British. Hamilton ordered Colonel Stephen Moylan to oversee the investigation of "a certain Mr. Bankson. . . . We suspect him to be a spy to Mr. Howe, though he offers himself as one to us." Moylan was urged by Hamilton to "take cautious methods to ascertain" Bankson's movements, to discover anything that may "throw light upon his designs." In classic Hamiltonian style, Moylan was urged to carry on his mission with "caution and address."[69]

Hamilton's ascension to a position where he could act unilaterally in Washington's absence is understandable in light of his role as a staff officer operating in the vortex of Washington's intelligence network. The first drafts of many of Washington's letters to his intelligence operatives are in Hamilton's writing, including those of a very detailed nature describing various methods of acquiring and conveying secret information. The force and vigor of Hamilton's later writings are found in many of these dispatches sent in Washington's name.

Exposure to the vagaries of the intelligence business was part of the formative experience of the young Hamilton, an exposure that reached its peak during a period from November 1778 to November 1779. During this critical period of the war, Hamilton was involved in a variety of intelligence matters:

November 29, 1778: Drafts a letter from Washington to Benjamin Tallmadge expressing concern over the "circuitous and dilatory" method employed by Tallmadge in conveying intelligence data, and the need for Tallmadge to designate an officer of great "discretion" who can deliver this "intelligence with expedition."[70]

February 19, 1779: Drafts a letter from Washington advising John Jay, the president of Congress, that Major General Alexander McDougall needs specie to support the operations of his espionage network.[71]

March 1, 1779: Drafts a letter from Washington to Jay urging public release of intelligence information obtained from Europe to boost citizen morale.[72]

March 3, 1779: Drafts a letter from Washington to Major General McDougall sending 150 guineas to be used for secret service funding.[73]

March 25, 1779: Drafts a letter from Washington to McDougall discussing the use of Elijah Hunter as a double agent and urging a policy of caution in dealing with any double agents.[74]

May 11, 1779: Drafts a letter from Washington to Jay thanking him for obtaining specie for "secret services." The letter notes the unfortunate necessity of employing "ambiguous characters" to obtain intelligence and of allowing spies to profit personally from their activities "both as an encouragement and cover to their mission."[75]

June 3, 1779: Drafts a letter to Jay containing intelligence received from McDougall and others that indicates that "the enemy had some important enterprise in contemplation."[76]

June 23, 1779: Drafts a letter from Washington to McDougall acknowledging the receipt of intelligence information and urging the "speediest" possible conveyance to a fellow general.[77]

July 5, 1779: Drafts a letter from Washington to Tallmadge reprimanding him for keeping secret documents at an advanced military post that were subsequently captured by the British. These papers apparently revealed the identity of an agent who, unless he was given "speediest notice of what has happened . . . will in all probability fall a sacrifice."[78]

August 6, 1779 (approximately): Deciphers a letter written in invisible ink from Samuel Culper, Jr., containing intelligence data on British military activities in New York City.[79]

November 1–2, 1779: Receives two letters from Washington containing intelligence received from the Culper Ring describing British troop movements. Hamilton was accompanying Brigadier General Louis le Bèque du Portail on a mission to Admiral Comte d'Estaing.[80]

Hamilton's awareness of and close access to the harsh world of clandestine operations is further revealed in a document written after the war's close. Hamilton wrote a certificate attesting to the courage of one of Washington's spies, who nearly lost his life after being captured by the British in New York City and remained imprisoned for 235 days:

> I was privy to the Petitioners being employed by the Commander in Chief in the manner he mentions. . . . I further certify that from the accounts repeatedly received at Head Quarters of the treatment he experienced there is no reason to doubt he suffered every thing he could bear without loss of Life.[81]

Hamilton's close proximity to American intelligence operations of the Revolutionary War can also be seen in his association with an American agent with the unlikely name of Hercules Mulligan. Mulligan was one of the first acquaintances of Hamilton upon his arrival in America in 1772. Hamilton had come to New York City from Nevis in the West Indies, and he arranged to stay with Mulligan through Mulligan's brother Hugh, a West Indies trader.[82] Hamilton and Hercules Mulligan went on to participate in one of the earliest instances of hostilities in the New York City area. A group of New Yorkers, including Hamilton and Mulligan, removed several cannon from a coastal battery while under fire from British warships anchored in the harbor.[83] The two men—along with Benjamin Tallmadge, the overseer of the Culper Ring, and Nathan Hale, America's first intelligence martyr—were part of a group of social acquaintances who formed the core of New York City intelligence operatives.[84]

The precise date at which Mulligan offered his services as a "confidential correspondent" of General Washington is difficult to determine, though the process appears to have begun some time in November 1776, following a meeting with Hamilton at Washington's encampment near Hackensack, New Jersey. Mulligan's responsibilities seem to have increased in the wake of Hamilton's appointment to Washington's staff on March 1, 1777.[85] His first intelligence success came in April 1777, when he warned of British general Howe's intended expedition to Delaware. He apparently cooperated with the Culper Ring but essentially remained a lone agent who capitalized on his familiarity with British officers, many of whom patronized his tailor shop.[86]

Although no intelligence dispatches exist bearing his signature, Mulligan is thought to have corresponded regularly with Washington through Hamilton. Mulligan's biographer believes him to be the source of a tip that warned the Americans of a plan to kidnap Washington in February 1781. He also points to two letters written by Hamilton during 1777 referring to intelligence received from New York City and believes Mulligan to be the agent responsible for acquiring the information.[87]

As Hamilton's friend and trusted secret agent, Mulligan received an honor reserved for those who had silently served their cause during the war. Following the British evacuation of New York, General Washington's first breakfast in the city was with Mulligan,[88] whose tailor shop went on to prosper partly as a result of his prominent connections.[89] His burial vault is but a few short paces from that of his old friend Alexander Hamilton.[90]

Before closing this discussion of Hamilton's role in wartime intelligence operations, it is worth noting two letters written by Hamilton that shed light on his attitude toward clandestine operations and the way they should be conducted. The first letter, written in October 1780, was sent to Hamilton's good friend John Laurens. The letter contains Hamilton's reaction to Benedict Arnold's treason and the events surrounding the execution of Major John André. In his letter to Laurens, Hamilton commented on the dirty but necessary business of intelligence and espionage:

> I speak not of André's conduct in this affair as a Philosophe, but as a man of the world. The authorised maxims and practices of war are the satire of human nature. They countenance almost every species of seduction as well as violence; and the General that can make most traitors in the army of his adversary is frequently most applauded. On this scale we acquit André, while we could not but condemn him, if we were to examine his conduct by the sober rules of philosophy and moral rectitude.[91]

The second letter was written to General Henry Knox in June 1782. Although not directly bearing on an intelligence matter, the letter reveals Hamilton's desire to shield the commander in chief from the actual implementation of repugnant acts done in furtherance of his objectives, a defense of the concept of plausible deniability. Washington had ordered the execution of a randomly selected British prisoner of war in retaliation for the execution of a captured American officer. Hamilton vehemently opposed this action but stated his position as to how it should be conducted if Washington was determined to see it through:

> If it is seriously believed that in this advanced state of affairs retaliation is necessary let another mode be chose. Let under actors be employed and let the authority by which it is done be wrapt in obscurity and doubt. . . . Let not the Commander in Chief considered as the first and most respectable character among us come forward in person and be the avowed author of an act at which every humane feeling revolts . . . appoint some obscure agents to perform the ceremony.[92]

Hamilton's experience as a staff officer at the center of command affirmed his belief in the need for an executive to move, when necessary, with secrecy and dispatch. He served by the side of a man burdened not only with the normal vexations of war, but with the necessity of waging it under a system notorious for its burdensome delays, excessive political wrangling, and sloppy execution. A biographer comments, "Hamilton was at the focus of these anxious developments, military, economic, and political . . . [his] later restless efforts to consolidate national gains may not be understood except by remembering problems of the war."[93]

Hamilton did not wait for the war to end to begin his efforts toward building a powerful executive office. As early as September 1780, he wrote to Congressman James Duane lamenting the sorry state of American government and presaging many of the themes on executive power that are found in *The Federalist*. The proposals to Duane were made in the hope of saving the country from "ruin":

> Another defect in our system is want of method and energy in the administra-
> tion. . . . Congress have kept the power too much into their own hands and
> have meddled too much with details of every sort. Congress is properly a
> deliberative corps and it forgets itself when it attempts to play the executive.
> It is impossible such a body, numerous as it is, constantly fluctuating, can
> ever act with sufficient decision, or with system.[94]

After his rise to prominence in the Washington administration, Hamilton did not hesitate to apply these lessons. He advocated the creation of a clandestine capability at the executive's disposal and a very limited role, if any, for Congress in overseeing its use. His influence can be seen in Washington's request for a secret service fund in his first annual message to Congress, a request with Hamilton's fingerprints all over it. Further evidence of Hamilton's belief in the importance of a secret service is found in a document written in June 1798; under the heading of "Further measures to be taken without delay," Hamilton laid out the steps necessary to put the United States on a war footing with France: "It is essential the Executive should have half a million of secret service money. If the measure cannot be carried without it, The expenditure may be with the approbation of three members of each house of Congress. But twere better without this incumbrance."[95] Thus the unrestricted use of executive power to direct secret initiatives was vigorously defended by two of the authors of *The Federalist,* in part as a result of their wartime careers in intelligence.

Building the Foundation

In 1787, Alexander Hamilton was joined at the Constitutional Convention by veterans of a number of American intelligence operations. Although to call them an intelligence lobby would be inaccurate, it is safe to assume that their experience inclined them toward the idea of a broad grant of executive discretion in controlling secret initiatives. In addition to the more notable veterans, such as Washington, Franklin, and Hamilton, several other delegates at the Constitutional Convention had strong intelligence backgrounds. Among them were Jonathan Dayton of New Jersey, a former field intelligence officer, and John Dickinson of Delaware, a member of the Secret Committee of the Continental Congress, which obtained military matériel covertly by flying foreign flags on its supply ships—often without permission of the nation whose flag they flew. Prominent Pennsylvania delegate James Wilson was a former member of the Committee on Spies and helped draw up the nation's first espionage laws. During the war, Wilson had served with Franklin and George Wythe on a special committee created to examine intercepted British communications. William Churchill Houston of New Jersey and Robert Morris of Pennsylvania were former members of the Committee of Secret Correspondence; Morris had also played a critical role in obtaining specie to finance intelligence operations. Two other Pennsylvanians, Major General Thomas Mifflin and Gouverneur Morris, were intimate participants in wartime intelligence activities. Mifflin had been a central figure in directing a portion of Washington's military intelligence network, and Morris had participated in counterintelligence activities in New York and would go on to become President Washington's first agent abroad. Elbridge Gerry of Massachusetts had deciphered the secret correspondence used by British agent Benjamin Church in the first year of the war. Additionally, nine other delegates had served on various state committees of safety charged with a number of minor intelligence functions.[96]

Perhaps the most influential delegate in attendance at the convention in Philadelphia was James Madison of Virginia. Madison, who would go down in history as the "father" of the American Constitution, had no intelligence background. He attended the convention as a thirty-six-year-old delegate from Virginia, having held a number of political posts, including membership in the Virginia legislature and the Continental Congress. While holding these positions, Madison had witnessed firsthand the ineffectiveness of the Articles of Confederation, which had "governed" the United States since 1781. The Articles of Confederation created little more than a "league of friendship," erecting an impotent national Congress whose very existence depended on the goodwill of the member states.

Throughout the 1780s, Madison led the effort to strengthen the authority of the national government over commerce, revenue, and, most important for our study, foreign relations. In September 1786, Madison joined with Alexander Hamilton in calling on Congress to convene a meeting of representatives from all the states for the purpose of rendering the federal constitution "adequate to the exigencies of the Union."[97] In May 1787, fifty-five delegates gathered at the State House in Philadelphia and spent a long, hot summer crafting a new government for the United States.

The dominant intelligence-related issue discussed at the Constitutional Convention was the likelihood of clandestine foreign penetration. The only mention of U.S. intelligence operations occurred on July 26, 1787, when Gouverneur Morris attacked a proposal from George Mason that sought to prevent persons with unsettled government accounts from holding office in the national legislature. According to James Madison, whose notes provide the sole account of the proceedings, "He [Morris] mentioned the case of the Commander in Chief"'s presenting his account for secret services, which he said was so moderate that every one was astonished at it; and so simple that no doubt could arise on it."[98] Morris used this example to show that a prohibition against persons with unsettled government financial accounts could prevent a distinguished person, such as Washington, from holding office.

As mentioned, the belief that foreign powers would continually attempt to interfere was the paramount intelligence issue discussed at the Constitutional Convention and in *The Federalist*. Indeed, the impact of the massive British intelligence operations against the United States can be seen in the delegates' repeated warnings of foreign meddling. For instance, on June 19, in response to William Paterson's plan for a national government, James Madison questioned whether the Paterson proposal would "secure the Union against the influence of foreign powers over its members." He did not say that these intrigues had yet occurred, "but it was naturally to be expected that occasions would produce [them]."[99] Ten days later, Alexander Hamilton warned of the dangers of the dissolution of the union and the formation of "partial confederacies" that would provide an opening for the "rival and hostile nations of Europe, who will foment disturbances among ourselves, and make us parties to all their own quarrels."[100] As Madison recorded, on July 5 Gouverneur Morris pleaded for unity among the states and warned of foreign interference in its absence: "How far foreign powers would be ready to take part in the confusions [Morris] would not say. . . . He drew the melancholy picture of foreign intrusions as exhibited in the History of Germany, & urged it as a standing lesson to other nations."[101] Two days later, Morris repeated his theme of protecting the interests of the nation over that of the states. He bemoaned the fact that great objects of national interest had constantly been sacrificed to the concerns of the states without recognizing a number of potential dangers, including the possibility that the states might "give themselves up to foreign influence." He pointed once more to the example of Germany, where "foreign influence disturbs every internal operation."[102]

The mode of electing the president prompted discussion about foreign infiltration of the American electoral process. In his famous address to the delegates on June 18, Hamilton had warned that "one of the weak sides of Republics was their being liable to foreign influence and corruption." He urged the adoption of a system that would best resist this influence by encouraging "stability and permanency" in government, including the election of an executive for life.[103] On July 25, Madison warned that electing the chief executive by the national legislature would encourage foreign powers to "make use of the opportunity to mix their intrigues & influence with the Election." Madison believed that no expense would be spared to gain an appointment of an executive favorable to foreign interests. Poland and again Germany were cited as examples of nations "much influenced by foreign interference," the former having "slid entirely into foreign hands."[104] That same day, Pierce Butler of South Carolina warned that the important point to remember in electing a chief executive was to avoid "cabal at home, & influence from abroad."[105] Hugh Williamson of North Carolina echoed the prevailing sentiment that the election of the president by the legislature "opened a door for foreign influence."[106]

The creation of the electoral college was in part the result of this concern over clandestine foreign intervention in the American electoral process. Hamilton's defense of the electoral college found in *The Federalist*, No. 68, noted:

> Nothing was more to be desired, than that every practicable obstacle should be opposed to cabal, intrigue, and corruption. These most deadly adversaries of republican government might naturally have been expected to make their approaches from more than one quarter, but chiefly from the desire in foreign powers to gain an improper ascendant in our councils. How could they better gratify this, than by raising a creature of their own to the chief magistracy of the Union?[107]

The issue of eligibility requirements for members of the United States Senate sparked additional discussion of the problem of foreign penetration. On August 9, 1787, the focus of the convention debate was the problem of balancing the rights of talented immigrants who wished to pursue a career in public service with the need to prevent foreign powers from penetrating the higher reaches of American government. Once again, the prospect of foreign intervention was consistently repeated by participants in the debate, with Charles Pinckney and Pierce Butler urging the necessity of a long period of citizenship prior to eligibility for election to the Senate. James Madison resisted the idea of incorporating such restrictions directly into the Constitution, in part because it would give the document "a tincture of illiberality." However, Madison did not deny the probability of foreign efforts at penetration; he simply saw a greater chance of their "bribes" being expended not on "strangers," but on "men whose circumstances would rather stifle than excite jealousy & watchfulness in the public."[108]

The debate over eligibility for membership in the House further revealed the delegates' concern over foreign intervention, with Elbridge Gerry expressing these fears in a very blunt manner:

> Foreign powers will intermeddle in our affairs, and spare no expence to influence them. Persons having foreign attachments will be sent among us & insinuated into our councils, in order to be made instruments for their purposes. Every one knows the vast sums laid out in Europe for secret services.[109]

Throughout the debates, the danger of foreign interference led certain delegates to propose rigid measures to prevent foreign-born citizens from holding congressional office. Such stiff restrictions (such as limiting congressional office holders to native-born Americans) were generally resisted by Madison and Hamilton. It should be noted, however, that the two prominent founders did share many of the concerns expressed by Gerry, Morris, and Butler. One sees this clearly expressed in *The Federalist*. For instance, in No. 15, Hamilton warned of the weakness of offensive and defensive alliances as a substitute for union, where the states would be subject to jealousies and rivalries "nourished by the intrigues of foreign nations."[110] In *The Federalist*, No. 59, Hamilton made clear his expectation that as its strength increased, attempts to penetrate America's government would intensify:

> It ought never to be forgotten, that a firm Union of this country, under an efficient government, will probably be an increasing object of jealousy to more than one nation of Europe; and that enterprises to subvert it will sometimes originate in the intrigues of foreign powers, and will seldom fail to be patronised and abetted by some of them.[111]

Madison echoed these concerns at various points throughout *The Federalist*. He spoke in No. 43 of the dangers of insurrectionary forces receiving "secret succors from foreign powers."[112] He also defended the power of the national government to come to the assistance of states in rebellion that might experience "domestic violence" as a result of "the intrigues and influence of foreign powers."[113] Moreover, he defended the "prudent" compromise reached over senatorial eligibility, noting that a requirement of nine years of citizenship balanced the need to attract meritorious aliens with the necessity to block any "channel for foreign influence on the national councils."[114]

Along with concern over foreign penetration of the U.S. government, the Constitutional Convention and *The Federalist* also considered the role of an American intelligence capability to penetrate foreign governments. In *The Federalist*, No. 70, Hamilton made the case for an energetic executive, one possessing the ingredients of unity, duration, adequate provision for its support, and competent powers, capable of acting with "vigour and expedition."[115] In his discussion of a unified (single) executive, Hamilton noted that the exercise of executive power by one man would be characterized by "decision, activity, secrecy, and dispatch."[116] In a later essay, Hamilton argued against a role for the House in the treaty process by noting that body's lack of "decision, secrecy and dispatch."[117] The executive's role as envisioned by Hamilton might be interpreted to include control of intelligence operations, but nowhere is this intent more clearly stated than by John Jay in *The Federalist*, No. 64.

Jay built his argument for executive control of intelligence in an essay primarily concerned with the shared responsibility of the president and the Senate in the treaty process. In this essay, Jay contrasted the president's need to act quickly with the Senate's deliberative quality; he pointed out that the president was often forced to act out of necessity to capitalize on shifts in foreign affairs. In order to exploit and be in tune with these, a president needed sources who would inform him of these potential opportunities in international diplomacy. Jay commented:

> They who have turned their attention to the affairs of men, must have perceived that there are tides in them. Tides, very irregular in their duration, strength and direction, and seldom found to run twice exactly in the same manner or measure. To discern and profit by these tides in national affairs, is the business of those who preside over them; and they who have had much experience on this head inform us, that there frequently are occasions when days, nay even when hours are precious. . . . As in the field, so in the cabinet, there are moments to be seized as they pass, and they who preside in either, should be left in capacity to improve them.

Jay noted that opportunities had been missed under the Articles of Confederation due to the "want of secrecy and dispatch." To take advantage of these opportunities, a number of "preparatory measures" had to be undertaken, measures that had to be concealed and implemented quickly. These preparations were to be conducted under tight presidential control. Secrecy was essential to guarantee the free flow of information that was to alert the executive to the available opportunity. Presidential "dispatch" ensured that any occasion would be fully exploited. It was at this critical juncture that the president's control of the "business of intelligence" would be most vital. As Jay explained:

> There are cases where the most useful intelligence may be obtained, if the persons possessing it can be relieved from apprehensions of discovery. Those apprehensions will operate on those persons whether they are actuated by mercenary or friendly motives, and there doubtless are many of both descriptions, who would rely on the secrecy of the president, but who would not rely on the secrecy of the senate, and still less than that of a large popular assembly. The convention have done well therefore in so disposing of the power of making treaties, that although the president must in forming them act by the advice and consent of the senate, yet he will be able to manage the business of intelligence in such manner as prudence may suggest.[118]

It is this position that would guide the first administration to operate under the new Constitution, an administration whose foreign-policy underpinnings were designed by the three figures whose careers in intelligence we have just examined: Washington, Hamilton, and Jay. All three were guided by what Madison called "the lessons of practice."[119] As "practicing" political and military men of their day, they were immersed in events that forged their advocacy of executive control of the secret instruments of foreign policy.

Hamilton and Jay shared Washington's belief that "there are some Secrets, on the keeping of which so, depends, oftentimes, the salvation of an Army: Secrets which cannot, at least ought not to, be intrusted to paper; nay, which none but the Commander in Chief at the time, should be acquainted with."[120] All three men extended this principle to apply not only to the salvation of an army during wartime but to the permanent peacetime protection of the nation they founded. This principle became a working part of the American government with the advent of the so-called secret service or Contingency Fund in 1790, recounted in the next chapter.

This is not to say that they eagerly embraced the often harsh methods required to conduct intelligence activity. They appear to have bemoaned the necessity to employ measures that stretched their sense of decency to the limit. Washington and Hamilton were aware that the price of nation-hood carried certain costs that would test a people's "moral rectitude." As America emerged as a nation on the world scene, dealing with the Old World powers would lead it down paths many wished it did not have to travel. Years later, a representative of the new nation sent to Napoleon's government was greeted with a fitting welcome: "You have come to a very corrupt world."[121]

The Contingency Fund

[I]f a desire was felt that any subject should be bruted about
in every corner of the United States, should become the topic
of universal discussion, nothing more was necessary than to
close the doors of the Senate chamber, and make it the object
of secret, confidential deliberation.

Senator (and future secretary of state)
JOHN FORSYTH of Georgia, *1831*[1]

∎ The creation of the Contingency Fund reflected a desire on the
part of the new nation to codify practices established during the
struggle for independence. The importance Washington placed
on secret agents during the Revolutionary War was later reflected in his
inclusion of a request for a secret fund in his first annual message to
Congress. In acceding to Washington's request, the First Congress gave
the executive a discretionary fund capable of providing him with the
financial resources needed to conduct intelligence operations. (However,
much of this fund was actually devoted to the facilitation of traditional
diplomatic functions.) A stable fund at the executive's disposal would
prevent the problem of erratic funding that had haunted Washington
throughout all his wartime operations. This chapter examines a period
from 1790 to 1831, during which the Contingency Fund was established
and became an important tool for presidential control of foreign-policy
making.

From its lowly origin in 1790, the Contingency Fund was understood to
be available, at least in part, for "secret services." A close reading of what

little congressional debate took place over the fund—and reaction to various early missions—reveals wide understanding that it could legitimately provide for those services necessary to facilitate the acquisition of intelligence. A capability was needed outside the established diplomatic corps for a variety of secret functions to the executive branch.

The Contingency Fund, according to Edward S. Corwin, uniquely demonstrates the notion of the president's prerogative in the field of foreign relations.[2] The fund was enacted into law on July 1, 1790, and was often referred to as the "secret fund," though its official title was "The Contingent Fund of Foreign Intercourse."[3] The initial budget allotment was $40,000, and by its third year of existence it had grown to $1 million—or 12 percent of the entire federal budget at the time.[4] Congress granted the president a great amount of discretion; the bill allowed him simply to acknowledge that he had spent the money but did not require that he state for what purpose or to whom the money was sent. According to Abraham Sofaer, "The President could therefore hire special agents, or pay for secrets, or support other sensitive activities without revealing his conduct."[5]

As part of his first annual address, on January 8, 1790, President Washington personally appealed to the First Congress to create the fund. The president noted that the interests of the United States required the facilitation of "intercourse with other nations." Accordingly, "a competent fund designated for defraying the expenses incident to the conduct of our foreign affairs" was required.[6] The president's request was directed by the House to a committee chaired by Congressman Theodore Sedgwick of Massachusetts. The following account is a summation of the main points in the House discussion as found in the *Annals of Congress*. The debate took place over a period of three days: January 19, 26, and 27, 1790.

Debates over the Bill

January 19, 1790

The significance of these early debates can be seen in the timeless nature of the questions raised regarding the appropriate scope of presidential discretion in appointing foreign agents.[7] The propriety of granting a blank check to the president for unnamed diplomatic appointments was the major focus of debate. Washington clearly requested an open-ended commitment of funds for future exigencies; nonetheless, the House resolution forming Sedgwick's committee apparently called instead for compensation for only those already employed in the diplomatic corps. This confusion led Sedgwick and at least three other House members to request that the secretary of state come before the House and clarify matters (I have uncovered no evidence that John Jay actually appeared before the House).[8]

As debate began on January 19, Congressman White supported the idea of granting the executive latitude to appoint foreign service officers.[9] White thought it might be "necessary to send ambassadors extraordinary to foreign nations." This could be best facilitated by giving the president a "general provision" to compensate designated individuals without delay.[10] Congressman Smith echoed this viewpoint by stating that it was not the province of the House to determine "when and where" foreign representatives should be sent.[11] The House should simply decide in a general way whether salaries and expenses should be appropriated. It would be the Senate and the executive who would make specific decisions to deploy them "on any occasion where they thought them necessary."[12] Roger Sherman disagreed with this limited understanding of the House's role in foreign-affairs appointments.[13] He thought it highly appropriate for the House to designate exactly how many ministers should be employed abroad. Congressman White reiterated his belief that emergencies might arise requiring swift executive action. These emergencies might occur before the legislature could convene to meet the crisis; hence, the swift dispatch of foreign envoys should be an executive function. Congressman Jackson stated that the president potentially could be embarrassed over the discretionary power given him to provide different levels of compensation to foreign envoys.[14] If Congress preordained the offices and amounts of compensation, the president would avoid having to make difficult choices.

Congressman Lee, a member of Sedgwick's committee, believed the president's request to be a general one and urged the House to act on this basis.[15] The request was for a fund to compensate persons "who may hereafter be employed in such [foreign] intercourse."[16] Lee then suggested that Sedgwick's committee respond to the president's request as he understood it, and the motion was adopted. The House had moved toward granting the president a generous amount of flexibility in appointing and controlling executive agents.

January 26, 1790

The House resumed debate on January 26, 1790, when it resolved itself into a committee of the whole. Sedgwick's committee had recommended a general appropriation that would allow for a broad grant of presidential latitude in deciding when and where to appoint executive agents. The House immediately adopted a proposal to make this an annual appropriation. However, many House members continued to express uneasiness over a broad grant of executive authority.

Congressman Lee believed that the appropriation could not be drawn on exclusively by the president, but only with the consent of the Senate as well. Congressman Smith objected that this restriction would diminish executive responsibility—that in the absence of an explicit constitutional prohibition, the "principle of expediency" necessitated presidential control.[17] Congressman Stone countered with a repetition of Lee's argument that the Senate should consent to any presidential action relating to intercourse with a foreign nation.[18] Congressman Huntington, expressing some frustration, argued that the subject had been debated in the course of the Sedgwick committee's deliberations and that it "was determined to vest the discretionary power in the president alone."[19] Huntington urged that circumstances (such as the Senate's being in recess) dictated that decisions in this area be left to the president.[20]

Congressman Sedgwick rose to state that to "diffuse" the authority to draw on the Contingency Fund weakened responsibility, if it did not destroy it altogether. Congressman Lawrence believed that the question focused entirely on the principle of expediency and that this was reflected in the content of the committee's bill.[21] Stone repeated his concern over the amount of discretion granted a president in disposing of public money and the perpetual nature of the expenses that he "hoped at some day would be found to be unnecessary."[22] Roger Sherman believed that the Constitution had given the Senate "joint" powers with the president for conducting foreign business; thus the bill giving the president sole discretionary power deviated from the principles of the Constitution.[23] Congressman Smith took note of the variety of duties that foreign agents may undertake; in a veiled reference to agents sent for intelligence purposes, he remarked that "many officers may be established in the diplomatic line without being concerned with making treaties" and continued that "the Constitution does not appear to trust that equal confidence in the Senate; for it gives the President the first and greatest influence."[24] A grant of this discretionary power, Smith claimed, was "absolutely necessary" for the execution of presidential responsibility.[25] James Madison stated his belief that the president "alone" could better perform the function under consideration than if he were "connected with a large body."[26] As debate was to finish for the day, Congressman Benson echoed Madison in stating that it was wrong to "blend" the Senate's powers with the president's.[27] The question under consideration was one of an executive nature.[28]

January 27, 1790

As debate resumed, Congressman Jackson voiced his belief that the House possessed the authority to place the discretionary power to disperse funds where it pleased. He proposed in this instance to give it to the House.[29] He feared that a grant of this power to one individual might lead to pressure in the future to grant this same person additional arbitrary power. At this point, a seemingly frustrated Congressman Boudinot expressed his view that the debate to that point had answered a recurring point of contention: the president, and the president alone, possessed discretionary power over expenditures for foreign envoys.[30] Congressman Scott tried to remind his colleagues that the focus of the debate did not concern who had the power to fix salary grades for diplomatic agents but whether discretionary power could be surrendered by the House to another body. Scott restated his belief that the expenditure of public moneys was strictly a legislative function; the Constitution was clear on this point.[31]

Congressman Smith argued that precedent already existed for the president unilaterally to dispatch and compensate envoys. He stated that it would be "improper to notice very particularly" the exact nature of this mission.[32] (Smith was possibly referring to the mission of Gouverneur Morris to London on October 13, 1789. However, diplomatic historian Henry Wriston states that Congress was not formally notified of the Morris mission until February 14, 1791. Either the Morris mission had already been revealed to some members of Congress, or Smith was referring to an as yet unknown case. The Morris mission established a number of precedents bearing on the subject of presidential control of secret foreign operatives. Washington went ahead and dispatched Morris without prior congressional notification and committed his administration to paying $2,000 without any congressional funds designated for such a purpose. As Henry Wriston notes, this demonstrated the "independent origin of the practice of sending agents.")[33]

Congressman Jackson repeated his contention that the House could lodge discretionary power anywhere it saw fit and that this power best belonged in the hands of the House. He left the door open to the possibility of giving this power to the president when future circumstances might demand it. Congressman Lawrence acknowledged potential "injustices" if the House attempted to fix with precision the salaries of all foreign agents, on the one hand, and granted a blank check to the president, on the other. Congressman Scott had the last word on the subject before the bill was adopted by the House: money for "secret services" could properly be allocated by the House with a degree of precision that the proponents of the Sedgwick bill seemed to ignore. He was confident of the ability of the House to act wisely in retaining its power to specifically appropriate funds for executive agents. At the end of this day, the House voted down Congressman Lee's amendment to require "the advice and consent of the Senate" for the appointment of executive agents.[34]

Passage of the Bill: Spring–Summer 1790

The course of the bill so aptly described by Congressman Scott as a secret service fund becomes difficult to follow after this point due to the rules of secrecy observed by the Senate. Yet a few bits of information are discernible. The Senate received formal notification from the House on April 30, 1790, of the passage of a bill providing the means of intercourse between the United States and foreign nations.[35] The bill was read for a second time on the floor of the Senate on May 3 and for a third time on May 26.[36] After this second reading, the Senate committee, apparently under the leadership of Caleb Strong,[37] appears to have voted to amend the bill by reducing the appropriation from $40,000 to $30,000.[38] On May 28, 1790, the House informed the Senate that it disagreed with the Senate amendment. The Senate then requested a conference committee meeting with the House and appointed as its conference managers Senators King, Read, and Izard.[39]

The conference committee managers for the Senate reported completion of negotiations with the House on June 23, with the senators apparently conceding to the will of the House on the major points of contention. Senate manager Rufus King reported that the House request for $40,000 would remain intact. Additional adjustments that were made in the conference committee meetings concerned maximum allowable amounts of compensation for regular diplomatic corps members, with the House again preferring a larger expenditure.[40] The Senate consented to the conference committee report on that day, though Senator William Maclay of Pennsylvania registered his dissent in his journal:

> The Intercourse bill . . . had been referred to a committee of conference so long ago that I had forgotton it, but the thing was neither dead nor sleeping. . . . The report increased the salaries and added ten thousand dollars to the appropriations. . . . The whole appropriation was $40,000, and they were voted with an air of perfect indifference by the affirmants, although I consider the money as worse than thrown away, for I know not a single thing that we have for a minister to do at a single court in Europe. Indeed, the less we have to do with them the better.

Maclay went on to state that the bill was "well spoken against."[41]

On July 1, 1790, "an Act providing the means of intercourse between the United States and foreign nations" became law. The act entitled the president, on his own, to spend a sum not exceeding $40,000 annually for the support of persons who served the United States in foreign parts and for any expenses incident to their business. The law provided that the president account for those expenditures that "in his judgement may be made public."[42] In essence, the president was granted an exemption from one of Congress's most impressive powers: the oversight of expenditures. By simply filing a "certificate" that should "be deemed a sufficient voucher for the sum or sums therein expressed to have been expended," the president could avoid a specific accounting of the activities of executive agents.[43]

Two Early Missions

The Washington administration wasted little time in dispatching agents to Europe both to gather intelligence and to engage in secret diplomacy. As noted, before the approval of the Contingency Fund, Washington had sent Gouverneur Morris to London. On August 11, 1790, six weeks after the approval of the Contingency Fund, the president dispatched David Humphreys to Portugal and Spain.

The Mission of Gouverneur Morris

The Morris mission was an attempt to measure British attitudes toward the new American government and perhaps indirectly to pressure Spain to show some flexibility toward American designs on western lands.[44] Washington's instructions to Morris urged him to conduct himself with "delicacy" in discovering the "Sentiments and Intentions" of the royal court at London. He believed that it was "most expedient to have these Inquiries made informally, by a private Agent."[45] Washington was uncomfortable with his direct role in ordering this mission but eager to have it proceed without delay: "This Communication ought regularly to be made to you by the Secretary of State, but that Office not being at present filled, my Desire of avoiding Delays induces me to make it under my own Hand."[46] On this day, October 13, 1789, Washington dispatched three letters to Morris and received one dated July 31 from him, at the time based in Dieppe, France. In his capacity as Washington's eyes and ears in Europe, Morris obtained intelligence on conditions inside Revolutionary France. Morris wrote in the July 31 letter, "I . . . send some Tables which contains the political military pecuniary and commercial State of this Country. I believe them to be tolerably authentic, as far as they go."[47]

Morris was eventually paid for his services in two separate payments of $1,000 taken from the Contingency Fund.[48] The mission was long completed when Congress was formally notified of Morris's secret undertaking on February 14, 1791.[49] Not everyone in Congress was impressed. One senator, William Maclay, expressed some blunt misgivings about the techniques employed by the new government's first intelligence gatherer: "He [Morris] has acted in a strange kind of capacity, half pimp, half envoy, or perhaps more properly a kind of political eavesdropper about the British Court, for sometime past."[50]

Abraham Sofaer has documented the "two-track" communication that existed between Washington and Morris. Establishing a precedent that would become something of a hallmark of presidential contact with executive agents, Washington and Morris maintained formal communication through the secretary of state's office while engaging in "private" correspondence of a more "detailed" nature free from congressional oversight. Despite Washington's disclaimer that Morris should deal with him through the secretary of state's office, Sofaer notes that "numerous [private] letters" continued back and forth between these two men, letters that "were invariably withheld from transmittals to Congress." Those missives sent to the secretary of state's office were generally bland, formal pronouncements of official events that were routinely forwarded to Congress.[51] Not only were congressional overseers locked out by this method of communication, but the Department of State and the secretary himself were often "out of the loop."

The Mission of Colonel David Humphreys

The journey of David Humphreys to Lisbon and Madrid in 1790 took place under an unusual amount of secrecy. Humphreys was no stranger to covert missions and intelligence gathering. As one of General Washington's key staff officers during the Revolution, Humphreys often had been called on to conduct clandestine operations. His most daring escapade took place on Christmas Day 1780, when he led a team seeking to kidnap two British generals.[52] Ten years later, President Washington asked him to undertake a delicate mission to preserve American neutrality in what appeared to be a coming confrontation between Britain and Spain. The goal of American policy was to play these two nations off each other in order to obtain access to the Mississippi from Spain and a favorable commercial treaty with England.[53]

Secretary of State Jefferson's instructions to Humphreys emphasized the confidential nature of the mission. In a letter to Humphreys dated August 11, 1790, Jefferson ordered Humphreys to rendezvous with Gouverneur Morris in London before heading to Lisbon, for the purpose of "communicating to us from thence any interesting public intelligence you may be able to obtain, and then take as early a passage as possible to Lisbon."[54] Jefferson emphasized the importance of concealing the true purpose of the Humphreys visit: "Thro' the whole of this business it will be best that you avoid all suspicion of being on any public business."[55] It was also suggested that, if necessary, Humphreys conceal the true nature of his mission to Madrid from Portuguese authorities. The Portuguese minister of foreign affairs, Chevalier Pinto, "need not know of your journey to Madrid, or if it be necessary, he may be made to understand that it is a journey of curiousity to fill up the interval between writing your letters and receiving the answers."[56] In fact, Humphreys was meeting the American chargé d'affaires, William Carmichael. Humphreys was to deliver letters and papers containing "special matters" for Carmichael's perusal. Jefferson warned Humphreys to maintain proper cover throughout his journey: "To every other person it will be best that you appear as a private traveller."[57]

Colonel Humphreys was apparently less than effective in concealing his true identity and expressed his concern in letters written to Washington and Jefferson. On October 28, Humphreys wrote to Jefferson that his presence in England prior to his departure for Lisbon had generated some curiosity; patrons in a coffeehouse had raised his name repeatedly "with speculations on the cause of my coming here at this time."[58] To Washington, he wrote that despite his efforts to keep clear of "all appearances of curious enquiry or mysterious reserve . . . somebody has written to Paris, describing a person, once a Colonel, in the American Army, as now employed here in intrigues relative to the Spanish War."[59] When the crisis between Britain and Spain eased, the sense of urgency over Humphreys's secret mission evaporated. However, Washington went on to appoint him the permanent minister at the royal court in Lisbon.[60]

Congress was formally notified of the Humphreys mission on February 18, 1791. Once again, Senator William Maclay expressed his discontent over this unilateral assertion of executive authority: "The President sends first and asks our advice and consent afterward." Henry Wriston states that there is no evidence indicating that Maclay's dissatisfaction was shared by other senators; this conclusion is obviously difficult to prove, since the Senate operated in secrecy and few senators kept journals similar to Maclay's. However, if we believe Maclay's statement that approval of the Contingency Fund was "well spoken against," then the Morris and Humphreys missions may well have generated an audible level of congressional disaffection.[61]

Hamilton and the Contingency Fund

Another important event related to the early history of the Contingency Fund occurred during the administration of President John Adams (1797–1801). At the time of the undeclared naval war with France from 1798 to 1799, President Adams appointed Alexander Hamilton as inspector general of the U.S. Army. This office placed him second in command to Washington, who was called back to duty by Adams to prepare for war with the French. Hamilton approached the impending crisis with his characteristic aggressive style, attempting with limited resources and little time to improve American military preparedness.[62]

In a letter most likely written in January 1799, Hamilton urged the immediate adoption of a series of measures designed to put the nation on a war footing. The letter, apparently circulated to the Adams cabinet and leading Federalists, called for an increase in the Contingency Fund budget: "It is essential the Executive should have half a million of secret service money. If the measure cannot be carried without it, the expenditure may be with the approbation of three members of each house of Congress. But twere better without this incumbrance."[63] The crisis between the United States and France eventually dissipated when Adams, over the objections of the "High Federalists," sent negotiators to Paris to arrange an accord. Yet Hamilton's plea for secret service funds is another example of the importance the founding generation placed on secret agents as essential factors in the achievement of American foreign-policy objectives.

Two Important Debates

The Contingency Fund generated little congressional debate or reaction for twenty-three years following its initial approval.[64] Presidential authority to withhold specific justification for expenditures was routinely approved for those cases where the executive deemed public exposure detrimental to the national interest.

Two debates did occur some thirteen years apart that shed some light on congressional attitudes toward the use of secret agents. The first took place in March 1818; the second, in February 1831.[65] Both debates revolved around the issue of presidential appointment powers during Senate recess and sought to clarify the line between "public" ministers and "private" agents, the latter being entirely at the president's disposal and often operating in secret from both the nation to which they were dispatched and the Congress. The question of Senate confirmation for those individuals who straddled this line generated intense discussion. An examination of these debates reveals congressional attitude toward these "private" agents and the amount of discretion given to the executive to direct their activities.

March 1818

In March 1818, some twenty-nine years after Morris had been sent to Britain, Speaker of the House and future secretary of state Henry Clay attacked the Monroe administration for the manner in which it had dispatched a mission to South America. A delegation consisting of Caesar Rodney, John Graham, and Theodorick Bland had been instructed to travel to Buenos Aires on a fact-finding mission and then to proceed to Chile if they deemed it appropriate. The mission was conducted in a very public manner with widespread newspaper coverage prior to the group's departure.[66]

In the course of what appears to have been a partisan attack on the mission, Speaker Clay gave a rousing defense of the Contingency Fund and the use of secret agents. While rebuking the Monroe administration, Clay provided another indication of the early political consensus that existed regarding presidential control over the appointment and direction of secret agents. Clay criticized the administration for believing it could acquire accurate information by dispatching three prominent citizens whose appointment was announced in the newspapers and "made known to the whole world."[67] Clay believed that this absence of secrecy meant that the envoys would be fed misleading data and prevented from "getting correct information of the real condition of things."[68] A successful mission could not be achieved with the object known in advance, for the arts of "deception and imposition" would prevent access to the truth. Clay then proceeded to give his definition of the qualities needed for successful intelligence gathering: "The proper course to have adopted was to despatch an individual unknown to all parties; some intelligent, keen, silent, and observing man, of pleasing address and insinuating manners, who, concealing the object of his visit, would see and hear everything, and report it faithfully."[69]

Clay then shifted the emphasis of his attack and in the process revealed his understanding of broad presidential control of the Contingency Fund, essentially viewing it as a presidential blank check. Clay stated that Monroe should have utilized the Contingency Fund (at this time budgeted at $50,000 annually), which was "confided to his discretion." The president was entitled to spend from this fund "without rendering to Congress any account of it." Furthermore, the purpose of such an expenditure "would not have been a proper subject for inquiry" on the part of the Congress.[70] Clay went on to say that he did not want to make further issue of the mission but wished to register his protest.

The administration's position was defended in a somewhat remarkable argument by Congressman John Forsyth, who stated that a public mission provided protection to the agents for what would normally be a risky undertaking.[71] An agent operating in secret might otherwise be "thrown into a dungeon."[72] Moreover, Forsyth believed that the use of secret service funds might have been proper in this case, though further appropriation would have been necessary due to the expensive nature of the mission. Congress would have had to approve a doubling of the Contingency Fund budget while the administration concealed the rationale for such a request. Critical of Clay's position, Forsyth nevertheless revealed what seems to have been the dominant understanding of the purpose of the Contingency Fund: the employment of spies. Forsyth asked, "Would the House have been willing to vote an addition to the secret service fund, for what might have been considered the employment of spies throughout the world?" It was better in this instance for the executive to proceed in an "open and frank manner."[73]

The abiding lesson from this debate came from Speaker Clay, who endorsed a broad interpretation of presidential control of a secret service fund. The position was not contested by Forsyth, whose objections to Clay's opinion were based solely on notions of what was expedient for the mission being discussed. In fact, in a later debate on a similar issue, Forsyth described the Contingency Fund—in terms resembling Clay's—as "that fund which was entrusted to the absolute discretion of the President."[74]

February 1831

The second debate took place in February 1831, with John Forsyth, now a U.S. senator, leading the discussion. Once again, a dispute over the status of the Senate's role in confirming treaty negotiators generated discussion about the Contingency Fund and the purposes for which it could be employed. The debate occurred in response to a newly completed treaty between the United States and Turkey. In this debate, clear congressional understanding is evident concerning the use of the Contingency Fund as a resource for intelligence activities. Senator Forsyth opened the debate by recounting his clash with Henry Clay in 1818 and then stated his belief in absolute presidential discretion over the Contingency Fund. Forsyth explained his rationale in supporting a broad grant of authority, focusing on the chronic inability of Congress to keep secrets. In a final note of frustration, Forsyth noted that "the art of keeping state secrets is no better understood now than it formerly was."[75]

In the course of this debate, executive agents were often referred to as spies. This was not simply sloppy use of language, but reflected the common understanding of their purpose.[76] One senator, Littleton Tazewell of Virginia, understood the Contingency Fund to exist solely for the purpose of paying spies. Forsyth saw the fund as a broader resource for presidential foreign-policy making, including the payment of secret treaty negotiators. While justifying the use of the Contingency Fund for diplomatic missions, Forsyth characterized foreign envoys as "privileged spies, sent abroad to lie for the benefit of their country." Forsyth rejected Tazewell's limitation of the fund to espionage activities alone, though he also noted the importance of that purpose. The Contingency Fund was created "for all purposes to which a secret service fund should or could be applied for the public benefit. For spies, if the gentlemen pleases." These persons, operating at times under cover, sought important political and commercial information, felt the "pulse" of foreign governments, and carried confidential correspondence to American envoys. Forsyth stated that frequent use had been made of this fund, for both open and covert purposes, with its importance never doubted. He felt he could not properly discuss specific examples, but insisted on pointing out its repeated utilization.[77]

The debate proceeded to a discussion of the propriety of using executive agents for services closely related to traditional diplomatic functions. For our purposes, it is not necessary to examine those questions. What is striking from this debate and the previous one is the agreement that existed over the Contingency Fund as a presidential spy fund. Disputes over the fund arose when presidents used it to compensate agents involved in treaty negotiations, an act viewed as an abuse of power by many senators anxious to protect that body's "advice and consent" responsibility. From the debate over the Sedgwick bill to the one in February 1831, the question of using the Contingency Fund for those "traditional" diplomatic functions concerned both the House and the Senate. To a modern reader of the debates, the degree of congressional acquiescence to total presidential control over the Contingency Fund as an espionage resource is of interest. Although Senator William Maclay and opponents to the Sedgwick bill expressed misgivings in the early confrontations, the fund seems to have been widely and routinely accepted as an appropriate tool for an energetic executive. By the 1830s, if one reads closely enough between the lines, the fund appears to have been regularly utilized in a manner suited to the more Byzantine aspects of foreign relations.

4 ■

Options Short of War

Thomas Jefferson's

Clandestine Foreign Policy

> All nations have found it necessary, that for the advantageous
> conduct of their affairs, some of these [executive] proceed-
> ings, at least, should remain known to their executive func-
> tionary only.
>
> THOMAS JEFFERSON to GEORGE HAY, *June 17, 1807*[1]

The presidency of Thomas Jefferson (1801–1809) provides a
classic case study in the broad exercise of executive control over
clandestine activity. Jefferson believed that the president alone
had the authority to make the difficult but often necessary decision to
employ surreptitious means to further American interests abroad. Those
seeking evidence of an alternative tradition in the American experience,
one emphasizing strict congressional oversight of clandestine operations
and an aversion to executive secrecy, will find an examination of the
Jefferson presidency a discouraging experience.

Thomas Jefferson served as an American envoy to France (1784–1789)
and secretary of state (1790–1794) before becoming president of the
United States. While holding those positions, Jefferson authorized a variety of missions designed to acquire information on the activities of foreign
governments; in a number of instances, he authorized covert operations

intended to influence the internal workings of those governments. Jefferson stretched the outer limits of his presidential power by authorizing a diverse range of covert activities, including bribing foreign leaders, toppling a foreign government, and providing indirect but tangible assistance to an insurgency designed to remove the Old World powers from the North American continent.

An examination of the clandestine activities of the Jefferson era raises basic questions about the propriety of secret operations undertaken by a democratic polity. Although opposed in principle to the idea of "intermeddling" in the domestic affairs of other nations, Jefferson occasionally overcame his scruples. What might appear at first glance to be an example of hypocrisy was actually a reflection of Jefferson's sincere belief that there was no distinction between the interests of the United States and those of liberty itself. His zealous devotion to the American experiment led Jefferson to countenance clandestine operations that other Founders, perhaps less convinced of America's unique role in the world, might have rejected. For Jefferson, the line between his enlightened New World and the uncivilized Old World was starkly drawn. When dealing with those on the other side of the line, he was capable of authorizing activities that he would not tolerate within his own political order. More often than not, he went right to the edge of this boundary and stopped, but on occasion he crossed it and went to great lengths to conceal his actions, particularly for the benefit of democratic opinion at home. All these actions were legitimate, Jefferson believed, and intended to hasten the day when new nations and peoples could be brought into the world of democratic enlightenment.

Revolutionary Beginnings and Clandestine Diplomacy

Thomas Jefferson's wartime clandestine activity was minor in comparison with that of contemporaries like Hamilton, Washington, and Jay. His primary contribution to the American intelligence effort lay in the area of propaganda and psychological warfare. For instance, one accusation Jefferson leveled against George III in the Declaration of Independence referred to the use of "large armies of foreign mercenaries to compleat the works of death, desolation and tyranny, already begun with circumstances of cruelty and perfidy." Conclusive evidence of the arrangement between George III and various German princes to provide manpower for the Revolutionary struggle was obtained by an American prisoner of war who had spent time in captivity in England and managed to acquire copies of the British–Hessian agreements. The documents reached American authorities in May 1776, in time for Jefferson to refer to the definitive evidence of George III's "perfidy" in the Declaration. During this period, Jefferson was appointed to a congressional committee that was asked to "extract and publish the [British–Hessian] treaties . . . to consider of an adequate reward for the person who brought the intelligence; and to prepare an address to the foreign mercenaries who are coming to invade America." Jefferson followed up this effort by authoring propaganda addresses to Hessian soldiers, urging them to desert their army in exchange for a reward of land offered by American authorities.[2]

Jefferson's other wartime intelligence function consisted of his membership on the Committee on Spies, whose members were asked by the Continental Congress "to consider what is proper to be done with persons giving intelligence to the enemy or supplying them with provisions." In August 1776, the Continental Congress responded to the committee's proposals and enacted the nation's first espionage act, which recommended the death penalty for foreigners convicted of espionage:

> Resolved, That all persons not members of, nor owing allegiance to, any of the United States of America . . . who shall be found lurking as spies in or about the fortifications or encampments of the armies of the United States . . . shall suffer death, according to the law and usage of nations, by sentence of a court martial, or such other punishment as such court martial may direct.[3]

Thomas Jefferson's postwar career as an American diplomat exposed him to the world of European power politics and demonstrated to him the benefits that could accrue from secret operations. Although the bulk of his time as minister to France was spent in the normal course of diplomatic activity, there were a few incidents that testify to Jefferson's belief in the utility of clandestine operations. At that early stage in his political career, Jefferson already had his eyes on the expansion of the United States, to the point where he covertly sought to acquire a map of South America commissioned by the Spanish government. He wrote about the incident:

> The Government of Spain at first permitted the map, but the moment they saw one of them come out, they destroyed the plates, seized all of the few copies which had got out and on which they could lay their hands, and issued the severest injunctions to call in the rest and to prevent their going abroad. Some few copies escaped their search. A friend has by good management procured me one, and it is arrived safe through all the searches that travellers are submitted to.[4]

In addition to acquiring the secret map, Jefferson obtained intelligence that the Spanish government had commissioned a study examining the prospects for a canal through the Isthmus of Panama. Jefferson prodded the American envoy in Madrid, William Carmichael, to obtain a copy of the survey. Carmichael was deeply involved in diplomatic intrigue in Madrid and was in a position to acquire the confidential report. Jefferson wrote to Carmichael: "With respect to the isthmus of Panama I am assured by Burgoine (who would not chuse to be named however) that a survey was made, that a canal appeared very practicable, and that the idea was suppressed for political reasons altogether. He has seen and minutely examined the report." Jefferson went on to add that the report "is to me a vast desideratum for reasons political and philosophical." Unfortunately for Jefferson, Carmichael was unable to obtain the survey.[5]

Jefferson's access to confidential material of the Spanish government was exceeded only by his knowledge of the inner workings of the Dutch government. He utilized the talents of Charles W. F. Dumas, an early defender of the American Revolution who cultivated a relationship with a prominent Dutch newspaper editor. Dumas used this relationship to plant stories favorable to American interests. In addition, he provided Jefferson with information acquired from within the Dutch government. Jefferson referred to this access in a letter written to James Monroe: "[W]ould it not be worth while to continue the agency of Dumas? . . . He is undoubtedly in the confidence of some one who has a part in the Dutch government, & who seems to allow him to communicate to us."[6]

Jefferson's reputation as a "revolutionary" drew to Paris believers from Mexico and Brazil seeking American support for independence movements in their nations. Although Jefferson kept these revolutionaries at arm's length, he had an ingenious way of walking a very fine line between promising direct U.S. involvement and offering indirect assistance and encouragement. In one instance, Jefferson urged a Brazilian revolutionary to persist in his cause and held out the prospect of assistance from private American citizens. Jefferson wrote Foreign Affairs Secretary John Jay:

> I took care to impress on him thro' the whole of our conversation that I had neither instructions nor authority to say a word to any body on this subject, and that I could only give him my own ideas as a single individual: which were that we were not in a condition *at present* [emphasis added] to meddle nationally in any war. . . . That yet a successful revolution in Brasil could not be uninteresting to us. That prospects of lucre might possibly draw numbers of individuals to their aid. . . . That our citizens, being free to leave their own country individually without the consent of their governments, are equally free to go to any other.

Jefferson noted in the same letter to Jay that he acted with caution while meeting a Mexican revolutionary. He suspected he was being lured into a trap, observing that "this gentleman was intimate at the Spanish Ambassador's" and though he appeared to be a man of candor, "that can be borrowed."[7]

Jefferson's interest in the prospects for Brazilian independence from Portugal persisted throughout his political career. During his later tenure as secretary of state, he pushed David Humphreys, his envoy in Lisbon, to procure all the available intelligence "as to the strength, riches, resources, lights and dispositions of Brazil. The jealousy of the court of

Lisbon on this subject will of course inspire you with due caution in making and communicating these inquiries."[8]

Jefferson's most pressing concern in Paris was not the fate of distant revolutionary movements but the activities of the European powers on the North American continent. He anxiously monitored the exploratory missions of the European powers probing the vast American wilderness. In one case, Jefferson ordered Captain John Paul Jones to spy on the French explorer Jean-François de Galoup, Comte de La Pérouse, who he feared was undertaking a mission to establish a French settlement on the west coast of North America. Jefferson wrote to Jay:

> You have doubtless seen in the papers that this court was sending two vessels into the South sea, under the conduct of Capt. Peyrouse. They give out that the object is merely for the improvement of our knowledge of that part of the globe. . . . Their loading however as detailed in conversations and some other circumstances appeared to me to indicate some other design. . . . Capt. Paul Jones being at l'Orient, within a day's journey of Brest, where Capt. Peyrouse's vessels lay, I desired him if he could not satisfy himself at l'Orient of the nature of this equipment that he would go to Brest for that purpose: conducting himself so as to excite no suspicion that we attended at all to this expedition. His discretion can be relied on.[9]

Not content to let the European powers have the upper hand in exploring unchartered North America, Jefferson sponsored the expedition of an adventurer named John Ledyard, whose goal was to travel across the Russian Empire and eventually reach the American Northwest. The expedition was derailed by Ledyard's arrest by the police of Catherine the Great, two hundred miles short of the Pacific Ocean.[10]

As secretary of state, Jefferson was in a position to direct the instruments of secret diplomacy, particularly through the use of the Contingency Fund. Jefferson urged the first American agents sent abroad, particularly Humphreys in August 1790 (Chapter 3), to employ secret communications and false cover to enhance their prospects for successful information gathering. Although he was not part of the administration when Washington submitted his proposal for the creation of the Contingency Fund in January 1790, Jefferson did play a part in later congressional action regarding the secret funds. For example, in a December 1792 letter to Washington, Jefferson suggested an amendment to the Foreign Intercourse bill that would reinforce the president's ability to conceal operations funded by the Foreign Intercourse Act of 1790. Payments made by the president under the authority of the act "for all such parts thereof as in his judgment may be made public to the Auditor of the U.S. and for all other parts, to such person as he shall appoint, prescribing for their government, in every case, such rules as the nature of the case shall in his opinion require."[11]

During his tenure as secretary of state, Jefferson began to lay the groundwork for a number of clandestine operations aimed at the Barbary pirates, conflict with the Indian nations, and the acquisition of territory bordering on what was then the southwestern United States.

Insurgents and Espionage: Jefferson's Territorial Expansion

Henry Adams stated that Jefferson's "greed for land equalled that of any settler on the border."[12] Despite Adams's hyperbole, there is no question that Jefferson engaged in tough diplomacy to enlarge the territory of the United States and that he utilized the resources of secret agents to assist in that effort. Jefferson's designs focused on the vast American West; and although he possessed a genuine interest in the scientific benefits of exploration, he placed even greater value on the political benefits to the United States of the exploration and ultimate acquisition of that territory. Some of his more noteworthy exploratory undertakings, such as the Lewis and Clark expedition, had an intelligence component that was as important to Jefferson as the discovery of new species of flora and fauna and unknown geographical wonders.

As early as 1791, Jefferson had thought to acquire Florida from Spain, preferably without resorting to war. He found the perfect solution that would deliver Florida to the United States while screening from view the American government's involvement in the acquisition. The Spanish governor had invited foreigners to settle in the territory, and many of the takers were American debtors fleeing their creditors. Jefferson was not pleased with that development but hoped to exploit the opening that Spain had given the United States. Jefferson wrote to Washington:

> I wish a hundred thousand of our inhabitants would accept the invitation. It will be the means of delivering to us peaceably, what may otherwise cost us a war. In the mean time we may complain of this seduction of our inhabitants just enough to make them believe we think it very wise policy for them, and confirm them in it.[13]

As secretary of state, Jefferson also ensured that the United States would provide a safe haven for revolutionaries escaping Spanish authorities. While negotiating a treaty with Spain in 1792—a treaty that included provisions for the mutual delivery of fugitives from justice— Jefferson made a strong exception for the return of "strugglers against tyranny" who fled to the United States. Jefferson told his chief negotiators:

> The unsuccessful strugglers against tyranny, have been the chief martyrs of treason laws in all countries. Reformation of government with our neighbors, being as much wanted now as reformation of religion is . . . we should not wish then, to give up to the executioner, the patriot who fails and flees to us.[14]

Both these examples demonstrate Jefferson's zeal for hidden-hand diplomacy that would enhance American security and extend the influence of American ideals.

Jefferson applied the same clandestine techniques to other frontier regions. As diplomatic historian Isaac Cox has noted, Jefferson was often at odds with his own president's policy of restricting western expansion throughout the continent: "Washington might issue his proclamation against Yazoo claimants, French revolutionists, and would be filibusters, but his secretary of state, Jefferson, sympathized with them and secretly abetted their efforts."[15]

One of the most controversial secret initiatives that the secretary undertook concerned a presidentially unauthorized mission by French explorer André Michaux, an agent of "Citizen" Genêt, the new minister of the French Republic's revolutionary government. Michaux's mission, operating under the cover of a scientific exploration, received assistance in 1793 from Secretary of State Jefferson, who wrote letters of introduction to the governor of Kentucky. Jefferson vouched for Michaux's character and urged the governor to cooperate with him, even though the secretary knew that Michaux carried instructions from Genêt to two American generals in Kentucky planning an attack on Spanish possessions in Louisiana.[16]

Michaux also carried proclamations to be delivered to Canada and Louisiana inciting the populace to revolt against British and Spanish rule. The only reservation Jefferson expressed to Genêt was that the attacking force rendezvous outside of U.S. territory to maintain the appearance of American neutrality. Jefferson took a big risk in assisting Michaux: the Washington administration had a policy of restraining Americans from attacking Spanish territory. Intelligence received from Kentucky at that time had hinted at a possible expedition launched from that state, and the administration had decided that General Anthony Wayne would be instructed to "intercept by force" any invasion force. Needless to say, one dissenting voice in the cabinet—the secretary of state—opposed the use of force to stop any invasion.[17]

Jefferson's concern for protecting the secrecy of Michaux's mission, which ultimately was without result, lasted long after it was disbanded. Writing some twenty years after its failure, Jefferson described Michaux's mission as primarily botanical; even at that date, he neglected to mention any political connection to the operation. According to Jefferson's biographer Dumas Malone, the incident represented an example of Jefferson's "evasiveness with respect to unpleasant matters."[18]

Jefferson's support of the failed Michaux operation did not mark the end of his effort to infiltrate the Louisiana Territory. After Jefferson's election to the presidency, sending an intelligence-gathering mission into the area became a top presidential priority. The selection of trusted presidential confidant Meriwether Lewis to lead the new mission reflected Jefferson's desire to conduct the operation under strict executive control. Additionally, there were a number of intriguing connections between Lewis and Clark's and Michaux's activities that merit attention. Lewis had requested in 1793 that Jefferson allow him to participate in the

Michaux mission, and Clark's older brother, George Rogers, had been named a general in charge of leading the invasion force. In both missions, science and exploration served as the cover story, though in the case of Lewis and Clark this entailed a much smaller and less ambitious operation.[19]

It should be said that the Washington administration had ordered a secret reconnaissance of the Missouri River in 1790, so Jefferson was not the first president to authorize an attempt to penetrate the western reaches of the continent. In the previous instance, Secretary of War Henry Knox had ordered the expedition to be conducted by American soldiers who should be dressed "like Indians in all respects," and under no circumstances should outside observers "discover any Connection with the troops." Knox instructed the general in charge of the mission to ensure that no written instructions were carried. The elaborate cover was designed to keep the Spanish in the dark about the origins of the mission.[20]

Although Lewis and Clark did not resort to disguises for their reconnaissance, they did keep the true nature of their mission a secret to all but those at the very top of the United States government. Jefferson had requested funding for their mission in a secret message to Congress on January 18, 1803. However, planning for the mission had been under way throughout 1802 as Jefferson began taking steps for acquiring at least part of the Louisiana Territory from France, which would be ceded it by Spain. Jefferson's carefully crafted rationale for the expedition, delivered in his message to Congress, emphasized its commercial and scientific benefits while excluding any reference to territorial designs or strategic considerations. A major concern for Jefferson was the possibility, should France and Britain go to war, that Britain would seize the territory. If the United States could claim lands far to the west by means of an expedition, then the Louisiana Territory would be boxed in by the United States and eventually fall into its hands.[21] The selection of William Clark for the mission is revealing, for Clark was a veteran military-intelligence officer who had conducted a detailed reconnaissance of Spanish fortifications along the Ohio River in 1795.[22] Not surprisingly, Lewis's letter of recruitment to Clark had included a stern warning about "the necessity of keeping this matter a perfect secret."[23]

The purchase of the territory by the Jefferson administration changed the rationale for the operation but reinforced the need for the U.S. government to get a better sense of the land it had acquired. Clark focused on the defensive measures that would be required to make certain that the territory could be protected by American forces. The simple transfer of the land from France to the United States did not mean that the British or the Indians would abide by the agreement.

As the two explorers made their way through the new territory, they encountered reports of British intrigue and submitted a report to the administration proposing restrictions on the activities of British traders and agents in the area. Clark charted locations for proposed American forts, some two-thirds of which were built in response to his recommendations. The Lewis and Clark mission was a success on many fronts, not the least of which was the strategic intelligence it provided for military planners to secure the area.[24]

There was one location within the territory acquired by the Louisiana Purchase that piqued Jefferson's interest more than any other: the city of New Orleans. Ten years before Lewis and Clark began their expedition, Secretary of State Jefferson had dispatched a spy to the city with instructions to operate under cover as a merchant. Jefferson turned to his friend James Madison to find the appropriate candidate for the job:

> We want an intelligent prudent native, who will go to reside at N. Orleans as a secret correspondent, for 1000 D. a year. He might do a little business, merely to cover his real office. Do point out such a one. Virginia ought to offer more loungers equal to this & ready for it, than any other state.[25]

For President Jefferson, the purchase of the Louisiana Territory was a tremendous diplomatic and personal victory no matter how much chance may have played a role in his success. However, Jefferson could not rest until the territory was firmly in American hands, for the signing of the agreement with Napoleon's government did not guarantee that Spain would turn control of the region over to the French. Under the terms of the retrocession agreement, France did not actually acquire control of the territory that it had just sold until November 30, 1803. Until then, the land remained under Spanish control, and Jefferson feared to the very end a move on that nation's part to keep the territory out of American hands. In preparing for such a possibility, Jefferson resorted to tactics designed to evict Spain from the region while concealing the American role. On September 14, 1803, Jefferson instructed Secretary of State Madison to inform the American consul in New Orleans, Daniel Clark, that he needed to engage in an intelligence mission to gauge Spanish intentions. Jefferson wanted Clark "to sound in every direction, but with so much caution as to avoid suspicion" in order to acquire any evidence of Spanish hesitation in handing over the land. The consul was to determine both the strength of Spanish forces there and the attitude of the citizens toward an American invasion force—whether they would take up arms on behalf of Spain or welcome the American action.[26]

Jefferson's concern for democratic sensibilities was reflected in this last request for intelligence; he wanted the takeover of the territory to appear as much as possible an event welcomed by the indigenous population. Moreover, while planning to seize the territory by force, Jefferson hoped to portray the assault as conducted primarily by the inhabitants of Louisiana and directed by France. Jefferson told Treasury Secretary Albert Gallatin that if Spain resisted, America would resort to force, but in a surreptitious manner. Jefferson proposed that any attack "should be made as much as possible the act of France, by including Laussat [the French Prefect of New Orleans], with the aid of [Daniel] Clark, to raise an insurrectionary force of the inhabitants, to which ours might be only auxiliary."[27] Once again, Jefferson revealed his penchant for operations that concealed American involvement in a controversial foreign-policy initiative, though in this instance the plans were not carried into effect.

Jefferson also cast a clandestine eye on East and West Florida, lands he claimed were given to the United States as part of the Louisiana Purchase. Their acquisition became a major focal point of the last years of Jefferson's administration and was a prominent foreign-policy objective of the Madison administration. Jefferson's desire for this territory led him at one point to consider bribing Napoleon to apply pressure on Spain to yield it. Napoleon had offered to deliver the land in exchange for $7 million, the bulk of which would be pocketed by the French. One of Jefferson's most ardent congressional supporters considered this action "a base prostration of the national character to excite one nation by money to bully another nation out of its property."[28] Nevertheless, under intense administration pressure, Congress met in secret session and appropriated $2 million to begin negotiating this deal. The funds were never delivered, as Napoleon withdrew his offer after a change in the European diplomatic situation altered his plans.

That was not the first time the Jefferson administration considered bribery an appropriate means of avoiding, as Henry Adams noted, "the expense and losses inevitable in a war."[29] Reflecting Jefferson's belief in the need for covert means to project U.S. influence short of war, bribery as a tool of foreign policy reached its peak in the administration's dealings with the Indian nations.

Jefferson's Clandestine Indian Policy

As in other areas, Thomas Jefferson formulated his policy toward the American Indian nations long before attaining the presidency. His policy was designed to allow the United States to expand peacefully while assimilating the Indian into the democratic experiment. Jefferson viewed a policy of bribing the Indians into ceasing hostilities and surrendering their lands as the cheapest and most reliable method of achieving this goal.[30]

Jefferson's advocacy of this approach emerged during the early years of the Washington administration. On at least three occasions, the secretary of state expressed his wish to see a shift in American policy from conventional warfare to bribery. Writing to Charles Carroll on April 15, 1791, Jefferson commented:

> I hope we shall give the Indians a good drubbing this summer, and then change our tomahawk into a golden chain of friendship. The most economical as well as the most humane conduct towards them is to bribe them into peace, and to retain them in peace by eternal bribes.[31]

Two days later, Jefferson repeated his desire to see a change in American policy in a letter to James Monroe: "I hope we shall drub the Indians well this summer, and then change our plan from war to bribery. We must do as the Spaniards and English do, keep them in peace by liberal and constant presents. They find it the cheapest plan, and so shall we."[32] In presenting his plan to President Washington, Jefferson delicately omitted the use of the word *bribery,* but asserted that a plan of "liberal and repeated presents" would save blood and treasure and at the same time fulfill American policy objectives.[33]

The implementation of this policy would have to wait for Jefferson's elevation to the presidency, but in the interim Washington's secretary of state advocated other covert techniques designed to counter Indian hostilities on the frontier. To check the Spanish-backed Creek Indians, Jefferson advocated dispatching a secret agent to other Indian tribes to encourage them to wage war against the Creeks. In one instance, Jefferson sought to encourage the Choctaws to ally themselves with the Chickasaws, who were in the midst of a war with the Creeks. Jefferson, along with Secretary of War Knox, proposed to Washington

> that an agent be sent to the Choctaw nation, to endeavor secretly to engage them to support the Chickasaws in their present war with the Creeks—giving them, for that purpose, arms and ammunition sufficient; and that it be kept in view, that if we settle our differences amicably with the Creeks, we at the same time mediate effectually the peace of the Chickasaws and the Choctaws; so as to rescue the former from the difficulties in which they are engaged and the latter from those into which we may have been instrumental in engaging them.[34]

Jefferson's proposal provides further evidence of his penchant for covert tactics, in this instance enticing surrogates to bear the burden of a war that advanced American interests. This plan had the added attraction of positioning the United States as the peacemaker capable of winning the goodwill of all the parties involved, thereby enhancing America's diplomatic position with them in the future.[35]

Ten years after he first proposed it, President Jefferson was able to shift American Indian policy to his approach and away from conventional warfare, which required a standing army and endless expense. The key man in President Jefferson's bribery scheme was his secretary of war, Henry Dearborn. When the administration sought to open a road between Georgia and Tennessee, Dearborn instructed one of his Indian agents that the recalcitrant Cherokee Indians would have to be "brought to reason" by bribing one or two prominent chiefs.[36] Later, the administration sought to acquire a large tract of land from the Chickasaw Indians, and again the administration's policy proved effective. Dearborn wrote one of his commissioners negotiating with the Chickasaws:

> [I]f any particular individual among the Chickasaws, and who may be opposed to the proposed Cession of lands, and who may have considerable

influence with the nation, can be induced to change the direction of his influence, by any reasonable means, the Commissioners will please to act in such cases, as circumstances may require.

Two chiefs involved in the negotiations were each given $1,000, and another was given a $100 annuity. This arrangement helped to facilitate the signing of a treaty that gave the United States a portion of the desired land.[37]

William Henry Harrison, governor of the Indiana Territory and future American president, was another principal figure in the Jefferson administration's bribery network. In settling conflicting territorial claims of various tribes in June 1804, Dearborn instructed Harrison to "take such measures and make such pecuniary advances to individual Chiefs or others as their respective cases require."[38] Harrison also played a part in one of Jefferson's ingenious schemes to separate the Indians from their land without the appearance of coercion. In a secret letter to Harrison, Jefferson expressed his desire to expand the number of trading houses throughout Indian country, hoping that prominent leaders would run up large debts. When the debts became too burdensome, the Indians would pay them off by yielding valuable land.[39]

For Jefferson, his policy of bribery and economic coercion was intended to save American lives and treasure. As he told Treasury Secretary Gallatin (in a slight variation from his letters advocating bribery), "The Indians can be kept in order only by commerce or war. The former is the cheaper."[40] He also seems to have been genuinely determined to lift the Indians out of their "primitive" state and bring to them the blessings of American democracy. It was with that goal in mind that Jefferson justified his conduct, whether toward hostile Indian nations or Barbary pirates. Jefferson repeatedly expressed his desire to see both groups join the "civilized" world; covert methods were part of the arsenal needed to achieve this goal.

Jefferson's "Hidden-Hand" Presidency: To the Shores of Tripoli

Thomas Jefferson bore a long-standing grudge against the Barbary powers—"these nests of banditti"—that dated back to his time as American envoy to France. As early as November 1784, he expressed his wish to cut "them to pieces by piecemeal."[41] During that period, he sought intelligence data on the naval strength of the Barbary states and urged an American envoy to "give . . . what information he can of their naval strength, resources and cruising grounds."[42] His elevation to the presidency sixteen years later allowed him to strike back at powers that had forced the United States to pay tribute to protect its merchant fleet. In his riposte, President Jefferson employed tactics ranging from traditional diplomacy to conventional warfare and covert action.

The four Barbary states—Morocco, Algiers, Tunis, and Tripoli—had harassed American shipping since the founding of the United States. This was part of a long-standing Mediterranean tradition encouraged by European powers, which were skilled at bribing the pirate states to hamper the shipping of their continental opponents. For the right price, maritime nations could buy themselves peace until the Barbary extortionists upped their demands; then the harassment would begin anew. For the United States, overt hostilities with the Barbary powers began in May 1801, when the pasha (or bashaw) of Tripoli declared war less than three weeks after Jefferson's inauguration. An inconclusive naval conflict endured for the next four years, in part because of Jefferson's determination to fight as inexpensive a war as possible.

Early in the Jefferson administration, serious consideration was given to a proposal to overthrow the pasha, the foremost troublemaker in the region. The idea was first suggested to the administration by James Cathcart, the American consul at Tripoli, in a letter written to Secretary of State James Madison on July 2, 1801. Cathcart told Madison, "I not only contemplate the obtaining a permanent and honorable peace, but likewise dethroning the present Bashaw, and effecting a revolution in favor of his brother Hamet who is at Tunis, and thereby insure the United States the gratitude of him and his successors."[43]

Cathcart's next step was to direct William Eaton, the American consul at Tunis, to "endeavor to ascertain how far said Hamet would be willing to engage in an expedition of that nature."[44] Eaton was a graduate of Dartmouth College who spoke a minimum of four Arab dialects fluently and thrived on the rough life of the soldier-adventurer.[45] He would go on to become the key American operative in this drama and a figure of legend to nineteenth-century American schoolchildren. Eaton's intelligence on the situation in Tripoli led him to write to Madison in September 1801 that "the subjects, in general, of the reigning Bashaw, Joseph, are very discontented, and ripe for revolt."[46] Eaton acquired additional intelligence on the situation in Tripoli from a Danish commodore, who stated that the citizenry was tired of the war with the United States and anxious to be rid of the reigning sovereign. Eaton reported that the people desired "the restoration of their rightful sovereign," who needed only to be presented to them at which time they would "rise en masse to receive him." Eaton reported to Madison that the exiled brother, Hamet, "desired to be advised" whether the United States would engage in operations on his behalf. Hamet was instructed by Eaton to remain patient and silent until approval for the operation was obtained from the American government, thus beginning the long and tortuous process of waiting for Jefferson to choose a course of action.[47]

A development took place at this time that endangered Eaton and Cathcart's plan. Cathcart had sought support for the operation from the Ottoman Turkish government; he hoped ultimately to win protection for

American interests in the region from both the restored sovereign of Tripoli and the Turks. Around this time, Hamet was denied asylum in one of the neighboring Barbary states and was forced to accept an offer from his hated brother, who apparently had received word of the American machinations. The pasha offered to permit his brother to rule over the provinces of Derne and Bengazi, a proposal that the lonely exile agreed to and one that Cathcart believed was a trap. In order to prevent the entire American operation from unraveling, Eaton was sent to persuade Hamet not to accept. Eaton's effort was successful; he convinced Hamet to remain in Malta until the operation could begin. Cathcart's hope—to effect a revolution in Hamet's favor and place him on the throne of Tripoli—remained intact.[48]

Madison, writing to Cathcart, expressed relief that Eaton had "prevailed" on Hamet to reject a deal from his brother and that he could "still be made use of against the Bashaw." Eaton had "prevailed" through an interesting form of persuasion—the ever-present reminder that Hamet's brother desired to kill him—accompanied by a $2,000 "gratuity." In this same letter to Cathcart, Madison wrote one of the more revealing statements made during the course of the entire operation:

> Although it does not accord with the general sentiments or views of the United States to intermeddle with the domestic controversies of other countries, it cannot be unfair, in the prosecution of a just war, or the accomplishment of a reasonable peace, to take advantage of the hostile co-operation of others. As far, therefore, as the views of the brother may contribute to our success, the aid of them may be used for the purpose.[49]

Throughout this period, the administration wavered between using force and acceding to the pasha's demands for tribute. The choice became more difficult due to the seizure of 308 American hostages, taken when the frigate USS *Philadelphia* ran aground while blockading Tripoli harbor. Concern over the hostages' fate appears to have been a major factor in American hesitation to proceed with the effort to overthrow the pasha, who made it clear that if the U.S. actions advanced too far, the hostages' lives would be in danger. That and the expense of the operation were the dominant concerns of the Jefferson administration and the naval officers on the scene as they wrestled with the question of how far they should go.[50] The thrust of the administration's position appears to have been that the operation, in concert with a conventional naval blockade, would serve to pressure the reigning sovereign to sue for peace on American terms. Restoring the exiled brother to the throne was a welcome secondary objective for the administration but by no means the primary goal. The exiled brother was an "instrument" to be used to coerce the pasha, a pawn to be disposed of if the political or diplomatic costs got out of hand.

The critical event in this saga occurred during a White House meeting between President Jefferson and William Eaton in 1803. Eaton had returned to the United States in the spring of that year in an attempt to restore the lagging effort to depose the pasha. For Eaton, this meeting was something of a last-ditch effort to preserve the operation. Late in 1802, the quirky Hamet, against Eaton's advice, had tried to do it on his own by returning to the city of Derne and announcing his intention to challenge his brother. A series of disastrous events for Hamet and the Americans had quickly reversed any hopes for success. The seizure of the *Philadelphia* and Hamet's inability to maintain his supporters in the isolated city caused him to flee into Egypt to avoid being captured by his brother.

For Eaton, the White House meeting became a critical test of the administration's resolve. Eaton met with Jefferson in the White House on December 10, 1803, two days after being told by Robert Smith, secretary of the navy, that the president would be receptive to his proposals. The only two participants at the meeting were Jefferson and Eaton; Secretary of State Madison's health prevented him from attending.[51] Jefferson must have been impressed with what he heard, for in the spring of 1804 he gave the go-ahead for the operation. The president noted in his diary on May 26, 1804, "Present the Secretaries and Atty. Genl. . . . Shall anything be furnished to the Ex-Bashaw to engage cooperation? Unanimously 20,000. D."[52] Additionally, Madison arranged the delivery of a thousand rifles from the War Department, removed Eaton from the State Department payroll, and placed him under direction of Secretary Smith, the foremost proponent of the Eaton plan within Jefferson's cabinet. The rationale for this move appears to have been to attempt to place Eaton under the tighter operational control of the naval officers on the scene as well as to distance the State Department from the activities he was about to undertake.[53] The administration's two-track policy was in place: diplomatic initiatives would be handled by the Department of State; the coup d'état and military assistance for it would be handled by the Department of the Navy.

Eaton returned to the Mediterranean as "Navy Agent for the Several Barbary Regencies."[54] In the immediate aftermath of this appointment, Madison wrote to Tobias Lear, the chief American diplomat in the Barbary region, and to Commodore Samuel Barron, commander of the Mediterranean squadron, outlining the administration's two-pronged effort to protect American interests. Madison left the door open to negotiation and the payment of ransom in exchange for the *Philadelphia* prisoners and a hands-off policy toward American shipping. But both men were told to consider employing the services of William Eaton and Hamet, if the appropriate moment arose. Lear was told:

[O]f the cooperation of the elder brother of the Bashaw of Tripoli, we are still willing to avail ourselves, if the commodore [Barron] should judge that it may be useful, and to engage which, as well as to render it the more effectual, he has discretionary authority to grant him pecuniary or other subsidies, not exceeding twenty thousand dollars.[55]

Barron received his instructions from the secretary of the navy, who echoed Madison's theme:

> With respect to the ex-Bashaw of Tripoli, we have no objection to your availing yourself of his co-operation with you against Tripoli, if you . . . consider his co-operation expedient. The subject is committed entirely to your discretion. In such an event you will, it is believed, find Mr. Eaton extremely useful to you.[56]

Barron went on to throw his support behind the mission, secretly dispatching a ship carrying Eaton to Alexandria; Eaton then went on to locate Hamet in Egypt. Barron had accepted Eaton's clearly defined goal: to cooperate with Hamet "against the usurper, his brother" and to reestablish him in the regency of Tripoli.[57]

Eaton established contact with Hamet in January 1805, a development immediately reported to Tripoli. The pasha attempted in vain to pressure the Egyptians into preventing Hamet from leaving the country, a sure indication of his concern over his brother's intentions.[58] On March 6, 1805, Eaton and Hamet began a quixotic, five-hundred-mile march across the Libyan desert with an army of approximately four hundred men. The insurgent force was composed primarily of Arabs loyal to or lent to Hamet by other Arab chieftains. A force of ten U.S. Marines helped "General" Eaton direct the operations of the ragtag army marching in the brutal desert environment. Hamet and Eaton arrived at Derne on April 25 and attacked it two days later, taking complete control of the city by April 29. At the height of his triumph, Eaton was unaware that the pressure of his operation was leading Joseph to sue for peace and ushering in the end of the American endeavor to restore Hamet to the throne.[59]

The peace overtures received from the pasha marked the end of Hamet's usefulness as an instrument of American policy in the region. Eaton received formal notification of this development on May 19, 1805, in a letter from Commodore Barron.[60] A critical concern for Barron was the pasha's threat to kill the American hostages if the operation continued. Furthermore, Barron believed that Hamet lacked the popularity and the resources to proceed on his own. In spite of these difficulties, even the most skeptical American observer was forced to admit that the operation had had a significant impact on the pasha. Tobias Lear, the negotiator of the treaty, found that Eaton's efforts "had made a deep impression on the Bashaw."[61] The only remaining problem for the United States was to extricate Eaton and the surviving Marines along with Hamet and his immediate entourage. This was accomplished by a quietly engineered evacuation that left behind most of the motley army to fend for itself.[62]

For the United States, the first attempt to intervene in the domestic political affairs of another nation was a success, at least in the short run.

Although Eaton and Hamet remained bitter that the effort to restore the latter to the throne had not been carried to completion, the United States had bought itself a temporary peace in the Mediterranean.

There are a number of interesting parallels between this first operation and subsequent American attempts to intervene in the domestic affairs of foreign nations. Although the overall effort was sanctioned at the highest levels, certain operational details were conveniently left to the discretion of those in the field. Eaton, as the main operative, may have oversold the extent to which the United States would go the distance for Hamet. Of course, Eaton had to engage Hamet in the scheme and could hardly let him think that the United States would end its help once its interests had been served. Jefferson was more than willing to allow his field agent to make these promises, while keeping enough distance to allow the administration to abandon the arrangement should U.S. interests require it.

Congressional criticism of the coup attempt focused on the fact that the Jefferson administration had failed to see the operation through to completion, not that an effort had been made to topple a foreign government. As Abraham Sofaer notes, "No one raised any question, however, concerning the legality or propriety of the joint action with Hamet. . . . The only significant complaint heard in Congress was that the President reneged on his alliance with Hamet, not that he had made one."[63]

In response, the Jefferson administration attempted to persuade its critics that it had entered into a limited alliance with Hamet and had made no guarantee of restoring him to his throne. The administration hoped to convince the Congress that Eaton had gone beyond his authority in his dealings with Hamet. Jefferson wrote to Congress:

> During the war with Tripoli, it was suggested that Hamet Caramalli . . . mediated the recovery of his inheritance, and that a concert in action with us was desirable to him. We considered that concerted operations by those who have a common enemy were entirely justifiable, and might produce effects favorable to both, without binding either to guarantee the objects of the other. But the distance of the scene, the difficulties of communication, and the uncertainty of our information inducing the less confidence in the measure, it was committed to our agents as one which might be resorted to, if it promised to promote our success.[64]

Jefferson then tried to explain the difficulties involved in maintaining presidential control: "In operations at such a distance, it becomes necessary to leave much to the discretion of the agents employed; but events may still turn up beyond the limits of that discretion."[65]

President Jefferson went on to state that he had merely authorized his agent to engage the "cooperation" of Hamet against the pasha. Jefferson referred to Eaton as "a zealous citizen" motivated by pure and patriotic beliefs who nonetheless exceeded his authority. The idea of placing Hamet on the throne was "a stipulation so entirely unauthorized, so far beyond our views and so enormous, [it] could not be sanctioned by our Government."[66] The coup attempt may have been "entirely unauthorized" after the fact, but the administration did not make its lack of commitment clear to Eaton while the overthrow effort was under way. Instead, the matter of defining "cooperation" was left in Eaton's hands.

It must be remembered that Madison had written to Eaton in May 1801 (as hostilities with Tripoli were just beginning), that "the means [of dealing with the pasha] must be left, in a great degree, to your knowledge of the local and other circumstances."[67] Eaton and Cathcart had responded with a clear declaration of their intent to overthrow the pasha in July 1801 and again in September. As noted, in July, Cathcart had proposed to Madison the "dethroning [of] the present Bashaw."[68] In this same letter, Cathcart wrote that he had instructed Eaton to "ascertain how far said Hamet would be willing to engage in an expedition of that nature."[69] Eaton had responded in September, "The idea of dethroning our enemy . . . will teach the other Barbary States."[70] In August 1802, Madison had written to Cathcart expressing his satisfaction that Hamet could "still be made use of against the Bashaw."[71] As late as June 1804, Secretary Smith had written to Commodore Barron that he could avail himself of Hamet's cooperation, "if you consider his co-operation expedient."[72]

The major American participants in this affair undoubtedly had different perspectives on Hamet's usefulness. For Jefferson and Madison, Hamet's value stemmed from his importance as a bargaining chip in their negotiations with the pasha. For the operatives in the field, the pressure of the immediate situation often required making commitments that decision makers in Washington probably preferred not to know. However, this operation was not the result of a rogue agent at work. For over three years, the Jefferson administration had kept Eaton in a position of meeting Hamet's every need, well aware that Eaton was the most vocal proponent—and possible originator—of the coup scheme itself.[73] Many accounts of this affair, including the authorized statement issued by Jefferson, ignore the crucial December 10, 1803, White House meeting between Jefferson and Eaton, followed that spring by the arms transfer to Eaton and the granting of a $20,000 expense account.[74] However, the chain of discretionary authority constructed by the White House allowed Jefferson the leeway to invoke the concept of plausible deniability later. The administration also had the perfect scapegoat in Eaton, whose character lent credibility to the charge of his being a reckless adventurer. It seems clear that Jefferson and Madison had tacitly approved a long-term effort to overthrow a foreign government, overcoming Madison's expressed reservation about meddling in other countries' domestic affairs.[75]

For the first—but no means the last—time in its history, the United States was confronted with the disturbing prospect of abandoning a surrogate force organized and equipped by American agents. Despite the relative success of this particular operation, most of those who played a part were acutely aware of the high cost to those "instruments" who were left to fend for themselves in the desert. Eaton's vivid recollection of the abandonment of the Arab army at Derne in the dead of night haunted him until his death and even disburbed many of the administration's most dedicated supporters. Eaton was direct in his account of the administration's actions: "It is impossible for me to undertake to say that the Bashaw has not been deceived. Nor can I reconcile . . . the manner of his being abandoned with those principles of natural justice and honor which have hitherto marked our character."[76]

The attractiveness of operations such as Eaton's is, of course, easy to understand; they offer an inexpensive, low-profile method of projecting force. Unfortunately, they are never as manageable as they appear in the planning. There is a difficulty in containing the operations and in finding agents with the proper political sensibilities who can also direct special military operations. There is the added problem of keeping the sponsored movement genuinely indigenous; this particular undertaking was burdened by Hamet's never-ending demands for further U.S. assistance and his willingness to let Eaton and his band of Marines direct his army. Ultimately, such operations cannot be simply abandoned when policy makers in Washington change their minds. Repercussions from the attempted coup were felt for years after the signing of a peace treaty, as bands of Hamet's supporters continued to harass the pasha long after the United States had withdrawn.[77]

The full story of Jefferson's complicity in an attempt to overthrow a foreign government has been pieced together by historians long after the participants were gone. Jefferson's skillful use of surrogates effectively distanced from the White House could—and did—serve as a model for all similar American interventions in the future. These operations represent Jefferson's belief, shared by most of his successors, that "the transaction of business with foreign nations is Executive altogether."[78] In few other areas is this exercise of executive power displayed in such a raw and highly volatile form.

Jefferson's Covert Legacy

Thomas Jefferson left the White House having enlarged the scope of presidentially authorized clandestine activity. As we have seen, Jefferson's notion of presidential control of secret operations was broadly defined, and the types of covert actions he was willing to authorize covered a wide spectrum.

Jefferson shared with other Founders a belief that foreign powers would spare no expense to penetrate the American government for pernicious reasons. This concern over foreign penetration, nurtured during the struggle for independence, acted as a powerful force on the founding generation in creating an American intelligence capability. Jefferson noted in a letter written from Paris in 1787 that "wretched, indeed, is the nation in whose affairs foreign powers are once permitted to intermeddle."[79] He repeated these concerns in a letter written to Madison in December 1787. While discussing some of his objections to the newly proposed Constitution, Jefferson expressed his belief that allowing the president unlimited terms of office meant he would be an "officer for life." Once this happened, "it becomes of so much consequence to certain nations to have a friend or foe at the head of our affairs that they will interfere with money and with arms."[80] Vice President Jefferson wrote to Elbridge Gerry in May 1797 complaining about foreign influence and intrigue in the United States and of the need to "find some means of shielding ourselves in [the] future from foreign influence, political, commercial, or in whatever form it may be attempted."[81]

Jefferson's experience as president only strengthened his convictions about interfering foreign powers, as evidenced by their plots with the frontier Indians or British attempts to exploit public dissent over Jefferson's unpopular trade embargo. After he left the presidency, Jefferson's fears were confirmed when he was informed of evidence concerning a British attempt during the embargo to "promote division & dissension in the year 1809 . . . by means of a secret mission to Boston, the object of which was to intrigue with the disaffected."[82] Despite the tendency of the Jeffersonian Republicans to overstate the seriousness of such events for political benefit, many of these activities represented legitimate threats to American security.

Jefferson was more than ready to counter those efforts with covert techniques of his own, as he alluded to in a letter to Spanish authorities in 1792. In response to their agitation among the Creek Indians, Jefferson blatantly threatened to use the same tactics against the Spanish: "It is not to a nation whose dominions are circumstanced as those of Spain in our neighborhood that we need develop the inconveniences of permitting reciprocally the unlicensed mission of Agents into the territories of each other."[83] Jefferson's willingness to engage in covert retaliatory operations included an effort to persuade the Madison administration to authorize a secret effort to avenge the British burning of the White House and the Capitol during the War of 1812. The operation would be conducted for classic Jeffersonian reasons: inexpensive retaliation could be achieved without the loss of American life, and American responsibility for the action could be concealed. An angry Jefferson wrote to Dr. Thomas Cooper: "The English have burned our Capitol and President's House by means of their force. We can burn their St. James's and St. Paul's by means of our money, offered to their own incendiaries, of whom there are thousands in London who would do it rather than starve."[84]

In the same letter, Jefferson declared that it was "against the laws of civilized warfare to employ secret incendiaries" but still promoted the idea that a nation must use those means at its disposal to defend itself—in this case, "our money and their [England's] pauperism." Although Jefferson's proposal was never adopted by the Madison administration, it is intriguing to speculate whether the overseer of the Eaton operation and the initiator of bribes to the Indian nations would have authorized such an operation had he been president in 1814.

Jefferson's penchant for executive options capable of projecting force short of war led him to support a policy of government-sanctioned piracy during the War of 1812. Jefferson advocated such a policy to Madison's secretary of state, James Monroe; concerns over cost and casualties were once again major factors leading him to make this recommendation. Jefferson was also aware of the imbalance in conventional forces between the United States and Britain and sought means that would allow the Americans to fight on more favorable terms. Jefferson wrote to Monroe, "Privateers will find their own men and money. Let nothing be spared to encourage them. They are the dagger which strikes at the heart of the enemy, their commerce . . . they will make the merchants of England feel, and squeal, and cry out for peace."[85] Although the commissioning of private ships to harass foreign merchant ships was a common activity in seventeenth- and eighteenth-century warfare, Jefferson's strong support of such a tactic once again reveals his attraction to nonconventional uses of force.

Jefferson's attraction to clandestine activity fits with the leadership style of a man who conducted much of his domestic politics through surrogates willing to engage in power politics to further his interests. A key to his success as an American political leader stemmed from his keen ability to motivate others to carry out his wishes while he remained above the fray.[86] One leading historian of the Jefferson presidency, Henry Adams, noted Jefferson's liking for secrecy, particularly in dealing with foreign powers:

> The necessary secrecy of diplomacy gave to every president the power to involve the country without its knowledge in dangers which could not be afterward escaped, and the Republican party neither invented nor suggested means by which this old evil of irresponsible politics could be cured; but of all presidents, none used these arbitrary powers with more freedom and secrecy than Jefferson. His ideas of presidential authority in foreign affairs were little short of royal. He loved the sense of freedom from oversight which diplomacy gave.[87]

Jefferson occasionally utilized private citizens for purposes of secret diplomacy if the situation required; he established a system of correspondence with his emissaries that operated not only beyond the realm of congressional oversight, but outside the reach of his secretary of state as well. He defended the practice in a letter to James Monroe: "I can make private friendships instrumental to the public good by inspiring a confidence which is denied to public, and official communications."[88] In one instance, Jefferson used a private citizen to carry a secret letter to the American envoy to France. The letter also contained a cipher for confidential correspondence between Jefferson and the envoy. Jefferson explained his rationale for the strict secrecy requirements:

> But why a cipher between us, when official things go naturally to the Secretary of State, and things not political need no cipher. 1) matters of a public nature, and proper to go on our records, should go to the secretary of state. 2) matters of a public nature not proper to be placed on our records may still go to the secretary of state, headed by the word "private." But 3) there may be matters merely personal to ourselves, and which require the cover of a cipher more than those of any other character. This last purpose and others which we cannot foresee may render it convenient and advantageous to have at hand a mask for whatever may need it.[89]

Jefferson utilized these unofficial methods of communication out of a belief that Congress lacked the capacity to keep secrets and that an energetic executive often had to undertake foreign initiatives free from cumbersome congressional oversight. Upon sending an executive envoy to Russia, Jefferson wrote the secretary of the treasury that it was more important to take advantage of a diplomatic opening than to wait for Senate approval of the mission and declared, "We think secrecy also important, & that the mission should be as little known as possible, till it is in Petersburgh, which could not be, if known to the Senate."[90]

Throughout his career, Jefferson held the line against Senate participation in foreign-policy initiatives or access to executive secrets. He wrote in his first year as Washington's secretary of state:

> The Senate is not supposed by the Constitution to be acquainted with the concerns of the Executive Department . . . nor can they, therefore, be qualified to judge of the necessity which calls for a mission to any particular place . . . which special and secret circumstances may call for. All this is left to the President.[91]

Jefferson's defense of executive secrecy placed him squarely in the tradition of Washington, Hamilton, and Jay, who shared Jefferson's belief that "all nations have found it necessary, that for the advantageous conduct of their affairs, some of these [executive] proceedings, at least, should remain known to their executive functionary only."[92]

Jefferson's public rhetoric in defense of democratic principles might appear to be at odds with his willingness to use techniques of intrigue and deception in dealing with foreign powers. Yet I believe that Jefferson saw no contradiction between his love of democratic government and his use of surreptitious means to advance its cause. His attraction to clandestine activity as a foreign-policy weapon was based on a desire to contain the cost of American participation in international affairs. In fact, he raised the possibility that low-intensity covert operations were tailor-made for nations leery of large, permanent military establishments. Jefferson also wished to preserve a deep-rooted American belief that the manner in which democratic nations conduct their foreign policy is fundamentally different from that of monarchical or authoritarian regimes. He understood the importance of shielding democratic sensibilities from activities such as bribery or surreptitious territorial acquisition; territorial desires could be fulfilled best through indirect methods, ideally by generating such "indigenous" and "spontaneous" uprisings as he sought in Louisiana. At the same time, Jefferson was convinced that American interests were threatened by the Barbary pirates, the Indian nations, and the European powers whose territorial possessions bordered the United States. He acted to counter those threats through a combination of diplomacy, conventional military force, and clandestine activity.

Jefferson's employment of covert operations was not an example of an extraconstitutional abuse of power but a simple exercise of the president's prerequisite to implement foreign policy. Jefferson's clandestine activities while president were natural appendages of the powers given him as commander in chief and as the nation's chief diplomat. Jefferson was "certain" that "in cases of military operations some occasions for secret service money must arise."[93] He also believed in the broad use of secret service funds to assist in achieving diplomatic advantage over hostile foreign powers or in some cases the employment of covert operations as a substitute for conventional military operations. Jefferson was aware that in the gray area of foreign relations traditional standards of conduct were often put aside as nations sought advantage over one another. He understood that secrecy was often essential in securing an advantage over one's foes, that the president had the unique and sometimes difficult position of deciding when clandestine operations were necessary. The apostle of limited, strictly defined central government at home interpreted a very broad grant of power for the central government's external relations, with an energetic executive guiding the course of those relations.

Any moral concerns Jefferson may have had over engaging in bribery or other underhanded activities thus were overridden. Perhaps more important, Jefferson appears to have had little difficulty justifying clandestine techniques against "uncivilized" nations in the hope that such tactics would assist in the expansion of the "empire for liberty."[94] Someday such tactics would be outmoded as all the nations of the world were brought into the democratic orbit. In the meantime, covert intermeddling was appropriate if the intention was to "civilize" Indians, Barbary pirates, or the British.

Jefferson viewed the world beyond America's shores as a hostile place where the people were oppressed by princes and priests and held in "primitive" bondage. He believed that the standards of conduct that characterized relations between enlightened democratic societies could not guide the conduct of relations with the amoral nations of the Old World.

It was his mixture of hard-nosed realism and idealistic belief in the superiority of democratic societies that fundamentally guided Jefferson.

In the thirty-three years between the time Jefferson wrote the Declaration of Independence and the time he departed from the White House, the nascent American government had authorized an astounding variety of covert missions. In war and in peace, a series of American leaders had sanctioned operations involving espionage and deception, kidnapping, bribing foreign leaders, using the clergy and media for intelligence purposes, overthrowing a foreign government, and assisting insurgencies designed to remove hostile powers from the American continent. Thomas Jefferson had numerous differences with Hamilton, Washington, and Jay over the many issues confronting the new nation, but he shared with them a firm belief that the protection of America's security interests depended on the unfettered capability of the president to conduct clandestine operations.

AGENTS
OF LIBERTY

The Covert Struggle
for the Americas

5 ■

The Era of
Covert Expansion
Part 1, 1809–1829

[A]pprize Gov[erno]r H[olmes] confidentially, of the course adopted as to W[est] F[lorida] and . . . have his co-operation in diffusing the impressions we wish to be made there.

JAMES MADISON to ROBERT SMITH, July 17, 1810[1]

As for the Floridas I swear, General, on my honor as a gentle-man, not only that we are strangers to everything that has happened, but even that the Americans who have appeared there as agents or leaders are the enemies of the Executive, and act in this sense against the Federal government as well as against Spain.

ROBERT SMITH to Ambassador LOUIS TURREAU, *October 1810*[2]

■ Thomas Jefferson's successors, beginning with his good friend James Madison, eagerly embraced covert operations as a tool of executive foreign-policy making. Covert techniques were used to acquire additional territory for the nation and to assist in the expansion of republican ideals throughout the Americas. This period could truly be described as a golden age of covert operations, as a deferential Congress paid limited attention to executive conduct in this area.

The Founding Father as Covert Operator:
The Madison Administration's Secret
Operations in the Floridas

President Madison's effort to acquire the Floridas appears to have involved two ambitious covert operations designed to generate "spontaneous" uprisings against Spanish authority in the region. Madison, who
served as president from 1809 to 1817, conducted his first operation in an
area known as West Florida, a strip of land whose boundary the United
States considered to lie between the Mississippi River in the west and the
Perdido River in the east. The second occurred in East Florida, a region
that stretched from the Perdido to the Atlantic Ocean, though its population was clustered in a narrow coastal region between the St. John's River
and the Atlantic.[3]

The operation planners employed the classic techniques of a large-scale
covert operation. The effort was designed in such a way as to portray U.S.
expansionism as a defensive action. Secret American support helped to
create an "indigenous" revolutionary government that "requested" American intervention to protect its interests. As in the case of William Eaton
and the pasha of Tripoli, an American administration once again granted
broad discretionary authority to its agents in the field, left a limited
"paper trail" to disguise its intentions, and eventually discarded its
agents due to shifting circumstances beyond its control. In addition, by
distancing itself from operational details and looking away at critical
moments, the administration was able to invoke the concept of plausible
deniability when circumstances required it.

These techniques worked to perfection in West Florida, while later in
East Florida the scale of the operation forced the United States to forgo
its covert designs, biding its time and ultimately acquiring the land
through a combination of conventional force and diplomacy. This quest
for the Floridas was based on the desire of both frontiersmen and government officials to gain access to valuable land holdings and waterways
controlled by the Spanish. It was also meant to eliminate the possibility
that Spain could incite Indian attacks on frontier settlements.[4]

The general goal of American policy makers was the acquisition of the
remaining Spanish territory adjacent to the United States. Jefferson
wrote to a member of the Senate in 1803 that "we shall certainly obtain the
Floridas, and all in good time."[5] That acquisition, along with the island of
Cuba, would give the United States "control . . . over the Gulf of
Mexico, and the countries and isthmus bordering on it, as well as all whose
waters flow into it . . . [filling] up the measure of our political well-
being."[6] James Madison was as determined as his illustrious predecessor
to extend the "empire for liberty" to the southern reaches of the continent.
Evidence of this intent can be seen in Madison's instructions to his penny-
pinching secretary of the treasury, Albert Gallatin, who recommended

limiting expenses for American diplomatic activity throughout Spanish America. Madison rebuked the secretary, "Everything relating to Spanish America is too important to be subjected to a minute economy; or even to unnecessary delays."[7]

Since Jefferson's first term, the United States had made a diplomatic claim to ownership of the West Florida territory as part of the Louisiana Purchase.[8] Jefferson's claim would be realized by his successors, James Madison and James Monroe. One French diplomat observed that "the acquisition of the Floridas is the object of all of Mr. Madison's prayers."[9]

"Spontaneous Revolution" in West Florida

Madison's secret operation in West Florida, though not so large as his later one in East Florida, was by far the more ambitious in terms of the raw exercise of presidential covert authority. Without congressional mandate, through the unilateral exercise of executive power, Madison dispatched secret operatives and as a result acquired a portion of West Florida from the Mississippi to the Pearl River. The authorization for this operation came directly from the White House, as the administration cunningly exploited the presence of a large number of American settlers in West Florida.[10] The forces that would ultimately topple Spanish authority in the region had been building for quite some time; Madison merely administered the final blow to an unstable Spanish colonial government.

The idea for the operation had originated with Governor William Claiborne of the Orleans Territory in concert with David Holmes, governor of the Mississippi Territory. Claiborne had advocated American intervention in West Florida as early as 1807.[11] Holmes, the other major player in the drama, had just been appointed governor of the Mississippi Territory in the spring of 1810. The conventional interpretation of this affair holds that the operation was launched following a meeting between Claiborne and Madison held in June 1810, though historian Isaac Cox suggests that collusion between the administration and insurrectionary operatives may have been at work earlier.

Even if the idea of earlier intrigue is rejected, it is clear that the planners of the operation well understood the administration's intentions. Any action undertaken prior to the formal White House approval of June 1810 was no doubt conducted under the aegis of an unwritten understanding between Madison and Holmes, the latter a fellow Virginian long known by Madison.

Governor Claiborne personally lobbied the president for his approval, while Holmes submitted reports to the administration detailing the level of unrest in the region and holding out the prospect of great gain for the United States.[12] As noted, Claiborne's proposal was formally adopted as American policy following a face-to-face meeting with President Madison in June. Claiborne persuaded the president that a powerful coalition in West Florida desired independence from Spain and union with the United States. All that was needed was a signal from the United States, and the coalition would spring into action. Having been convinced to approve the operation, the president authorized Claiborne to find the appropriate operative to conduct the mission.[13] The agent chosen to spark this pro-American rebellion was William Wykoff, Jr., a prominent plantation owner and political figure who was well acquainted with a number of Americans living in Spanish-held territory. Claiborne wrote from "the house of the President" on June 14, 1810, asking Wykoff to undertake a secret mission designed to generate a movement for independence and a request for American intervention: "I am persuaded under present circumstances, it would be more pleasing that the taking possession of the country be preceded by a request from the inhabitants. Can no means be devised to obtain such request?"[14] To help achieve this objective, Claiborne proposed that Wykoff "prepare for this occasion the minds of the more influential characters in the vicinity of Mobile."[15] Claiborne went on to note that Wykoff's expenses associated with the mission would by compensated by the United States and that if Wykoff was so inclined he should protect the secrecy of his mission by not signing any of his correspondence.[16]

Meanwhile, David Holmes was also busily assisting the cause of insurrection. He is credited with being the ever- "wakeful eye," the most important operative in this drama, who monitored and generated the "internal convulsions" that gripped West Florida in the summer of 1810. When in early July a convention was held in the most populous section of West Florida to form a governing body that would "cooperate" with Spanish officials, Holmes wrote the administration, "You may ready conjecture how this business will eventuate." At the next meeting of the convention, Holmes sent an agent into the assembly who portrayed himself as an innocent observer of the proceedings. Not surprisingly, the agent acted as more than a disinterested bystander. Holmes's correspondence with the administration included reports on the activities of the convention delegates, while conveying information on possible British operations designed to counter American efforts.[17]

Isaac Cox has noted that Madison personally and aggressively directed the operation. For reasons that are not quite clear, Robert Smith, now secretary of state and a veteran of Jefferson's covert operation against Tripoli, was unable or unwilling to supervise it. A week after Claiborne's first communication with Wykoff, Smith did dispatch a letter to Wykoff, ordering him to proceed into the Floridas. He was sent for "the purpose of diffusing the impression" that an effort to achieve independence from Spain would be welcomed and would lead to the incorporation of the region into the United States.[18] Cox notes that it quickly became apparent that Smith was "unequal to the task" of directing these secret operations;

therefore, Madison "had to assume direct executive control."[19] On July 17, 1810, while visiting his family home in Montpelier, Virginia, Madison directed Smith to notify Governor Holmes in Mississippi to keep "a wakeful eye to occurrences & appearances in W. Florida, and in transmitting information concerning them." Additionally, the president instructed Smith to "apprize Govr. H. confidentially, of the course adopted as to W.F. and to have his co-operation in diffusing the impressions we wish to be made there."[20] Smith followed Madison's instructions almost word for word in his letter to Governor Holmes and included a copy of Claiborne's June 14 letter to Wykoff, noting that it was "written under a sanction from the President."[21]

Madison's covert operation in West Florida was a remarkable success. The plan approved in the White House meeting between President Madison and Governor Claiborne was efficiently conducted and generated minimal diplomatic repercussions. Claiborne had suggested in his first letter to agent Wykoff that a "spontaneous" call be issued to assemble a convention of delegates who would form the nucleus of the insurrectionary force.[22] This was the course of action adopted by the "revolutionary" movement. The operation directed by Holmes, Claiborne, and Wykoff that began in late July with the assembling of American "dissidents" led in late September to a military assault against Spanish forces by the "insurgents" and, finally, to a request for annexation by the United States. As with most covert operations, there was some tension between the authorities in Washington and the surrogate force in the field. Madison quickly broke with the West Florida revolutionaries when they began to demand a loan of $100,000 and large tracts of land as compensation for their efforts. Madison refused to recognize the newly independent West Florida government; issuing a proclamation on October 27, 1810, he claimed the territory for the United States as part of the Louisiana Purchase.[23] As Governor Holmes put it, in a most understated way, the desires of the American government were "in a great measure effected."[24]

With one great exception—the June meeting between Claiborne and Madison—the bulk of the deceptive activities associated with this operation were conducted at a discreet distance from the Madison White House. At the peak of the operation, on October 9, 1810, Secretary of State Smith met with the Spanish consul general assigned to Baltimore to discuss the latter's concern over attacks by private American citizens against Spanish West Florida. Smith sought to persuade Spain that the United States was not involved in these aggressive actions, and the meeting appears to have focused on the unsanctioned acts of American soldiers of fortune, whom Smith dismissed as rogue plotters operating in defiance of U.S. law. Smith told the envoy that the president condemned the actions of American citizens "which might tend to compromise the peace and good understanding" between Spain and the United States. Smith further informed the consul general that the administration would "punish to the utmost extent of the law" any private American citizen committing hostilities against "the subjects and territories of Spain." Smith successfully covered up the involvement of the U.S. government's "official" effort under way at the very moment the two diplomats were meeting. As Madison's biographer Irving Brant notes, Smith's statement "no doubt represented Madison's attitude toward lawless American adventurers, but it fell far short of disclosing the encouragement he was giving to revolt" in West Florida.[25]

Smith's cover-up continued weeks later when he met with General Louis Turreau, the French ambassador to the United States. As we have seen, Smith told Turreau that American officials were "strangers to everything that has happened."[26]

The administration's effort to conceal its involvement in West Florida included an attempt to alter the historical record of the affair by postdating a packet of documents relating to the insurrection. The documents had been sent by Holmes to Secretary Smith on October 3, 1810—at the height of the operation—but were postdated by the State Department to October 17, 1810. Madison and Smith wished to make it appear that they did not have the material in their possession until after Smith's meeting with Ambassador Turreau. The material had arrived at the State Department by October 27 and was well known to Smith at the time of his October 31 meeting with the ambassador. A second packet mailed by Holmes on October 17 did not arrive until early November, after the Turreau meeting. When the administration submitted the material for publication in *American State Papers,* attached was a note that read "Transmitted with the letter of Governor Holmes to the Secretary of State, of October 17, 1810." Years later, an enterprising historian discovered the original file, dated October 3, 1810, in the Department of State.[27]

The absence of any congressional role in the affair is one of the most intriguing elements of this saga. The covert acquisition of West Florida represented, in Irving Brant's words, "expansion by Executive Order."[28] Madison himself seems to have been somewhat unsettled by the prospect of acquiring West Florida through the exercise of unilateral executive authority. He expressed these concerns in a letter to Jefferson written in October 1810:

> The crisis in West Florida, as you will see, has come home to our feelings and our interests. It presents, at the same time, serious questions as to the authority of the Executive. . . . And the near approach of Congress might subject any intermediate interposition of the Executive to the charge of being premature and disrespectful, if not being illegal.[29]

To ensure that Congress would remain in the dark until the West Florida operation had achieved its goal, Madison suppressed until mid-December any public mention of his October 27 proclamation authorizing

American authorities to take control of the region. In one of the earliest examples of presidential news "management," Madison withheld any information on activities in West Florida long enough to solidify America's hold there and to allow proadministration newspapers enough time to editorialize in favor of the acquisition.[30] Furthermore, as Irving Brant comments, "Secrecy, maintained amazingly well . . . enabled Claiborne and his troops to do their work before opposition could be organized by the land speculators or by the Spanish in Pensacola. It presented European ministries with a *fait accompli.*"[31] This tactic had the additional benefit of allowing Madison to present the West Florida acquisition as a fait accompli to Congress as well.

The reaction within Congress was essentially supportive of the administration's initiative, and very little attention was paid to possible American involvement in igniting the insurrection. One critic was Senator Outerbridge Horsey of Delaware, who appears to have sensed that the Madison White House was not entirely truthful in its account of events. The senator was skeptical that a revolutionary movement would overthrow one foreign master and then immediately request the intervention of another. Horsey asked:

> If these proceedings [the formation of a revolutionary government] are not all a sham, the territory in question is now in possession of a people claiming to be sovereign and independent; and is it supposable that this people can behave so dastardly as to submit, without a struggle, to the incursion of a hostile army?[32]

Horsey's comment is the only suggestion during the debate that the "insurrection" may not have been as spontaneous as the administration suggested. His skepticism regarding the origins of the revolutionary government was not shared by other critics of the administration, however, who tended to focus their attention on the constitutional and legal questions surrounding Madison's issuance of the October 27 proclamation.

Madison's West Florida policy was defended by Senator John Pope, who offered a somewhat contradictory account of an innocent administration responding to the wishes of the citizens of that area. Pope stated that the president, under authority granted during the time of the Louisiana Purchase, had been given the power to take possession of this territory at his "discretion." According to Pope:

> [Madison] did not think it proper to seize upon it by force, but to wait for the occurrence of events to throw it into our hands without a struggle. . . . If the President had refused or hesitated to meet the wishes of the people of West Florida by extending to them the protection of the American Government . . . he would have been charged with imbecility.[33]

Responding to unnamed critics who indelicately referred to the measure legitimizing the occupation and retention of West Florida as "an act of robbery and war," Senator Pope stated that the step was justified in the name of "national security."

Although overtly defending a bill supporting the occupation and retention of West Florida, Pope might have been making a case for clandestine operations. On the one hand, he proclaimed that the "principle of necessity and expediency" should be used in only the most extreme cases and with great caution; seizing the property of others by force tended to "relax the morals of the people, by destroying that criterion of right and wrong, observance of which is so necessary to the purity of our Republic." But on the other, Pope declared that the European powers conducted their affairs in a manner noted for "perfidy and rapacity." Therefore, Pope stated:

> [W]e ought not, as regards them [the European powers] to be over nice or squeamish upon questions of this sort. Shall we sit here with our arms folded until the enemy is at our gates? If we waste our time in abstract questions of right and wrong, we shall lose our independence.[34]

There may have been a variety of reasons for Congress's acquiescence toward Madison's West Florida policy. Some senators may have accepted the administration's version of events at face value, while skeptics may have lacked solid evidence to support the accusation of a sham insurrection alluded to by Horsey. No doubt some administration supporters were simply satisfied with the results and refused to quibble with success. But it is probable that the most important factor in achieving congressional acceptance was Madison's skillful manipulation of newspaper coverage and his delay in formally notifying Congress until success was ensured. This deception paid a handsome dividend as congressional participation was limited to an after-the-fact ratification of Madison's actions.

The ease with which Madison pulled off the West Florida covert operation may have influenced his decision to use similar techniques to acquire Spanish-held East Florida. The dust from West Florida had barely settled before Madison dispatched an agent named George Mathews to investigate the possibilities of acquiring the remainder of Florida. The similarities between Mathews and fellow covert operator William Eaton of Barbary fame are striking, not the least of which was their expendability in the eyes of their respective commanders in chief. In both Tripoli and East Florida, shifting diplomatic circumstances forced two American presidents to disavow any knowledge of the activities of their agents. And in both instances, they were portrayed as rogue operatives and left twisting in the wind.

East Florida: Executing "a Trust of Such Interest and Delicacy"

The East Florida operation of George Mathews was a classic case of an executive agent undertaking a mission under ambiguous and somewhat open-ended presidential instructions. The suggestion for hiring Mathews as an executive agent had come from Georgia senator William H. Crawford. He had written to Madison on September 18, 1810, that former Georgia governor George Mathews would be up to the task of dealing with "the delicate trust" of securing the territory of West Florida, and Mathews consequently played a limited role in the affair.[35]

In the early autumn of 1810, at Madison's behest, Mathews met with the Spanish governor of West Florida, Don Vicente Folch. In the wake of this meeting and beset by a province under revolt, Folch indicated to Madison his willingness to transfer West Florida peacefully to the United States in November 1810.[36] However, Folch's communication raised, at least in Madison's mind, the possibility that Spain might yield East Florida as well.[37] Madison decided to try for all of Florida at once, not content simply to secure his hold on West Florida. Isaac Cox states that "the President and the Secretary, therefore proposed to give Folch's appeal a wider scope than that official intended. East and West Florida were joined in their proposed policy and [George] Mathews and [Colonel John] McKee [an Indian agent recruited by the administration to assist in the mission] were associated as agents to carry it out.[38]

Believing that the governor would acquiesce to a request for the entire region, the administration moved quickly to seek congressional approval to acquire East Florida if circumstances warranted. To assist in winning congressional support, Madison attempted to create an emergency atmosphere by raising the specter of a British threat to East Florida.[39] This chilling prospect was included in Madison's secret message delivered to Congress on January 3, 1811. This requested approval of a resolution allowing the president "to take temporary possession of any part or parts of the said territory [East Florida]." The effectiveness of the threat can be seen in the passage of the secret legislation less than two weeks after the administration warned of foreign danger on America's southern frontier. On January 15, 1811, Madison signed a resolution and an act that read in part:

> That the United States, under the peculiar circumstances of the existing crisis, cannot, without serious inquietude, see any part of the said territory pass into the hands of any foreign power . . . the President of the United States be, and he is hereby, authorized, to take possession of, and occupy, all or any part of the territory.

In the event of foreign (i.e., British) interference, Madison was authorized to acquire East Florida as long as that met with the approval of "the local authority of the said territory." As historian Kenneth Porter has remarked, local authority "was a term capable of being liberally construed." Congress also requested the president to continue negotiating for the peaceful acquisition of the region and provided $100,000 to support Madison's activities, funds that immediately would be put to use. In contrast to his actions in West Florida, Madison had solid congressional backing for his attempt to acquire East Florida.[40]

Madison's selection of George Mathews to "negotiate" with Folch was an interesting choice. The former Georgia governor had an alleged history of meddling in the affairs of East Florida. According to historian Julius Pratt, "In the closing months of 1810 . . . [Mathews had] communicated with residents of the Spanish province and with individuals on the American side of the Saint Mary's river, with the purpose of stimulating in East Florida an independence movement."[41] Pratt quotes from a letter written on January 7, 1811, a week before the passage of the secret statute, in which government officials from Spanish East Florida reported that Mathews had "official instructions to assist a revolutionary movement in East Florida." According to historian Paul Kruse, "There is reason to believe that considerable progress had been made in inciting a revolution in East Florida before the secret act and resolution of January 15, 1811, were passed."[42] Whether or not Madison was aware of these activities before engaging Mathews's services is difficult to state with certainty. Mathews's alleged prior clandestine experience only adds to the controversy surrounding his mission.

Sometime in January 1811, President Madison met with Mathews at the White House to launch the mission.[43] Shortly thereafter, on January 26, 1811, Mathews and McKee received their written instructions from the administration. Their orders were, as one historian put it, "remarkably vague and general."[44] The written instructions from Secretary of State Robert Smith merely confirmed the fact that Mathews had received verbal instructions from the president; as Smith did not repeat them, we will never know their full nature. Smith's letter urged Mathews and McKee to "repair to that quarter [Florida] with all possible expedition, concealing from general observation the trust committed to you, with that discretion which the delicacy and importance of the undertaking require."[45]

When Mathews and McKee finally met with Folch in April 1811, the Spanish governor vowed to resist U.S. efforts to cement its hold on West Florida. Folch told Mathews that the president's actions in West Florida had deeply insulted him and that he would not peaceably negotiate a transfer of that territory or any part of Spanish Florida. When negotiations with Governor Folch halted, Secretary of State James Monroe (who had succeeded Smith on April 3, 1811) extended his thanks to Mathews and McKee for their efforts and told them that Governor Claiborne (of the Orleans Territory) would handle matters related to West Florida from that point on. However, the breakdown of negotiations did not mean that Mathews's business in Florida was finished. Instead, Monroe asked Mathews to turn his attention toward East Florida "if he thought he could accomplish anything there."[46] Mathews could not resist this invitation and began (or perhaps resumed) a surreptitious campaign to which the administration silently assented for seven months. For Mathews, and perhaps the administration that sent him to the region, the goal had shifted from a peaceful acquisition of East Florida to one relying on a "spontaneous" request for American intervention from the "local authorities."

Despite the ostensible concern with West Florida, East Florida actually appears to have been the focal point of Mathews's concern from the time he first arrived on his mission to see Governor Folch at his headquarters in Pensacola. In one of his earliest letters to Secretary Smith, Mathews reported:

> On my arivil hear I found the gentlemin hows names I give you will disposid to Sarve our government but thare has not one Solder arived or one armed visil or a gun Boat in this rivar, from this cause its thought not propar to attemp Eny thing at present . . . by the 20th of April . . . I hope to have it in my power to carey the Presedents wishes into afact . . . from the prospect of things hear E. F. is growing of more importens to the U.S. evarey day . . . you will plase to assure the President evary exershin in my power will be made to carey his wishes in to afact.[47]

Mathews wrote to the secretary on April 24, 1811, and recommended the United States hire a clergyman who would act as an American "asset" in Pensacola. Mathews and McKee had known this priest since 1797, and they claimed that the cleric had "a friendly disposition towards the United States, and has been esteemed by all who have had the pleasure of his acquaintance. We think it would be policy as well as justice to invite him to return and to make a provision for his support."[48]

Mathews and McKee laid the groundwork for an intelligence network throughout the Floridas, seeking to measure and at times shape the attitude of the citizenry toward the United States. McKee informed the State Department that he had sent a "trusty man to Pensacola" whose long residence and familiarity with the citizenry gave him a great opportunity to obtain information.[49] At one point, McKee also noted that Mathews had crossed into East Florida to reconnoiter a "site which he thinks calculated for a military post."[50] Mathews and McKee eventually acquired intelligence sources in Mobile, New Orleans, and Pensacola.

From the time of his appointment as Madison's secretary of state, James Monroe served as the president's operational point man for the Floridas. Monroe received a steady flow of reports from McKee, who assisted Governor Claiborne's effort to solidify the American hold on West Florida, portions of which still remained in Spanish hands. One report sent to Monroe included a letter from a spy who requested anonymity: "The author is a gentleman of unquestioned veracity with considerable means of acquiring intelligence, and the communication was made in confidence that as little publicity as possible would be given it."[51]

The Spanish kept McKee busy tracking down a number of wild rumors. It seems they were busily engaged in a disinformation campaign designed to mislead American agents on their military strength in the region.[52] McKee spent a considerable amount of time investigating reports of Spanish intrigue with the Indians. In one report to the administration, he noted that he was informed on "good authority" that a vessel had arrived from Mexico with somewhere between $5,000 and $7,000. He launched an investigation to see if the money had made any change "in the disposition of the Chiefs."[53] When such reports persisted, McKee told Monroe that he had sent a man to Pensacola "who is likely without creating suspicion to ascertain and counteract any intrigue that may be carrying on there with the Creeks."[54]

In the meantime, Mathews wrote—or had someone write for him—from his post on the East Florida border that he was thrilled with the appointment of James Monroe as secretary of state: "I will not recite all the motives I have for joy on this occasion" he wrote the new secretary.[55] From then on, Monroe received a steady stream of correspondence from his agent, sometimes simple letters of two or three sentences recounting the movements of foreign ships and the latest rumors circulating in the area or short notes to let his superiors in Washington know he was still on the job. Monroe was apparently anxious to acquire East Florida and wrote to Mathews that he was to continue his efforts, "especially if you entertain any reasonable hope of success there."[56] On June 28, 1811, Mathews had written to Monroe:

> I have obtained assurances upon which I can rely, that I shall be furnished, from time to time, with the earliest information relative to affairs in Florida. It is my intention to pass into the province the moment my health will permit—by being a spectator of what is going on I can better foresee and provide for events, than by the best information I can obtain here.

Mathews also added that he was "daily more and more convinced in a belief of the vast importance of Florida to the U. States."[57]

Isaac Cox notes that Mathews "spent the summer of 1811 alternately fighting malaria and encouraging insurrection."[58] His letter to Monroe written on August 3, 1811, marks a dramatic event in the evolution of this story: Mathews's intentions regarding East Florida had clearly gone beyond a negotiated acquisition of the region. In this letter, Mathews requested a covert shipment of supplies to insurrectionary forces in East Florida: "I ascertain that the quiet possession of E. Florida could not be obtained by an amicable negotiation with the powers that exist there . . . the inhabitants of the province are ripe for revolt, they are however incompetent to effect a thorough revolution without external aid." However, with arms and horsemen's swords in their possession,

> I am confident they would commence the business and with a fair prospect of success. These could be put into their hands by consigning them to the Commanding officer at this post subject to my order. I should use the most

discreet management and prevent the U. States being committed and altho I cannot vouch for the event, I think there would be but little danger.

Mathews asked that the administration respond to his request as quickly as possible and handle his letter with the utmost secrecy. He requested that it be confided to the proper department, "for I can foresee that much injury to my operation would ensue" if lower-level clerks had access to it.[59] As Paul Kruse has observed, "This letter, written more than seven months before the invasion was actually attempted, fully disclosed General Mathews' revolutionary designs upon East Florida. Not to have checked the plans after such a notice made the government a party to them. The letter went unanswered."[60]

In order to clarify that he was conducting himself in a manner consonant with the administration's intent, Mathews visited Senator Crawford, who had recommended him to Madison. On October 14, 1811, he wrote from Crawford's home in Oglethorpe County, Georgia, that he had given the senator a copy of the August 3 letter. Mathews was still waiting for a reply and repeated his contention that the United States must act: "Should we seize upon them at this juncture the same disposition to act in our favor continues among a certain portion of its inhabitants." Mathews added that if it was inconvenient for the administration to send the arms he requested, the American gunboats in nearby waters could easily "furnish arms and accoutrements that would render great facility to the business."[61] Subsequent correspondence from Mathews to Monroe repeated his request for supplies of arms to assist a rebel force.[62]

Mathews added in his October 14 letter that he had heard rumors that the administration was considering the removal of his authority. He asked that if the rumors were true: "I must entreat you to give me the earliest notice, for altho' I am ever ready to devote my best abilities to my country, yet I do not wish to remain in its employ any longer, than I can render it useful & acceptable services."[63] There is no record of a response from the administration. Probably the stakes had risen to the point where the administration could no longer afford to leave a paper trail should the operation be exposed; tacit approval was indicated by the administration's silence.

Mathews was further reassured by the administration's stonewalling in the face of a sharp diplomatic protest made by Great Britain. In September 1811, the British government obtained detailed information from Spanish sources describing the activities of George Mathews. To Secretary Monroe, the British minister at Washington, Augustus Foster, protested that Mathews was trying to produce revolution by "using every method of seduction to his purpose, offering to each white inhabitant, who would side with him fifty acres of land, and the guarantee of his religion and property."[64] After a two-month delay in responding, Monroe simply outlined the reasons why the administration viewed Florida as a desirable acquisition. This response made no mention of Mathews, a clear indication that the administration had no intention of stopping him.[65] In the wake of this indirect endorsement, Mathews escalated the campaign to topple Spanish authority in East Florida.

Mathews's top priority in the spring of 1812 was to engage the cooperation of American military authorities on the Florida border. The naval commander who assisted Mathews had received what could be interpreted as a signal of administration complicity in Mathews's designs. On March 28, 1812, before the news of Mathews's invasion reached Washington, Secretary of the Navy Paul Hamilton wrote to Captain Hugh Campbell asking him to give all his attention to affairs on the Florida border: "It is particularly important to have an officer of great skill and experience at St. Mary's [River], because it will most probably be a scene of active operations." The naval officer's career was not damaged by his timely assistance in providing gunboats for Mathews's initial assault.[66] The same cannot be said for the commanding army officer in the region, Major Jacint Laval. By refusing to cooperate, and thus effectively negating any chance of capturing St. Augustine, Laval's military career was ruined. He briefly was placed under arrest for his actions and ended his career as a military quartermaster. As Julius Pratt notes, "There can be little doubt which officer had acted more in accord with the wishes of the government."[67]

Mathews launched his revolution on March 13, 1812, when a force moved into Florida while "local" revolutionary authorities declared their independence and sought the support of freedom-loving men everywhere. They hoisted a new flag for East Florida, designed by a member of Mathews's staff, and with the assistance of U.S. naval gunboats captured the town of Fernandina.[68] Following the surrender of Fernandina, Mathews moved on to demand the surrender of St. Augustine.

The raising of a "revolutionary" force had presented something of a problem for Mathews, for it appears that the populace in East Florida was not so ripe for revolt as he might have hoped. Mathews's overtures seem to have had little impact on a population that was prospering economically and giving shelter from American authorities to runaway slaves and various Indian tribes. The force that Mathews ultimately assembled was composed predominately of Georgians and a handful of wealthy but discontented American plantation owners. The predominately Anglo composition of the insurrectionary force made it difficult to portray the operation as an indigenous uprising. One historian of the affair has noted that not a single Spanish soldier defected to the rebel cause despite lucrative offers.[69] The major flaw in the operation, one that set it apart from the successful effort in West Florida, was thus the apparent lack of any genuine groundswell of opposition to Spanish authority in East Florida. What was intended to have been a West Florida–style secret mission to foster rebellion discreetly instead became an overt American-sponsored military invasion.

Realizing that he had overestimated the level of support for American intervention and underestimated the willingness of Spain to resist, Mathews was forced to plead for additional U.S. military support. Mathews wrote to Monroe on the second day of his operation:

> The time has arrived when something must be done, and if ever you expect the Floridas send on immediately the companies of artillery and infantry I requested in my former letter and recall Major Laval . . . and if the President has confidence in me leave no discretion in the officer commanding in complying with my requests or orders.[70]

I believe that Mathews's admission that he could not achieve the seizure of East Florida without additional overt American military support pushed the administration over the edge. Months of silent acquiescence by the Madison White House came to an end. The cornerstone of the clandestine foreign policy of Jefferson and Madison was to project American influence through tactics short of war. Mathews, like Eaton before him, had promoted the type of overt military commitment that ran against a basic tenet of Jeffersonian-era foreign policy. Although the furtherance of American interests might require occasional covert assistance of the type seen in West Florida, the use of conventional forces in the absence of some evidence of indigenous support contradicted too many American ideals. Mathews's inability to conceal his actions and to generate a spontaneous, internal rebellion had rendered the operation too costly in the eyes of his overseers in Washington.

It was unfortunate for Mathews that just four days before he launched his operation, the administration released to Congress evidence that Britain had interfered covertly in the internal affairs of the United States. In order to score a propaganda victory over the British and the administration's Federalist opponents, Monroe and Madison had paid $50,000 out of the Contingency Fund to a disgruntled British agent who turned over correspondence relating to his secret activities in New England. The agent, John Henry, had traveled to Boston in January 1809 to measure, and perhaps to inflame, the level of discontent with Jefferson's trade embargo. The moral outrage of the Madison administration over the exposure of a British clandestine operation appeared somewhat hypocritical in light of the widespread awareness of Mathews's activities.[71] Mathews and many of his contemporaries believed that it was the release of the Henry papers that prompted his recall.[72] It would appear, however, that the Henry papers merely hastened the end of an operation that was certain to have been curtailed anyway; Mathews had enlarged the scope of his activities to the point where the administration no longer could plausibly deny responsibility for his actions.

Mathews was formally relieved of his duties on April 4, 1812. In his letter to Mathews, Monroe noted the contrast between the operations in West Florida and in East Florida. In West Florida, the United States "did not take possession until after the Spanish authority had been subverted by a revolutionary proceeding," and the threat of foreign intervention forced America's hand.[73] The actual message to Mathews was discernible between the lines: he had failed to generate unrest in East Florida as effectively as Holmes and Claiborne had done in West Florida. The recall letter also contained what one historian has interpreted as a veiled threat from Monroe to Mathews to keep quiet.[74]

By removing Mathews from his position, the administration eliminated the most public symbol of its controversial East Florida mission. Mathews's tactics had made him a target of British and Spanish diplomatic protests and Federalist party criticism. Yet despite this pressure and the ominous indications of the coming of the War of 1812, the administration still did not abandon its effort to acquire East Florida. Mathews's replacement as the president's special agent in the region, Georgia governor David Mitchell, was instructed to delay the evacuation of the rebel army from East Florida. The administration was determined to take advantage of the gains that Mathews had achieved, particularly by keeping the rebel army intact. Mitchell notified the Spanish governor of East Florida that any attempt to drive out the "patriots" who had rallied to the American cause would not be tolerated: "You alone will be answerable for all the consequences which may result from such a proceeding."[75] The administration appears to have hoped for some Spanish provocation that would allow U.S. forces to intervene under the pretext of protecting American lives.

On June 19, 1812, Congress entered the deliberations on future American policy in the region when the House debated a proposal from Congressman George M. Troup of Georgia to give the administration the authority to maintain an American military presence at Fernandina. (Fernandina had been occupied by U.S. forces in the wake of Mathews's seizure of the town.) The administration's position was supported in the House but rejected in the Senate. Nevertheless, Madison's determination to hold East Florida was so strong that he chose to ignore this congressional setback; Governor Mitchell was instructed to hold his ground. As one historian of the East Florida affair has asserted, Monroe's orders essentially asked Mitchell to risk his own neck by continuing the occupation of East Florida.[76] Monroe instructed Mitchell on May 27, 1812:

> It is not expected, if you should find it proper to withdraw the [American] troops, that you should interfere to compel the patriots to surrender the country, or any part of it to Spanish authorities. . . . Indeed, in consequence of the compromitment of the United States to the inhabitants, you have been already instructed not to withdraw the troops, unless you find that it can be done consistently with their safety, and to report to the Government the

result of your conferences with the Spanish authorities . . . holding in the mean time the ground occupied.[77]

Again in February 1813, the administration's request to preserve the American presence in East Florida was rejected by the Senate. Yet only after the second defeat did the administration abandon hope that events would aid its cause. Unfortunately for Madison, there had been neither Spanish reprisals against the rebel army nor British moves in that area as a result of the War of 1812. Thus the administration finally ceased its clandestine attempt to acquire East Florida; the pressure against Spain merely assumed a more overt diplomatic and military character, culminating in the American acquisition of the region in 1819.

The East Florida affair represents one of the earliest instances of significant congressional and media opposition to an operation that had covert undertones. This opposition was possible only because Congress and the press were given an unusual opportunity to comment on the mission while it was under way. The widespread awareness of the operation was due in part to the administration's bungled attempt to score propaganda points with the Henry papers. On his earlier trip to Boston, Henry had met with prominent Federalists, and with the release of his papers, the administration sought to tar the Federalist party with charges of treason. This effort in turn caused the Federalists to make the high-profile Mathews mission a partisan issue.

Although many pro-Madison newspapers dealt with the East Florida affair by ignoring it, describing it as a case of a rogue agent at work, or expressing regret that the region had not yet fallen into American hands, a number of opponents denounced the administration's tactics.[78] One prominent newspaper, the *Charleston Courier,* condemned Madison:

[T]he farce of receiving the Province from a handful of insurgents, assuming to themselves the glorious name of the Spanish patriots in the mother country, is disgraceful in the extreme. If Florida must be ours, let the arms of the U. States take it, and not receive it second hand.

In Congress, the assault on the administration's action was led by Senator William Hunter of Rhode Island:

Does a really deep, honest, spontaneous revolutionary movement exist there? Is it not, on the contrary, an artificial, concerted, contrived, petty, patched-up, miserable treason, paid for by our money, fomented by our people? Who caused this movement? Was it not solely occasioned by American interference—by American instigation?

The administration, not General Mathews, deserved the blame for events in East Florida, Senator Hunter added. "I cannot but believe that he [Mathews] thought he acted with perfect good faith to the Government. . . . He considered himself the victim of a temporizing, vacillating, insidious policy."[79] Congressional criticism of Madison's Florida policy did not have a great effect on the chief executive. Henry Adams described Madison's attitude toward his controversial policies and his critics: "He ignored caution in pursuit of an object which seemed to him proper in itself; nor could he understand why this quiet and patriotic conduct should rouse tempests of passion in his opponents, whose violence, by contrast, increased the apparent placidity of his own persistence."[80]

Senator Hunter's sympathy for George Mathews, the key figure in the East Florida affair, was shared by many outside observers. Counting on Mathews's patriotism and loyalty to the office of the presidency to keep him from revealing publicly his version of events, the administration continued to place the blame on him. However, Mathews's patience wore thin in the summer of 1812. He set out on a trip to Washington, allegedly saying that he would be "dam'd if he did not blow them all up." He appears to have had in mind the release of what his personal secretary called "back stairs" instructions. Fortunately for the administration, Mathews died in Augusta, Georgia, en route to Washington, on July 24, 1812.[81]

The Covert Madison

Often described as the father of American constitutional government, James Madison merits special attention. We can understand more about the nature of executive authority in America by examining the exercise of that authority by one of the Constitution's most important drafters. Additionally, it is useful to examine Madison's actions as chief executive in light of the conventional assumption that the use of covert operations by American presidents is primarily a Cold War phenomenon. As we have seen, Madison-era covert operations offer striking similarities to those of his twentieth-century successors.

Although this section focuses on covert operations in the Floridas, it should be noted that Madison had already acquired training in the world of secret operations long before launching his Florida missions. As Jefferson's secretary of state, he had assisted in the effort to overthrow the pasha of Tripoli during the Barbary Wars. As president, Madison appears to have continued Jefferson's policy of bribing Indian chiefs to obtain territorial concessions.[82] Madison revealed his familiarity with the unseemly necessities of foreign relations by procuring, at public expense, a prostitute for a foreign envoy. He probably had this particular event in mind when he noted that "appropriations to foreign intercourse are terms of great latitude and may be drawn on by very urgent and unforeseen occurrences."[83] During Madison's presidency, intelligence reports and other secret government documents were also given added protection by a formal system of classification (consisting of "secret," "confidential," and "private").[84]

In addition, as intelligence historian Edward Sayle has noted, the United States allied itself with pirates in the War of 1812, when General Andrew Jackson utilized the resources of Jean Lafitte to scout, to spy, and occasionally, to fight for the United States. This "unholy alliance . . . with gangsters," as Sayle calls it, would not mark the last time the nation called on such elements for assistance in the Gulf of Mexico. In 1815, as a reward for their efforts on behalf of the United States, Lafitte and his men were given full pardons for their past activities by President Madison after the American victory at the Battle of New Orleans.[85]

Important as these events are in the history of American intelligence activity, none match the significance of Madison's actions in the Floridas. The dispatch of secret American operatives to that region followed precedents set by William Eaton's operation against the Barbary pirates. Once again, particularly in the case of George Mathews, an agent was sent on a mission with vague instructions (at least vague *written* instructions) and granted broad discretionary authority. In both cases, the agent apparently was asked to achieve an objective without burdening the executive with specific operational details. Both men were left for prolonged periods in positions of responsibility while they made commitments and undertook initiatives allegedly at odds with the administration's policy. Both men were asked to perform the role of scapegoat for controversial executive initiatives, confronting them with a choice between personal vindication and patriotic duty. The Barbary and East Florida operations demonstrate the importance of a president's weighing all the possible consequences of initiating covert operations. Like Jefferson before him, President Madison does not seem to have considered in advance whether he was prepared to support his surrogate forces with overt U.S. assistance should that become necessary. Jefferson and Madison appear to have vacillated over that point; moreover, both demonstrated a degree of naïveté about their ability to shut the operations down when they believed circumstances required it. They both ultimately chose to engage in damage limitation and to abandon their surrogate forces when these encountered difficulties. As was true in the Barbary coup attempt, repercussions from the East Florida operation were felt long after policy makers in Washington decided to terminate the operation. Henry Adams termed the situation in Florida after the withdrawal of the American presence there as one of "anarchy," which had been introduced by the United States and "could never be mastered except by the power that created it."[86]

One is left with the question of why the West Florida operation was a model of a successful covert operation, while the East Florida operation was an embarrassing failure. There were crucial differences in their execution, differences partly the result of circumstances beyond the agents' control. Madison's agents in West Florida achieved their objective quickly and with a minimum of direct U.S. involvement. The long arm of the American government was well concealed, and events moved at such a pace as to keep Congress and foreign powers from meddling. Furthermore, the operatives in West Florida had an easier time due to a high level of indigenous support for an insurrection against Spanish authority and sympathy for union with the United States. In East Florida, Mathews faced more hostile elements eager to maintain the protection of the Spanish government. As a result, Mathews was forced to assemble what amounted to an invasion force to secure the region.

Were the covert operations in the Floridas justified? Of course, there was the "problem" of East Florida's serving as a safe haven for runaway slaves and various hostile Indian tribes, a constant source of irritation to southern governors (though at the same time, many Americans profited from a bustling smugglers' market on the Florida border).[87] Yet there was no apparent threat to America's security on its southern frontier from either Spain or Britain. Americans believed nonetheless that Spanish Florida represented a danger. Foreign-policy historian Alexander De-Conde has described the American attitude toward Florida as "a pistol held by an alien hand pointed at the heart of the nation."[88] Beyond the perceived threat to America's physical security, European possessions in the New World represented something of an ideological challenge to the United States. This was a source of frustration to a series of American presidents beginning with Jefferson, continuing with Madison, and reaching its peak with the presidency of Madison's successor, James Monroe. The doctrine that bears Monroe's name could accurately be described as official American policy long before he became chief executive.

Madison's determination to rid the Floridas of this reactionary European presence led him to manipulate and mislead Congress. He did his utmost to sustain the rebel army in East Florida in spite of congressional refusal to sanction his policies. He withheld notification of Congress of his actions in West Florida for weeks, until his control over that region was complete. When notification was made, he overstated British designs on the region in order to stampede Congress into supporting his objectives in East Florida. He sought, as Isaac Cox put it, "to create the impression that the British were so manipulating affairs on our southern border as to justify the occupation of East as well as West Florida."[89] On this point, Mathews and McKee could possibly be accused of "cooking" their intelligence reports in order to manipulate their superiors in Washington. Both men reported rumors of massive British and Spanish troop movements to the region, along with information of black troops prepared to attack America's southern frontier. In any case, the administration seemed too willing to believe the allegations, the majority of which were unsubstantiated.[90]

Madison's predecessor in the executive office had sanctioned covert operations against nations with which the United States openly had engaged in hostilities. Madison, however, authorized a covert operation in West Florida and appears to have acquiesced to a similar mission against

East Florida; both actions were directed against Spain, a nation with which the United States was at peace.

Ironically, many chroniclers of Madison's presidency view him as a model of restraint in his exercise of executive authority. One observer sees Madison as the ultimate "republican" chief executive who serves as a refreshing contrast to the "imperial" presidents of the late twentieth century. According to this account, Madison's avoidance of the type of "executive excess" found in such Cold War presidents as those cited by the Church Committee sets him apart from his modern successors.[91] One can accept this interpretation of Madison's presidency only if one believes that he was unaware of the activities of his secret operatives in the Floridas. Madison must then be seen as a bumbling and detached chief executive misled and manipulated for months on end by "rogue agents."

An examination of Madison's presidency actually reveals that contemporary opponents of covert activity who invoke the legacy of the Founders are either deliberately disingenuous or simply unaware of the persuasive evidence that points to the endorsement of these operations by this preeminent Founder. The events discussed in this chapter demonstrate that James Madison believed covert operations were an essential part of America's foreign-policy arsenal. An honest assessment of proposals to eliminate or severely restrict the ability of the president to conduct secret operations can only be viewed as a fundamental rejection of this Founder's understanding of executive power. Contemporary critics of presidential control over covert activities interpret executive power in a manner that was not envisioned and, most important, not practiced by our most prominent Founding Father.

Covert Operative in Latin America

Joel Poinsett and American Intervention in Argentina and Chile

The operations of Joel Poinsett in Latin America, which spanned three administrations, represented an attempt on the part of the United States to assist the cause of republican government by removing the presence of Old World powers from the Americas. The operations extended into remote corners of Latin America and followed the by-then well-established pattern of vaguely worded presidential instructions coupled with loose supervision of the respective agents' subsequent activities. As we have seen, this approach allowed the president, should circumstances require, to state that an agent had exceeded his authority. By giving the executive a cover story that distanced him from the actions of his agents, the president was able to advance American interests and ideals without generating diplomatic or military reprisals. Nowhere was the use of this strategy more apparent than in the part-public and part-covert actions of Joel R.

Poinsett, an executive agent whose revolutionary zeal for the democratic cause led one of his biographers to dub him the "apostle of liberty in South America."[92] Poinsett helped to create and direct political movements in Chile and Mexico pledged to the adoption of the American model of government and hostile to European interests.

The first of Poinsett's missions began in the fall of 1810, the peak period of the Madison administration's infatuation with covert operations. Poinsett was instructed to travel to Buenos Aires and, if possible, Santiago, Chile, and Lima, Peru. Poinsett's instructions from Secretary of State Robert Smith matched the level of intentional ambiguity found in the instructions to Madison's other covert operatives. Smith instructed Poinsett on August 27, 1810:

> The real as well as ostensible object of your mission is to explain the mutual advantage of commerce with the United States . . . to diffuse the impression that the United States cherish the sincerest good will towards the people of Spanish America as neighbors . . . that this disposition will exist, whatever may be their internal system or European relation, with respect to which no interference of any sort is pretended.

And yet the classic Madison ambiguity can be found in two lines from the secretary's letter that could be construed as leaving the door open for a more active role for the agent. After the reference to nonintervention, Smith noted that the occurrence of "a political separation from the parent country" would be a most welcome development in the hemisphere and would "coincide with the sentiments and policy of the United States." All nations of the Americas had an interest in maintaining "that system of peace, justice, and good will, which is the only source of happiness for nations." Poinsett was to "take such steps, not incompatible with the neutral character and honest policy of the United States, as the occasion renders proper."[93] As diplomatic historian Henry Wriston has observed, Poinsett's mission was unusual:

> [T]his was getting into diplomatic contact very early. There had, as yet, been no declaration of independence. . . . Poinsett was not sent to deal with a viceregal government, but with a legitimist party in revolt. He was to intimate very plainly that the United States would be glad to see revolt develop into revolution and independence.[94]

Apparently, Madison's concern over a possible British response to Poinsett's mission led him to insist that it proceed in secret. In January 1811, portraying himself as an Englishman and traveling on board a British merchant ship, Poinsett left for Buenos Aires.[95] After his arrival, Poinsett was immediately confronted with two obstacles he would face throughout his Latin American missions: the opposition of the Catholic Church to the spread of republican government, and the active presence of British agents who were buying influence wherever necessary. Poinsett's views on the Catholic hierarchy's resistance to republican "revolution" would lead him to engage in a number of operations designed to wean the people from their dependence on the Church. Poinsett believed that the Catholic clergy "were sent into this world with the spirit of fanaticism and persecution, to confirm the people in ignorance and superstition, by inculcating blind obedience to the sovereign."[96]

British operatives were an additional impediment to the arrangement of favorable commercial and political relationships with the United States. One prominent character in revolutionary Buenos Aires was described by Poinsett as "bankrupt in fortune, and devoid of honor . . . he is a fit subject to be corrupted by the british cabinet." Another revolutionary figure was a more reasonable man: "Ugarteche is a lawyer of reputation in Buenos Ayres and disposed to be useful to the American interests."[97] British operatives in the region were well aware of Poinsett's covert efforts to win support for American interests. One British naval officer took note of Poinsett's activities:

> They [leaders in Buenos Aires] have been led to expect that great benefit will be derived from taking this step [independence], by some citizens of the United States of America, who have been very busy in the politics of these people . . . a Mr. Poinsett . . . is particularly diligent and active in propagating doctrines and opinions prejudicial to the British government and subjects.[98]

The American objective of displacing British influence in the region was complicated by the tendency of revolutionary movements in South America to look to Britain for assistance in pressuring Spain to ease its grip on the region.[99] At the time of Poinsett's arrival in Buenos Aires, a revolutionary junta had been established but was riddled with faction and instability. Poinsett appears to have attempted to widen the gap between this junta and the nominal Spanish government, urging the former to issue an outright declaration of independence. Although Poinsett met with some success in arranging for favorable commercial terms for the United States, his efforts to arrange a complete break from Spain were resisted. When reports of a favorable revolutionary situation reached him from Santiago, Poinsett then decided to move on to Chile.[100]

President Madison had formally enlarged Poinsett's operational sphere to include Chile and Peru, and it was in those countries that Poinsett's skills at revolutionary agitation and counterinsurgency met their greatest test. In 1810, a revolutionary junta had overthrown most of the structures of Spanish authority in Chile. Between 1811 and 1814, the revolutionary movement undertook measures to establish self-government while nonetheless professing loyalty to the Spanish king. Spanish rule was restored briefly between 1814 and 1817, but Chile's independence was ultimately established in 1818.[101] Months before his departure for Chile, Poinsett received a letter from the new secretary of state, James Monroe, which reinforced the notion that the Madison administration welcomed revolution in Latin America:

The disposition shewn by most of the Spanish provinces to separate from Europe and to erect themselves into independent States excites great interest here. As Inhabitants of the same Hemisphere, as Neighbors, the United States cannot be unfeeling Spectators of so important a movement. The destiny of these provinces must depend on themselves. Should such a revolution however take place, it cannot be doubted that our relations with them will be more intimate and our friendship stronger than it can be while they are colonies of any European power.[102]

Poinsett wasted no time in ingratiating himself with the Chilean revolutionary junta. He became an "authorized councillor" to the president of the junta and assisted in the drafting of the provisional constitution of 1812, a document written in his home. Additionally, Poinsett presented a plan of organization for the Chilean police. The same British observer who had monitored Poinsett's activities in Buenos Aires now noted that the leadership of the Chilean junta was "entirely governed by Poinsett." As he had done in Buenos Aires, Poinsett urged the Chilean government to declare complete independence from Spain, a bold step that it was reluctant to take. In the midst of this activity, Poinsett settled a potentially fatal dispute between two brothers in the ruling junta, one of whom believed that the United States was becoming too influential in Chilean affairs.[103]

This intervention in the internal affairs of a foreign power was conducted for the most part with the consent of the ruling government in Chile, though much of it involved clandestine maneuvering with factions in the Chilean hierarchy. In one dispatch, Poinsett discussed the forces in the Catholic Church that obstructed his efforts at reshaping Chilean society:

I have purposefully omitted speaking of the Clergy and Friars; the most powerful engine of political intrigue in these countries, but the most difficult to manage and varying in influence according to the election of their provincials and chiefs. . . . These chapters agitate the minds of the people in a most extraordinary degree.[104]

Poinsett's efforts at "managing" Chilean internal affairs were generally known by his superiors in Washington. As one of his biographers has remarked:

He [Poinsett] probably thought his instructions might be interpreted so as to justify his course, and that his actions would not be disavowed. His reports, though never fully describing his intimate connections with the affairs of the country, were on the whole candid. It is possible that some of them never reached the State Department.[105]

Poinsett's most controversial actions took place after an invasion force of Peruvians loyal to the Spanish Crown attacked and seized Talcahuano, an important harbor in southern Chile. While serving as an agent of President Madison, Poinsett was given the rank of general in the Chilean revolutionary forces and led a charge against Peruvian royalist forces at the Battle of San Carlos. He then directed a successful attack on the city of Concepción, freeing ten American whaling vessels seized by royalist forces. In two letters to Secretary Monroe, Poinsett defended the latter action by stating that he was merely protecting American property.[106] Poinsett's high-profile activities had not gone unnoticed by the British, who at one point stationed warships off of Chile in part to "counteract" the efforts of "Mr. Poinsett."[107]

Much to Poinsett's frustration, the revolutionary forces he had supported suffered some military setbacks and began to turn against one another. Yet before surreptitiously leaving for the safety of Argentina in April 1814, he received news that his friends in the Chilean junta had returned to power. Pleased with the news, Poinsett still opted not to return to Chile and left for the United States after a tour of duty spanning nearly four years.[108]

Shortly after his return, Poinsett received a letter from Secretary Monroe that expressed his approval "of the ability and zeal with which" Poinsett had "discharged" his duties.[109] The written record appears to indicate that Poinsett never fully informed Monroe of some of his more ambitious endeavors on behalf of the Chilean junta. However, it should be noted that the written record is far from complete because Monroe ordered the State Department to deliver to Poinsett many of the most important files from his Chilean mission.[110] The administration provided other forms of assistance to Latin American revolutionary movements that lend credence to the idea that Poinsett's conduct was discreetly welcomed by the administration. Throughout this period (1809–1817), Madison allowed Latin American agents from revolutionary movements to operate freely in the United States and to purchase supplies. Moreover, Secretary of State Monroe met with a Mexican revolutionary, José Bernardo Maximiliano Gutiérrez de Lara, in the winter of 1811/1812 and provided him with material assistance. Following this meeting, de Lara organized an expedition that captured San Antonio and proclaimed a short-lived provisional republic of Texas.[111] The administration also established contact with these agents through a network of influential private American citizens.[112]

Perhaps the most convincing evidence of the administration's satisfaction with Poinsett's conduct can be seen in the assignments that later were sent his way. Indeed, Poinsett was offered a second mission to Chile and Argentina in 1817 by the new president, James Monroe, but he rejected it out of a belief that the quality of revolutionary leadership in South America was too low. In a letter to a personal friend, Poinsett outlined his reasons for his refusal and offered some suggestions for American agents sent in his place to Argentina and Chile. One leading Chilean revolutionary was described as "easily led . . . a skillful agent can render him subservient to all his views—he must be managed . . . gently." As for

Buenos Aires, "the American party is still powerful there & only wants a leader of firmness and talents—When I first arrived in Buenos Aires we had no party, and we were not known at all." It would appear that President Monroe wanted somebody for the new mission who could, in the words of Poinsett, "play the game" as adeptly as the latter had some few short years before.[113]

Although he rejected this mission, Poinsett's career as an "apostle of liberty" was far from complete. In fact, his most controversial assignment lay ahead.

Poinsett and American Intervention in Mexico

At the behest of President James Monroe, Joel Poinsett took advantage of the skills he had acquired in Argentina and Chile and put them to use in Mexico. Monroe called on Poinsett to undertake a confidential mission to Mexico in 1822 to investigate the level of popular support for Mexican emperor Augustín de Iturbide. Monroe believed that Iturbide had betrayed the principles of republicanism that had led Mexico to declare its independence from Spain in 1821. In the months immediately following independence, Iturbide had effected something of a counterrevolution, restoring the Catholic Church to its position of prominence in Mexican society. Once again, Poinsett would record his disgust with the alliance of the Church and monarchist elements in Latin American society. After a meeting with members of the emperor's family, Poinsett noted that the royal family had no idea how "ridiculous this miserable representation of royalty appears to a republican." Poinsett's prediction that Iturbide lacked any popular support and would soon be deposed came true shortly after his return to the United States in January 1823. It appears that Iturbide was overthrown partly through the assistance of the Scottish Rite Masons. As will be seen, the lesson of this group's participation in the coup would not be lost on Poinsett.[114]

Poinsett's accurate analysis of the situation in Mexico impressed his superiors in Washington and led to his appointment by President John Quincy Adams (1825–1829) as the American ambassador to Mexico in 1825. He appears to have been designated as the point man for the administration's effort to restrain growing British influence in Mexico. Prior to his departure, Poinsett had received instructions from the new, expansionist secretary of state, Henry Clay. While briefing Poinsett, Clay showed him a copy of instructions sent to an American agent in Colombia. These instructions applied to Poinsett's mission as well: the envoy was instructed "to show on all occasions an unobtrusive readiness to explain the practical operation and the very great advantages which appertain to our system."[115]

Upon arriving in Mexico, Poinsett took note of the influence of British agents on the Mexican government: "The British government has anticipated us. . . . Their [commercial] treaty is made, and . . . no doubt appears to be entertained of the result."[116] Poinsett was forced to counter this rising tide of British influence by working behind the scenes with opposition political leaders. He engineered a restructuring of that party by encouraging the formation of a York Rite Masonic Lodge, a group that became the core of the opposition's political machinery. The membership of the York Rite Masons would go on to include two members of the Mexican cabinet, two senators, a group of congressmen, and prominent members of the military.[117] On more than one occasion, Poinsett informed his government of his effort to build a pro-American political party in Mexico through this lodge. As early as October 12, 1825, Poinsett wrote to Secretary Clay that he "found it necessary to form a party out of such elements as the country afforded or to leave the English masters of the field."[118]

Poinsett's choice of the Masons as the vehicle with which to build a pro-American political party lends credence to the idea that Secretary Clay and perhaps President Adams had sent Poinsett to Mexico with this very purpose in mind; in the 1820s, Masonic lodges in Mexico, Colombia, and Cuba were centers of rebellion against colonial rule. Spain believed that the American government encouraged the Masons' subversive activities in these countries. It was particularly convinced that a Philadelphia Masonic lodge directed the actions of a proindependence lodge in Havana. These accusations of official American sanction of Masonic intrigue become somewhat more credible when one considers Poinsett's activities in Mexico and the fact that Secretary Clay was a prominent Mason, well positioned to monitor the activities of that secret society and perhaps request its assistance.[119]

Regardless of who inspired the idea, the creation of a pro-American Masonic lodge worked very well. Mexico soon became an intense political battleground with forces loyal to Britain and the United States vying for control. These were controlled by Poinsett and his British counterpart, Henry Ward. Believing that the other had upped the ante and forced the parties to go beyond the traditional bounds of diplomacy, each accused the other of foul play. Ward told his superiors in London that "nothing could have been further from my wishes, on Mr. Poinsett's first arrival, than to enter into any contest of this description."[120] The "contest" included the aforementioned manipulation of Mexican political parties along with the dissemination of propaganda hostile to each nation's interests.

As the October 1825 letter to Clay reveals, Poinsett's correspondence to his superiors directly referred to his effort to organize a political party through the vehicle of the York Rite Masons. In January 1826, Poinsett wrote to Clay that he was being attacked for his "agency" in bringing about a change in the political alliance between the executive and the two major Mexican political parties.[121] Three days afterward, Poinsett wrote to Clay that "Masonry is beginning to flourish" and bear "good fruit."[122] The administration received additional corroboration of Poinsett's activities from Secretary of State Clay's son, who traveled to Mexico in 1827. After meeting with Secretary Clay in May 1827, President Adams noted in his diary that Clay's son had arrived in Mexico and that the secretary of state "thinks Mr. Poinsett has indiscreetly connected himself with party movements and political Masonry in Mexico."[123]

Other prominent members of the American government were also aware of Poinsett's meddling in Mexican politics. In a letter written to Rufus King, the American ambassador to London, Poinsett boasted of a "large party of the Brotherhood" dining "joyfully" at his house. On a later occasion, he informed Senator Martin Van Buren, "They [York Rite Masons] were excluded from that participation in Government to which they thought themselves entitled, and as they felt conscious of their superior strength, were resolved to overthrow their adversaries. . . . [Poinsett considered it his] duty to interfere, and to advise a milder course." Poinsett suggested that the Mexican opposition unify their party, establish a press to present their case, and use the electoral process rather than force to achieve the change they desired.[124]

Poinsett's influence over the country's politics was so extensive that the Mexican president and other prominent political figures began to condemn his actions publicly, some demanding his recall. The pro-British newspaper *El Sol* stated that Poinsett was emulating his conduct in Chile and referred to him as "the scourge of the American continent."[125] Poinsett informed the administration of this development and offered to withdraw from his position. He also "frankly avowed and explained his conduct" in two private letters written to President Adams in April and July 1827.[126] In one of the letters, Poinsett noted that he was moderating his course of action but believed that he was acting as a force for restraint on the opposing parties, which would have torn themselves apart in his absence.

Adams and Clay, well aware of Poinsett's track record, nevertheless left it to Poinsett's discretion as to when he should leave. Poinsett's biographer believes that the president preferred that he remain until after the Mexican elections of 1828.[127] As another historian has observed, "He decided to stay on in Mexico because of the condition of internal politics, in which he was not supposed to be interested."[128] Poinsett remained in Mexico until October 1829; amid a series of revolts and further accusations of meddling, the Mexican government then formally requested his recall.

Joel Poinsett's activities in Latin America extended from 1810 to 1829. Madison, Monroe, and John Quincy Adams utilized his services and those of others to spread the gospel of democracy. This era also saw the United States locked in pitched competition with Great Britain over the future economic and political shape of the Americas. Poinsett noted the international character of this competition in one dispatch to Clay: "The English are active" in Peru, and "able men" were needed to counter their influence in that nation and Guatemala as well.[129] Both sides used both overt and covert means to win the allegiance of the Latin American nations, with Britain often marshaling greater resources and talent to thwart American efforts.

Joel Poinsett was the ideal covert operative for his time, an agent capable of broadly interpreting executive instructions in furtherance of objectives too sensitive to be acknowledged publicly. Poinsett appears to have been motivated not only by a desire to secure favorable commercial and political arrangements for the United States, but also by an even stronger drive to extend the blessings of the American experiment. Poinsett and his executive overseers shared with other American covert operatives of their era a belief in, to use Poinsett's words, "the progress of liberal principles."[130]

6 ▪

The Era of Covert Expansion

Part 2, 1829–1849

The experience of every nation on earth has demonstrated
that emergencies may arise in which it becomes absolutely
necessary for the public safety or the public good to make
expenditures the very object of which would be defeated by
publicity. . . . In no nation is the application of such sums
ever made public.

JAMES K. POLK, 1846[1]

Andrew Jackson and Anthony Butler:
Bribery in Mexico

President Andrew Jackson (1829–1837) replaced the controversial envoy to Mexico, Joel Poinsett, with Colonel Anthony
Butler in October 1829. Butler's top priority was to acquire "the
object so interesting to our government": Texas.[2] Jackson believed that
the acquisition of Texas was "necessary for the security of the great empo-
rium of the West," New Orleans, and that "the god of the universe had
intended this great valley to belong to one nation": the United States.[3]
Butler was sent to negotiate the acquisition of Texas for the United States
and told that he had $5 million at his disposal. Butler concluded that the
quickest way would be to bribe prominent Mexican political figures to

concede the area to the United States. Butler spent a tumultuous six years attempting to "persuade" Mexican authorities to concede Texas, all the while candidly informing President Jackson and his assorted secretaries of state of his various schemes.

One of the earliest dispatches Butler received from President Jackson clearly implied that bribery was an approach that Butler might consider. Jackson wrote in October 1829, "I scarcely ever knew a Spaniard who was not the slave of averice, and it is not improbable that this weakness may be worth a great deal to us, in this case."[4] Jackson also coached Butler on how to deceive the president of Mexico and other high government officials. He was to show "very confidentially" Mexican officials a copy of some general instructions that did not mention the topic of purchasing Texas. Jackson hoped that this "voluntary act" of Butler would win the confidence of the officials. Jackson noted:

> It is important, that these instructions are shown to them of your own mere will, & begging at the same time that it may not be known to us—but in such a manner as to induce a belief that it must be kept a profound secret from your own government, as on that event, it would destroy you. When you have read this P.S. and my private letter you will burn them both, first, if you please, taking notes from them—not being accustomed to diplomacy these might be stolen from you & made a handle against this government.[5]

In a strategy calculated to let strong Mexican sentiment against the United States run its course, Butler bided his time until the summer of 1831. On June 23, he wrote to the president, "As the influence of money is well understood and as readily conceded by these people as any under Heaven, I have no doubt of its doing its office." Butler asked for the authority to offer up to $7 million if necessary, but Jackson replied that the amount must not exceed $5 million.[6] Butler's discussions with Mexican officials dragged on inconclusively into 1832. In July of that year, he informed the president that his effort at ingratiating himself with the minister of foreign affairs was about to bear fruit. He added, "The amount to which I am limited for the purchase by my instructions will very probably be in part applied to facilitate the Negotiation, in which case we shall provide for that portion of the payment by a secret article."[7]

Unfortunately for Butler, the foreign minister was removed from office as a result of a revolution in Mexico, and the new administration took a much harder line against relinquishing Texas. As Butler told Jackson, the new Mexican president was "strait laced" on the subject of Texas, and that attitude left him with limited options. Butler stated:

> I have one road however by which I hope to reach him and vanquish his scruples, should they remain as it is said they formerly were, and I have besides the very Man provided to do the underworking with him. . . . I may meet with difficulties and great ones. . . . But I will succeed in uniting T—

— to our country before I am done with the Subject or I will forfeit my head. I know them all well, and I know how to manage them.[8]

Butler then proposed to Jackson that the president offer the near-bankrupt Mexican government a $5 million loan, which Butler believed Mexico would never be able to repay. The nub of the proposal was that the United States would take a mortgage on Texas for security. When his idea was rejected by the administration, Butler returned to various bribery schemes to achieve his objectives. He told one member of the Mexican government that he would receive $200,000 if he could force his government to yield Texas. On another occasion, Butler wrote to Jackson that he expected to use $1 million of the $5 million allotment to purchase influence.[9] In response, the president wrote back:

Provided you keep within your instructions and obtain the cession it is not for your consideration whether the government of Mexico applies the money to the purchase of men or to pay their public debt. It is not for you to inquire how they will apply the consideration for the cession which we shall pay—all we want is a good and unincumbered cession of Territory that will give us a good and permanent boundary.[10]

Butler appears to have justified his actions on the grounds that he was simply practicing "business as usual" in Mexico. He recounted for Jackson one instance of a prominent Mexican instructing him on the need to win the support of another individual "who must be brought over to us in this affair." The man inquired whether Butler had command of money; he replied, "Yes, I have money." The man went on to say that this individual was so important that he might require $200,000 to $300,000, and other persons might require additional sums. When asked whether he could command those amounts, Butler answered, "Assure me of the object, and the money shall not fail." Butler concluded his letter by telling Jackson that if his arrangement worked out, he could conclude a treaty in six hours.[11]

Jackson was angry that his agent had sent an uncoded letter in the regular mail describing his bribery plots. Jackson was astonished "that [he] would entrust such a letter, without being in cypher, to the mail" and repeated that whatever Mexican officials did with the $5 million was of no concern to the United States. However, Jackson did warn Butler that he should avoid giving the Mexican authorities any grounds for charging him with "tampering with their officers to obtain the cession thro corruption."[12] Butler replied to this apparent reprimand by reminding the president that he had kept Jackson posted all along about his tactics. He also stated his belief that he was acting within the president's directives:

More than two years since I wrote informing you that the best if not the only mode of attaining our object in relation to Texas would be to interest certain persons here through the application of money to lend their aid in negotiating the treaty. You replied that my instructions authorised me to apply a

given sum in procuring a cession of Texas and that if I kept myself within the
sum limited and procured the territory it was a matter of no consequence to
the Government how the money was disbursed. Now I beg you Sir to weigh
these expressions of yours, and then say whether they admitted of a different
construction than that which I gave to them?

Butler emphasized again before the close of the letter that resort had to be
made to "bribery" or "presents" to conclude a settlement.[13] Jackson apparently overcame his misgivings about Butler's carelessness, for he left
him in Mexico for over a year and a half after this exchange of correspondence, recalling him—at the request of the Mexican government—on October 31, 1835.

Butler believed throughout his tenure in Mexico that the United States
stood to lose if it refrained from certain dubious actions designed to
influence Mexican officials. Having been coached by Joel Poinsett prior to
the latter's departure from Mexico, Butler was aware of the actions of
British agents in that nation. Butler believed that these bought influence
in the Mexican government and worked against American interests. In
one dispatch to President Jackson, Butler noted that the Mexican foreign
minister "is a British Agent with a large salary and cannot but be more or
less under control of that Influence. He is a shrewd artful Man.—But I
know him."[14] This justification of U.S. conduct as a response to British
intrigue was repeated throughout America's expansionist era, but it is
difficult to measure the veracity of some of the charges leveled against the
British. No doubt, many of the stories were inflated accounts designed to
win government support for controversial initiatives favored by agents in
the field. However, it would be a mistake to believe that Britain did not
actively intervene in Mexican affairs, projecting its influence through all
possible means.

The level of Jackson's involvement in the various bribery schemes
launched by Butler is still a subject of some dispute. Jackson's biographers have generally viewed Butler as a rogue agent, though many freely
admit that the president should have exercised more control over him.
There is a tendency to portray Jackson as a chief executive distracted by
other pressing business while Butler ran amok in Mexico.[15] It does appear
that whatever doubts Jackson had regarding Butler's conduct were the
result of the latter's failing to get the job done without direct guidance
from Washington and his incautious habit of putting his proposals in
writing.

An example of Jackson's desire to maintain a plausibly deniable account of his administration's actions in Mexico was described by Butler
himself seven years after the end of his tour of duty there. Butler wrote to
the former president in response to a pamphlet then circulating that
leveled charges against Butler's conduct. The former presidential agent
had soured on his old friend, and he recalled for Jackson much of the
bribery correspondence described in the preceding pages. Butler also

recounted a meeting between the two men in June 1835. By that time, Butler had been in Mexico for approximately five years, and Jackson knew very well of his penchant for intrigue. Butler recalled Jackson sanctioning his actions in a private conversation and referring him to the secretary of state with the words, "Settle it with Mr. Forsyth and manage the affair as you please but do not let me know it."[16] The fact that Jackson sent Butler back to Mexico until he was formally recalled at the end of October 1835 lends an air of credibility to Butler's account. If Jackson was genuinely at odds with a policy of bribing foreign leaders, one would assume that he would not have sent the foremost advocate of such a policy back to Mexico City.

It takes a tremendous leap of faith to state, as one historian of the Butler affair has written, that there appears "no sufficient reason to accuse Jackson of . . . countenancing Butler's underhanded intrigues for influencing his negotiations."[17] It is clear that Andrew Jackson wanted Texas for the United States and was not terribly concerned with what Mexican officials did with their $5 million payment. The Anthony Butler mission to Mexico is an important example of a president desperately seeking a solution to a foreign-policy problem while hoping to spare himself and his office any embarrassment over the means employed to solve it.

Covert Action Comes Home: Daniel Webster's Secret Operations Against the Citizens of Maine

The sudden death of William Henry Harrison on April 4, 1841, led to the inauguration of his vice president, John Tyler. Tyler completed Harrison's term, serving as president until 1845. In concert with his secretary of state, Daniel Webster, Tyler would engage in one of the most blatant abuses of presidential covert authority in American history: a covert campaign designed to influence domestic political sentiment within the United States. This campaign was financed in part out of the Contingency Fund, with another substantial portion of financial assistance provided (with the administration's consent) by the British secret service.

The setting for this event involved negotiations between the United States and Britain over the disputed boundary between the state of Maine and Canada. Secretary of State Webster was caught in the uncomfortable position of trying to prevent hostilities while attempting to avoid being accused of appeasement. Webster sought to lay the groundwork by defusing the partisan nature of the question in the state with most to gain or lose from the negotiations: Maine. By influencing public sentiment there, Webster hoped to win the consent of the state's commissioners for compromise as well as to persuade the rest of the nation of the propriety of this path. Maine's political figures were pressing for possession of the entire disputed territory and demanding assistance from the federal government to repel foreign invasion. In the middle of the heated issue were

President Tyler and Secretary Webster, both vulnerable to attack from Whigs and Democrats alike. This was the context in which Webster, with Tyler's approval, opted to utilize secret service funds to influence the electorate in Maine to support a negotiated compromise.[18]

The operative selected by Webster to oversee the delicate operation was Francis O. J. Smith, a former congressman from Maine. The idea for the operation seems to have originated with Smith, who had made a similar proposal to President Martin Van Buren in December 1837. Van Buren apparently ignored it, but Smith received a much warmer reception from the Tyler administration. The proposal appears to have been first presented to Webster at a meeting in the secretary of state's home in May 1841. Smith followed up with a written statement to the secretary on June 7, 1841, outlining a covert propaganda compaign directed at the citizens of Maine that he had "hinted at in our conversation [in May]." Smith bluntly outlined his program: "Now my plan is, to prepare public sentiment in Maine for a compromise of the matter" by convincing the people of that state that its honor and pride would be upheld in accepting a compromise. This goal could be achieved "if it can be made to seem to have its origin with themselves. This, however, is the most delicate part of the enterprise." But Smith was sanguine: "Public sentiment upon this matter can be brought into right shape in Maine, by enlisting certain leading men of both political parties . . . and through them, at a proper time hereafter, guiding aright the public press."

Smith believed that his proposal offered a way for the administration to secure its objectives quickly and inexpensively. War with Britain had to be avoided, and the achievement of so lofty a goal required extraordinary measures. As Smith put it:

> A few thousand dollars expended upon such an agency will accomplish more than hundreds of thousands expended through the formalities and delays of ordinary diplomatic negotiations & surveys . . . —and, what is more—it would avert all occasion for such a national calamity. . . . I would have it commence with the proper enlistment of the services of a few judicious cooperators at different points in Maine, and extending their circle gradually, without display or the betrayal of official authority as opportunity might be created—drawing silently in the voluntary and patriotic aid of men of influence.

Smith concluded by stating that for the "interest and quiet of Maine . . . it should be attempted." But he politely warned the secretary and the president that this effort would require all their attention and that they should not underestimate the nature of the project they were about to authorize: "[T]he persons immediately engaged in it should feel if it was a subject worthy of their whole time and effort to accomplish it, both in a personal, political and national point of view." Smith added in a final note of optimism that "success would warrant almost any expenditure."[19]

The plan was approved quickly by Tyler and Webster, for Smith was busy at work in Maine less than a month later. He requested a salary of $3,500 a year, along with expenses and the authority to hire surrogate agents. Smith had already been given a $500 advance to submit the plan of June 7, and his $3,500 salary would be received upon completion of his mission.[20] The source of this money, the Contingency Fund, had been created for secret *foreign* operations.

For the next ten months, Smith campaigned to build public support for a negotiated settlement of the border dispute. His campaign was very much a grass-roots effort, with businessmen, lawyers, journalists, and pastors throughout Maine subject to various forms of lobbying. In one letter to Webster, Smith described his efforts at meticulously building support county by county for a negotiated settlement:

> After I shall have procured the signatures of certain leading men of both parties in this county, I shall employ the necessary persons to visit every town in the county, & obtain the principal men in each to cooperate, and at once proceed to the execution of a similar operation in each of the other counties.[21]

A favorite target of Smith was the major newspapers throughout the state, many of which had been vocal opponents of any concession to the British. Personal meetings were held with editors throughout the state, and Smith himself anonymously wrote a series of articles that appeared under the title "Northeastern Boundary—Why Not Settle It?" published by the *Christian Mirror* of Portland. Other Maine newpapers reprinted the article or published similar articles. Smith told Webster that he had placed his articles in "a politically neutral, but extensively circulated religious paper" from which he hoped to "secure their reprint in the party newpapers of this State on both sides." Smith's greatest prize was winning the support of the Democratic party press in the state, the *Eastern Argus*. This newspaper had influence on journalistic opinion outside of Maine; at the height of Webster's negotiations, newspapers throughout the country reprinted portions of Smith's articles, which portrayed a unified citizenry in Maine willing to compromise with Britain. The stories caused editors in the rest of the nation to alter their position on the boundary dispute, bowing to the wishes of the people of Maine.[22]

Smith sought to remove the boundary question as a divisive partisan issue. As he put it, he tried to "divest [the] subject of party interest, and party excitement."[23] By moving as rapidly as possible (indeed, long before Webster had even begun his negotiations with the British), Smith succeeded in depoliticizing the problem and in bringing Maine into line with the administration's position. At the same time, "divesting" the issue of its political content could go only so far. Smith believed that a well-organized cadre would be needed to push the appointment of sympathetic commissioners through the state legislature. These appointments were of critical importance to a successful treaty negotiation, for Webster had taken the unusual step of inviting Maine to appoint commissioners to take part in the negotiations.[24]

Smith employed a number of operatives to lobby state legislators. There were four principal players in the operation, among them prominent Harvard scholar Jared Sparks. Other members of the team included a federal judge from Massachusetts named Peleg Sprague, a Maine political figure named Albert Smith, and a former Maine agent, C. S. Daveis, who had in the past defended his state's interest on the boundary question in Washington.[25] These men made certain that the issue did not, as Smith put it, "expire from stagnation." He wrote to Webster at one critical point that an infusion of dollars at just the right moment would keep the boundary question alive and at a level that avoided the "belligerent spirit" of most party conflicts.[26]

In the spring of 1842, upon the arrival of Lord Ashburton from Britain, Webster's covert campaign intensified. Ashburton had been granted full powers to negotiate a treaty in the disputed border region. Shortly after Ashburton's arrival in the United States, Webster wrote to Smith, "I verily believe the time has come for a vigorous effort for ending that controversy."[27] The "vigorous effort" took the form of a mission for Sparks, to whom Webster proposed "a confidential errand" whereby the Harvard scholar would meet with Governor John Fairfield and show him maps of dubious authenticity, purportedly from the original negotiations of 1782 and 1783. The maps cast great doubt over Maine's claims to the disputed border region. Webster sent Sparks to Augusta, the state capital, with the reminder of "the absolute necessity of secrecy" and urged him to be as candid as possible with the governor, relying on the latter's "discretion & caution."[28] One historian has described the maps in Sparks,s possession as "terror inspiring" and "well calculated to produce apprehension in the minds of politicians as to the outcome of any future arbitration."

The administration's point was clear: settle this dispute as speedily as possible before the British find out about the maps and make demands for further American concessions. The combination of Smith's intense lobbying and Sparks's scholarly presentation of the damaging cartographic evidence led Governor Fairfield to call for a special session of the state legislature. The governor urged the state's legislators to appoint commissioners who would accept a certain amount of accommodation based on an exchange of an equivalent amount of territory between the parties. Webster's campaign to shift public sentiment had paid a handsome dividend as both the House and the Senate cast votes favoring the governor's proposals. This outcome signaled a massive shift in public sentiment in favor of a more conciliatory approach.[29]

This campaign to alter public sentiment was funded in part by a most unusual source—Lord Ashburton. Webster's motivation for permitting the payment remains a mystery. It is possible that money in the president's Contingency Fund was at a low point or that President Tyler was determined to keep expenditures for the operation to a minimum.[30] Most likely, the British funds were needed to bribe Maine political figures and community leaders. A certain comfort may have been found in using foreign money to achieve that end should the operation's cover have been exposed; Ashburton would have had a better chance of surviving such a revelation than Webster and Tyler. In any case, Ashburton made a payment of $14,500 to a source he described as "my informant," most likely Daniel Webster. Ashburton's informant told him that "without this stimulant Maine would never have yielded, and here [in Washington?] it has removed many objections in other quarters."[31]

After a summer of torturous negotiations between the secretary of state and Lord Ashburton, the United States Senate, swayed in part by Jared Sparks's maps, ratified the Webster-Ashburton Treaty on August 20, 1842. The vote was 39 to 9 in approval, the largest majority the Senate had ever given a treaty.[32] On the eve of Webster's triumph, Francis Smith wrote to the secretary from Maine, congratulating him on his apparent success and including a bill for services rendered: "I feel gratified in the result, from a conviction of many years standing that a new mode of approaching the subject, and such a one as you have adopted, would accomplish it while another forty years of circuitous diplomacy would have availed nothing." Smith politely requested compensation for his operatives, who assisted in "adjust[ing] the tone and direction of the party presses, and through them, of public sentiment." He enclosed a voucher with a blank space next to his name and those of his assistants. Webster wrote in "$2,000" next to Smith's name and "$500" next to "services of assistants and their incidental expenses."[33]

Yet the tactics employed by Webster to secure treaty ratification would later haunt the Tyler administration when, in 1846, the chairman of the House Foreign Affairs Committee attempted the retroactive impeachment of the former secretary of state. Committee chairman Charles Ingersoll of Pennsylvania hurled a variety of charges against Webster, many of them without foundation. However, one accusation was on target: that Webster had utilized secret service money to "corrupt" the press in Maine. Ingersoll had gained access to the secret records of the State Department and had found Smith's letter of August 12, 1842, which referred to adjusting the "tone" of the party presses. Ingersoll's call for an investigation was accepted by the House, and a select committee was created to investigate the charges. Former president Tyler was called to testify along with Francis Smith, the key operative in the affair. Tyler willingly testified and was remarkably candid in defending his administration's conduct. Tyler stated that the administration simply had wanted to be "heard and understood . . . and the only way which seemed opened to it was, by the employment of persons to make known its views by all proper means."[34]

The bulk of the questions directed at Tyler focused on accusations of financial improprieties regarding Webster's handling of the Contingency Fund.

Francis Smith testified under oath that his team of agents in Maine had utilized their talents to obtain "interviews with leading and influential men of their party, to induce favorable action on the subject of the compromise of the boundary . . . and procuring a favorable expression thereto on the part of the press."[35] By a 4 to 1 vote, the five-member investigating committee cleared Webster of all charges of misconduct. The majority report did not deem it "necessary or expedient" to "inquire into the propriety of employing agents for secret service within the limits of the United States, and paying them out of the contingent fund for foreign intercourse."[36] The lone dissenter, Congressman Jacob Brinkerhoff of Ohio, was the only member willing to grapple with the significance of the evidence presented to the committee. Brinkerhoff's minority report stated in part: "It would appear that the object of his [Smith's] agency in Maine was to institute and prosecute a systematic course of electioneering; and, by correspondence and confidential communication with the leading and influential political characters of both political parties, so to influence the public mind."[37]

It was actually no surprise that there was only one dissenter in the committee, for the investigation was crippled in part by Webster's powerful political clout in Congress. Moreover, the House had requested that President James K. Polk turn over documents related to payments made by Webster out of the Contingency Fund from March 4, 1841, until the secretary's retirement from office. Polk responded with a spirited defense of the need to preserve executive secrecy regarding the use of secret service funds. He told the House that President Tyler had exercised the authority granted him by a series of legislative acts extending back to the First Congress in July 1790. Tyler had "solemnly determined that the objects and items of these expenditures should not be made public." Polk believed that it would be inappropriate for him to break a solemn decision made by his predecessor, that "break[ing] the seal of confidence imposed by law, and heretofore uniformly preserved, would be subversive of the very purpose for which the law was enacted, and might be productive of the most disastrous consequences."[38]

Polk went on to defend covert activity as an essential component of executive power:

> The experience of every nation on earth has demonstrated that emergencies may arise in which it becomes absolutely necessary for the public safety or the public good to make expenditures the very object of which would be defeated by publicity. Some governments have very large amounts at their disposal, and have made vastly greater expenditures than the small amounts which have from time to time been accounted for on president's certificates. In no nation is the application of such sums ever made public. In time of war or

impending danger the situation of the country may make it necessary to employ individuals for the purpose of obtaining information or rendering other important services who could never be prevailed upon to act if they entertained the least apprehension that their names or their agency would in any contingency be divulged.

Polk noted one exception to his belief that records of presidentially authorized covert activity should be off limits to congressional investigators. In the case of an impeachment of an executive officer, "the power of the House in the pursuit of this object would penetrate into the most secret recesses of the Executive Departments."[39] Still, as there was no formal impeachment under way, Polk did not feel compelled to turn the material over to the House. Polk had spared Webster and Tyler any further embarrassment, no doubt over an honest commitment to principle.

Daniel Webster's final thoughts on the subject are worth noting. In a letter written shortly after the publication of Polk's message to Congress, the former secretary of state noted that he was quite "willing to trust all these things [papers, accounts, letters] with the public. Perhaps, indeed, that would be rather best, for me. But such a publication I cannot but think wd. be injurious & disreputable to the Govt." Webster went on to note the importance of preserving broad executive discretion over the use of secret service funds. Should the investigating committee conclude that the expenditures had been undertaken with the president's approval, "then very short work should be made of the whole business." The committee would have no business examining the objects of the expenditures "because to the extent of that fund, the discretion of the President is absolute. . . . If the Comee. find, that the disbursement was authorised by the President, they ought not to report facts, or particulars."

Webster appeared to take issue with Polk's suggestion that in cases of "great & dangerous delinquincy" this strict secrecy may be lifted:

I do not say this is my opinion. Indeed I cannot [see] the probability of any such case. But if this be admitted, to any extent, still it is clear, that when it is ascertained that no law is broken, nor the authority of the President transcended, it becomes quite improper to make an official disclosure . . . of the names of individuals connected with secret transactions.[40]

Because of Polk's position, Webster slipped through the noose of impeachment. The hard evidence linking Webster to a broad campaign to alter public sentiment and to accept British secret service money would remain hidden for 130 years. But extraordinary evidence was left behind for such a highly questionable operation, and it was uncovered by historian Frederick Merk. Merk has written that the Tyler–Webster program to influence Maine's position on the boundary question undermined existing federal–state relations through the use of secret service funds. The secret operation consisted of "federally subsidized underground electioneering to manage the sentiment of a state of the Union," Merk concludes.[41] Merk acknowledges that the effort was directed toward the worthy goal of preserving the peace between the United States and Britain. Yet the disturbing question—how a man of such stature as Webster could have authorized such a dubious operation and have been undisturbed by it—remains. In a letter written to his friend Jared Sparks, Webster boasted of his "grand stroke":

> [We managed to] get the previous consent of Maine & Massachusetts. Nobody else had attempted to do this; it had occurred to nobody else; it was a movement of great delicacy, & of very doubtful result. But it was made . . . & it succeeded, & to this success the fortunate result of the whole negotiation is to be attributed.[42]

The delicate balance between the need for executive secrecy in the conduct of foreign relations and the importance of protecting certain basic principles of a democratic society was violated by President Tyler and Secretary of State Webster. The position of President Polk—that confidentiality was essential to maintain the credibility of the president's control of a secret service capability—was upheld by the Congress at the time: records related to secret service activities should not be open to congressional investigators, with perhaps the formal exception of an impeachment inquiry.

This event marks an important watershed in the development of executive control of covert operations; an ambitious congressman had discovered a genuine abuse of the Contingency Fund but was unable to muster enough support to push the inquiry beyond a superficial level. Thereafter, presidential dominance of these operations was beyond question. As one historian of secret presidential diplomacy has noted, the closing of the Webster inquiry was something of a turning point, for "the question of executive agents was not again under discussion. It was not, indeed, until 1870 that another debate involving special agents took place."[43] Congress gave in at a point when a fundamental abuse of the president's secret service funds had occurred. A vigorous investigation might well have unearthed the fact that British secret service money had been used to influence domestic political sentiment with the consent of an American secretary of state. Even short of this revelation, the exposure of a *domestic* covert mission authorized by the president might well have been enough to damage fundamentally the concept of executive hegemony over clandestine operations. From that point, presidential domination of such operations would not be challenged seriously until the mid-1970s.

President Polk's Intervention in Mexican Affairs

James K. Polk, whose spirited defense of executive control over secret operations stalled a congressional inquiry into the machinations of Tyler and Webster, was also a great believer in secret diplomacy and covert operations. During his presidency (1845–1849), he authorized two missions to Mexico that directly interfered in its domestic political affairs. The first was an attempt to install a government sympathetic to American demands for the annexation of a contested region bordering Texas; the second involved the dispatch of an agent, operating under nebulous instructions, who ended up intriguing with leading members of the Catholic Church to halt the Mexican war effort. Polk's campaign against Mexico also witnessed the creation of a "spy company," composed primarily of Mexican outlaws. One student of Polk's conduct in office has remarked on the president's "decided proclivity for secrecy" and his belief that the solution to the Mexican government's intransigent position on territorial concessions awaited "the simple solution of bribery."[44] This section will begin by examining Polk's secret operations designed to resolve a simmering dispute with Mexico over the Texas border.

The Mission of Robert Stockton

President Polk, like Tyler before him, dispatched to Texas secret agents who involved themselves in inciting hostilities there. One of the more controversial operatives Polk sent was Commodore Robert Stockton.[45] Given orders to monitor the situation in Texas and to report on developments there, Stockton immediately set out to warn Texans of the possibility of hostile Mexican designs on their land. Stockton sought to rally Texans, and their president, Anson Jones, to preempt the Mexicans and march to the Rio Grande. Most accounts of Stockton's activities in Texas are based on an allegedly biased account written after the fact by a bitter President Jones, who accused Polk of having sent Stockton to instigate hostilities. Jones's account tends to be dismissed as the bitter reminiscences of a frustrated politician. However, I suspect that Polk, in a manner comparable to that of many of his predecessors, may have dispatched Stockton to Texas with a vaguely defined mandate to defend American interests aggressively. There is documentary evidence revealing deeper administration awareness of Stockton's activities than is generally acknowledged, most explicitly a letter sent by Stockton to Secretary of the Navy George Bancroft on May 27, 1845:

> Since my last letter I have seen Mr. Mayfield late [Texas] Secretary of State, who says that if the people here did not feel assured that the Boundary line would be the Rio Grande three fourths and himself amongst the number would oppose the annexation—But I need hardly say another word on that subject; its importance is apparent. But it may perhaps be as well for me in this way to let you know how I purpose to settle the matter without committing the U. States. The Major Genl will call out Three Thousand Men & "B.F. Stockton Esq." will supply them in a private way with [arms?] & ammunition.[46]

Although Stockton's plan of intrigue never came to fruition, it was not because the administration squelched the proposal, but because Texas president Jones rejected the idea. Stockton, ostensibly ordered to "monitor" events in Texas, had instead proposed to contribute to an already volatile situation by arming the local militia through private means and seizing the disputed region between the Nueces and Rio Grande Rivers by force "without committing the U. States."

Despite being notified of such plans, the administration did not recall Stockton, reprimand him, or issue clarifying instructions. Instead, he was rewarded with a future assignment in the hotly disputed territory of California. As historian R. W. Van Alstyne notes, Anson Jones's accusation that Polk tried to "inveigle him into manufacturing a war" with Mexico is difficult to refute in the light of Stockton's activities.[47] Nonetheless, President Polk received the pretext he needed to seize the contested territory; within months of Texas attaining statehood, the Mexicans were finally drawn into conflict after being successfully maneuvered by U.S. forces into firing the first shot.

The Return of Santa Anna

Another of President Polk's early secret initiatives directed at Mexico involved an attempt to return an exiled dictator to power in the hopes of achieving a favorable settlement of American territorial demands. On the eve of war with Mexico, a visitor named Alexander Atocha arrived to meet with Polk at the White House. Atocha told Polk that if the United States assisted the return to power of General Antonio López de Santa Anna from his exile in Havana and provided the general with a $500,000 payment to "expedite" his return to Mexico, the boundary dispute with the United States would be resolved in a manner favorable to American interests. Atocha stated that Santa Anna would cede New Mexico and portions of California for $30 million and recognize the American claim to the Texas border extending to the Rio Grande. In order to give the arrangement an air of credibility and "save face" for the Mexicans, the United States would have to arrange for a suitable show of force before Mexico announced any concessions.

Polk waited until after the outbreak of hostilities with Mexico before he decided to send an emissary to Santa Anna to determine if the offer merited American cooperation. The emissary, Alexander Slidell Mackenzie, arrived in Havana under the pretext of investigating the outfitting of privateers. Secrecy was so tight that even the American consul in Havana was unaware of the true nature of Mackenzie's mission. The unusual conversation between the American envoy and the exiled dictator covered such topics as the restoration of Santa Anna to power, settlement of the Rio Grande border dispute, and compensation for territorial cessions. The strangest part of the conversation occurred when Santa Anna advised the American envoy as to how the U.S. military could best proceed against his former army. This intelligence was quickly delivered to General Zachary Taylor at his battle headquarters in Mexico. Mackenzie informed Secretary of State James Buchanan that Santa Anna was anxious to work out an agreement with the United States. Clearing the way for Santa Anna to return home, the tight naval blockade of Mexico's ports was lifted long enough to let Santa Anna slip through.[48]

The American press did not accept the administration's account that Mackenzie had traveled to Havana to investigate the outfitting of privateers. Before their meeting, a number of newspapers reported that Mackenzie was actually going to Havana to confer with Santa Anna. In the weeks following the unusual discussion, newspapers recounted rumors and reports of the "mysterious mission of Captain Slidell Mackenzie to Havana." By the late fall of 1846, copies of American newspaper reports of an alleged agreement between Santa Anna and the Polk administration had reached Mexico City. These reports were the end of any possible deal with Santa Anna, as any conciliatory action on his part toward the United States would now be viewed as an act of treason. Surely to the dismay of the Polk administration, Santa Anna rallied the Mexican people to continue the war against the United States, perhaps prolonging the conflict for more than a year.[49]

President Polk had been made to look like a fool, and the press and Congress soon began to probe the administration's role in returning Santa Anna to power. In January 1848, Congress requested that Polk submit all relevant correspondence from the Mackenzie mission. Polk, harkening back to the stance taken during the congressional investigation of Tyler and Webster's abuse of the Contingency Fund, refused to yield. The president noted in his diary on January 8, 1848: "Another question of some importance arose as to the importance of sending to the House a communication made by Alexander Slidell Mckenzie of the U.S. Navy, made in July, 1846, to the Department of State. This communication is of a highly confidential character." Polk went on to describe in his diary (for the first time, eighteen months after the fact) the exchange between Mackenzie and Santa Anna. He recorded that Mackenzie was to determine if his restoration to power would lead Santa Anna to seek peace with the United States. If the general was so inclined, Mackenzie was to inform him that he would be allowed to slip through the blockade and return to Mexico. Polk expressed irritation at the fact that Mackenzie had "reduced to writing" a purported message from the president to Santa Anna when "I had sent him no message." Polk was worried that if Mackenzie's message appeared in print, it would "exhibit me in a ridiculous attitude." Polk also appears to have been concerned that the release to Congress of Mackenzie's correspondence regarding the "highly confidential" meeting would reflect a lack of good faith on the part of the American government. The president believed that "if it was made public the judgement of the world would condemn [us], & that no Government would ever again trust us." The cabinet agreed that Polk could not, "without impairing the national honour and character, communicate Mr. McKenzie's despatch to Congress."[50]

Polk's covert involvement in the effort to restore Santa Anna to power was a disaster. His obsession with preserving the secrecy of that operation as well as many others seems to have been based in part on avoiding political damage to himself and his office. In fact, his refusal to turn over to Congress documents related to the Santa Anna affair may well have saved his presidency. If the press and congressional opponents had been able persuasively to accuse him of being hoodwinked in restoring America's archenemy to the throne, the damage to Polk could have been catastrophic. The Polk–Santa Anna operation represents a classic lesson in the substantial political risks involved in intervening covertly in the internal affairs of foreign nations. The problem in this case—and with clandestine missions before and after Polk's time—was one of control: control over one's own agents and their indigenous collaborators. Between the planning and the implementing of any secret operation, a number of variables enter the equation. Being duped is an ever-present hazard.

President Polk's "proclivity for secrecy" was partly an outgrowth of the man's character. His secretary of the navy once noted, "He is withal the closest man I ever met with, keeping his mouth as effectively shut as any man I know."[51] A future secretary of the navy, Gideon Welles, said of Polk, "His secretiveness was large, and few men could better keep their own counsels. No man was the depository of his secrets, further than he chose to trust them for his own purpose, and hence he had no confidants except from calculation and for a purpose."[52]

Polk's irritation with journalistic and congressional revelations of secret executive initiatives was reinforced by events such as the Santa Anna affair. In fairness to Polk, it must be said that more than personal considerations influenced his desire to keep that operation secret. Premature disclosure of the mission may have destroyed any chance for a favorable, and peaceable, resolution of the Mexican–American conflict. In addition, Polk believed that strict secrecy was essential to keep British diplomats and agents off balance about his intentions, to prevent them from frustrating his initiatives. The final and perhaps most important rationale concerned the administration's use of secret agents to bribe Mexico for territorial concessions. As historian Anna K. Nelson has commented:

> The Polk administration did not enter official negotiations with Mexico as one would another sovereign state of equal or greater strength. . . . Instead it assumed that Mexico's reluctance to part with her empire or admit defeat in war was a matter awaiting the simple solution of bribery. Having little respect for the Mexicans or their rulers, Polk engaged in executive diplomacy by secret agent. As these agents were often promising money for land, Polk

did not want their activities known to the world at large—most particularly not to the Whig members of that world.[53]

Another typical example of Polk's use of secret operatives to conduct his foreign policy can be found in the mission of Moses Beach and Jane McManus Storms in November 1846. These secret operatives journeyed to Mexico City under false cover for the ostensible purpose of negotiating a treaty and ended up conspiring with the Catholic Church to disrupt the Mexican war effort.

The Intrigues of Moses Beach and Jane McManus Storms

President Polk designated Moses Beach a confidential executive agent on November 21, 1846. The editor of a New York newspaper called *The Sun*, Beach had come to the attention of Secretary of State Buchanan through the efforts of Jane McManus Storms, a correspondent and editorial writer for that paper. Storms accompanied Beach on his mission and may well have been the key operative in the drama.

For the first time since the Revolution, journalists were utilized as secret operatives by the American government. Ironically, their selection to carry out the most secret operation of Polk's presidency served to keep the press corps in the dark. As historian Anna Nelson has observed, "It can only be assumed that the usually suspicious press paid absolutely no attention to one of their own."[54]

Polk met with Beach at some point in early November 1846, and Buchanan met with him several times before Beach's departure to Mexico.[55] On November 21, 1846, Beach received his official instructions from the secretary of state:

> The trust confided in you is one of great delicacy and importance. In performing the duties which it imposes, great prudence and caution will be required. You ought never to give the slightest intimation . . . that you are an agent of this Government. . . . Be upon your guard against their wily diplomacy and take care that they shall obtain no advantage over you.[56]

The apparent purpose of the mission, as much as can be determined from the scant written record, was that Beach would attempt to lay the foundation for a peace agreement between the United States and Mexico. Beach also had some personal business initiatives he wished to pursue, including the possibility of creating a national bank in Mexico City and plans for a canal. However, there is the possibility, difficult to determine with any certainty, that the business proposals served as a convenient cover story for Beach's true objective. For reasons to be described, it is probable that the primary purpose of the Beach–Storms mission was to allow a representative of the Polk administration to establish contact with disgruntled elements in Mexican society—particularly the Catholic

Church and members of the Mexican congress. These contacts would allow the agents to measure the level of disaffection in Mexico and pass along assurances of American sympathy for the concerns of the dissident groups—especially the Catholic Church.

Beach's secret journey to Mexico suited Polk's liking for unconventional foreign-policy initiatives: the mission was the most ambitious clandestine effort launched by the Polk administration. Perhaps the most intriguing element of the operation was the assistance that Beach and Storms received from prominent Catholic clergymen in the United States, Cuba, and Mexico. Storms seems to have been the key to obtaining this assistance, and it was she who apparently recommended a tried-and-true approach for the mission: using the powerful clergy to influence the Mexican government to end the conflict with the United States. Two Texas acquaintances of Storms were in contact with unknown figures in Mexico, perhaps prominent members of the Mexican Catholic hierarchy or disgruntled members of the Mexican congress. These acquaintances informed Storms and Bishop John Hughes of New York City of their Mexican contacts, and the bishop urged that the information be forwarded to the Polk administration. Storms sent the information via her numerous contacts in Washington and was able to meet directly with Secretary Buchanan and President Polk, apparently persuading them of the importance of a Beach–Storms mission to Mexico.

Beach and Storms left for Mexico in late November 1846, accompanied by Beach's daughter, who historian Anna Nelson suggests may have accompanied the pair in order to conceal further the purpose of the trip.[57] The group made its first stop in Havana, where it received letters of introduction from the Cuban clergy to their Mexican counterparts. Beach also managed to obtain a British passport from the British consulate in Havana. Despite those precautions, Beach was arrested as a spy after his arrival in Mexico and briefly detained. Doubts apparently persisted about Beach's citizenship, forcing Storms to file a false affidavit swearing that Beach was a British subject.

Following Beach's release, the trio eventually made its way to Mexico City, where Beach and Storms seem to have made effective use of their letters of introduction from higher clergy in Havana to the Catholic hierarchy of Mexico. As Anna Nelson states, "Certainly the leading Bishops were willing to be 'persuaded' to refuse 'aid, direct and indirect,' in the prosecution of the war."[58] Its property being sold by the government to finance the war effort, the Mexican Church was growing increasingly disenchanted with the conflict with the United States.

Beach capitalized on this discontent, as his report submitted to Secretary of State Buchanan in June 1847 reveals. Beach told the secretary that he had succeeded in convincing the Church to withdraw its support for the war, support it had given in the hope of crushing the military's grip on Mexican society. Beach added that some prominent bishops "promised to dispose their most reliable friends in [Mexico's] Congress to advocate peace at the proper moment, and meanwhile to thwart and paralyze the measures of the bona fide war party." Beach believed that the bishops had met with some success in this initiative; but after the government succeeded in its effort to sell Church property to raise revenue, "I urged them to an organized resistance." When American general Winfield Scott landed American forces at Vera Cruz, the bishops made "a most important diversion in his favor by raising the standard of civil war. . . . This occupied five thousand men and all the arms, munitions of war . . . for twenty three days; effectively preventing them from assisting Vera Cruz."

At the height of the rebellion, Beach was informed by the clergy that $40,000 would be required to continue the revolt. As General Scott had just landed at Vera Cruz and might be delayed for some time, Beach "deemed that almost any outlay would be justified. The rebellion was therefore kept up, until the sudden appearance of General Santa Anna closed the affair." With the arrival of Santa Anna in the capital, Beach found it "expedient to leave instantly for the coast."[59]

Storms also submitted reports to Secretary Buchanan, six in all, urging him to maintain contacts with the Mexican Catholic Church. According to Anna Nelson, the letters written to Buchanan in the months following the mission contained suggestions on dealing with the Catholic clergy in Mexico and raised the possibility of dispatching a "Lt. Meade," a Catholic, on a mission to the country.[60]

The complete story of the Beach–Storms journey to Mexico is shrouded in secrecy, as Moses Beach remained uncommunicative about his activities until his death. The extraordinary secrecy surrounding this journey can be seen in the fact that five months after his return from his mission, Beach publicly denied that it had ever taken place. Moreover, at least one report written by Beach from Mexico City describing his activities and submitted to Secretary Buchanan has disappeared. It was the arrival of this report that prompted Polk to record in his diary a fairly lengthy entry regarding Moses Beach and his mission. Polk noted (misspelling his agent's name throughout the entry):

Mr. Beech was in Washington in November last & had several interviews with Mr. Buchanan & one with me. He was then on the eve of leaving for Mexico on private business, but from his intimacy with General Almonte expressed the opinion that he could [exert] a favourable influence on him and other leading men in Mexico, with a view to the restoration of the peace. . . . The object of constituting him a secret agent was that he might collect & furnish useful information to his government.[61]

President Polk's diary contains several other references to Beach, one dated May 11, 1847, in which the president stated his satisfaction with the intelligence that his secret agent had delivered to him in a White House meeting:

Mr. Moses Y. Beach, Editor of the N. York Sun, called and had a long conversation with me on Mexican affairs. He had recently returned from the City of Mexico, where he had gone several months ago in the character of a secret agent from the State Department. He gave me valuable information.[62]

An article that appeared in Beach's own newspaper, *The Sun,* represented a rare exception to the silence surrounding the mission. The article, written considerably after the mission, described Beach's effort to encourage the forces of secession in certain Mexican states and to free American prisoners by bribing a prison warden. The newspaper reported that a reward had been offered for Beach's capture in Mexico, with Mexican newspapers full of stories about a "Yankee spy" who was plotting against the nation.

The Beach–Storms mission to Mexico revealed once again the American government's respect for the power of the Catholic Church in Latin America. The same body that had been viewed as an impediment to the expansion of republican government during Joel Poinsett's time was enlisted as an ally in the U.S. effort to win territorial concessions from Mexico. Although there is nothing that establishes concretely that Polk dispatched Beach and Storms to capitalize on religious and political disaffection with the war, the evidence between the lines is quite compelling. In contrast to some of his clumsier predecessors, Polk avoided creating a paper trail that would conclusively resolve the question. Both the Mackenzie and the Beach missions demonstrated Polk's penchant for issuing oral instructions and his aversion to putting in writing anything that was capable of falling into the wrong hands. As diplomatic historian Henry Wriston has noted in reference to the secret plan to return Santa Anna from exile, Polk avoided direct written contact with the exiled leader: "There was, of course, no possibility of official intercourse with an exile. There was too great a hazard in dealing with Santa Anna to allow of any project being committed to paper."[63] The level of executive secrecy that characterized Polk's tenure in office would not be matched again until the nation's entry into its twentieth-century world wars.

A Legacy of Secrecy

James K. Polk's deft hand in conducting secret operations confronts students of his presidency with a number of vexing questions, among which one looms large: Did he secretly provoke hostilities in California that were designed to acquire that region for the United States, replicating the efforts in Mexico? Polk's conduct in office has given rise to the accusation that he issued misleading or ambiguous written orders to his secret operatives in California. In addition, it is believed by some historians that even his written orders were superseded by oral instructions directing his operatives to generate hostilities that would create the excuse to seize the region for the United States. These controversial accounts of Polk's conduct in office, particularly his alleged complicity in instigating the Bear

Flag Revolt in California, are subject to such dispute that no satisfactory resolution could possibly be rendered in this study. There may well be something to these charges: certainly, Polk would enjoy the legacy of unanswered questions surrounding his covert foreign policy.[64]

As a result of Polk's war against Mexico, the United States took its first steps toward incorporating an intelligence function within the nation's military. The United States entered the war with few intelligence assets to guide its operations in Mexico and in characteristic American fashion had to improvise. With the approval of President Polk and Secretary of War William Marcy, General Winfield Scott created the Mexican Spy Company, composed of "contraguerrillas" or "contrabandistas"—native Mexicans, many of whom were bandits acting as insurgents for the U.S. Army. The officer in charge of the spy company, Lieutenant Colonel Ethan Allen Hitchcock, worked out an arrangement whereby "for a sum of money yet to be determined, the robbers shall let our people pass without molestation and that they shall, for extra compensation, furnish us with guides, couriers and spies." Approximately two hundred bandits were recruited to assist the American military, many of whom had been "liberated" from Mexican jails and asked to reward their liberators by providing them with intelligence services. Additional intelligence was provided by another ring of spies who assisted General Scott in his capture of the city of Vera Cruz. Francis M. Dimond, the former American consul at that city, was given a military commission and dispatched to Havana, where he recruited agents to send into Vera Cruz. Beyond merely providing intelligence, members of the spy company engaged in insurgency operations often directed at other guerrilla bands that harassed the American military.[65]

The Mexican War was a proving ground for a number of American military figures whose mettle would be tested in the upcoming Civil War. The rudimentary intelligence apparatus created to assist the American army in Mexico would be disbanded, only to be revived once again to protect the nation in a time of great danger. The principles of executive secrecy and discretion over secret operations energetically defended by James K. Polk would serve as a model for the type of clandestine military and diplomatic operations conducted by the Lincoln administration.

By 1849, an activity utilized haltingly by Thomas Jefferson had evolved into a routine tool of American foreign policy. Rooted in Washington's wartime actions during the American Revolution, covert activity now was being employed for purposes of peacetime expansion and, in one instance, domestic pacification. The qualified approval that James Madison had given to "intermeddling" during the Barbary Wars had been replaced by Madison and his successors with an endorsement of peacetime intermeddling of ill-defined limits.

III

COVERT
ACTIVITY
AND THE
"IMPERIAL"
PRESIDENCY

7 ▪

Civil War and Aftermath
The Birth of the Modern
Intelligence Bureaucracy

The service stipulated by the contract was a secret service. . . . Both employer and agent must have understood that the lips of the other were to be for ever sealed. . . . This condition . . . is implied in all secret employments of the government in time of war, or upon matters affecting our foreign relations.

JUSTICE STEPHEN FIELD,
Totten, Administrator, v. *United States, 1875*[1]

▪ During the Civil War, President Abraham Lincoln (1861–1865) used his vast network of spies and agents of influence to turn public and official sentiment in Europe and North America against the Confederacy. Lincoln understood that influencing public opinion was a vital element in the Union war effort. In the aftermath of this successful effort, the United States took its first tentative steps toward becoming a world power, one in need of a permanent intelligence service capable of monitoring events around the globe. This led to the creation of the Office of Naval Intelligence (ONI).

Throughout this period and the other eras examined in this study, American presidents operated on an ad hoc basis in dispatching secret agents abroad. Sensitive operations were generally conducted for the president by his secretary of state, as in the example recounted in this chapter of the mission undertaken in Hawaii in the 1890s. Nonetheless, with the creation of the ONI, the United States laid the foundation for its first intelligence bureaucracy. The pressure of increased world responsibilities, particularly those of two world wars, dictated that secret operations could no longer be conducted on a haphazard basis. This pressure led to the creation of the Office of Strategic Services and its renowned successor, the Central Intelligence Agency.

Agents of Propaganda

Abraham Lincoln's Covert Campaign for the Hearts and Minds of Europe

The American Civil War generated a struggle thousands of miles from the battlefields in the United States, a conflict between Union and Confederate operatives for the political and economic support of the nations of Europe. The Lincoln administration's agents tried to deny the Confederacy the weapons, markets, and diplomatic support it desperately sought there. The administration's effort was directed by Secretary of State William Seward, who supervised the Union's intelligence operations at home as well as clandestine efforts abroad. Seward's European network not only monitored the activity of its Confederate opposites, but also took affirmative steps to ensure that European public opinion would support the Union war effort. This goal was achieved through the bribing of European journalists and the use of prominent American clergymen to lobby their European counterparts. At the same time, a campaign to disrupt the supply of ships and other war matériel to the Confederacy was conducted through the use of bribery and sabotage. A fitting tribute to the effectiveness of Seward's agents was paid by one of their greatest opponents, Confederate agent James D. Bulloch. Bulloch wrote in 1863:

> The extent to which the system of bribery and spying has been and continues to be practised by the agents of the United States is scarcely credible. The servants of gentlemen supposed to have Southern sympathies are tampered with; confidential clerks and even messengers from telegraph offices are bribed to betray their trust.[2]

Seward's chief operative in Europe was Henry Shelton Sanford, whose position as ambassador to Belgium concealed the hidden nature of his assignment as the director of the U.S. secret service in Europe. Secretary Seward's instructions to Sanford indicated the open-ended nature of his assignment: "You need not consider yourself as being restricted . . . from repairing at any time to points in Europe which you may deem your presence necessary, or likely to conduce to the public interest."[3]

Sanford arrived in Paris in April 1861 and immediately began planning his strategy of clandestine conflict. Seward had written him that "the most important duty of the diplomatic respresentatives of the United States in Europe will be to counteract by all proper means the efforts of the agents of that projected Confederacy at their respective Courts."[4]

Sanford gave priority to disrupting Confederate efforts in London and in Paris, cities he described as "the keys of the position." He pleaded with Seward "to provide sufficient secret service funds when Congress meets," "sufficiency" in Sanford's view meaning essentially unlimited funds. Sanford, in concert with the American consul in London, began building a network of agents whose objective was clearly defined: nullify the efforts of their Confederate counterparts in Great Britain. Sanford hired a British police detective whose private operatives fanned out to monitor the major ports and industrial centers where Confederate agents were beginning to sign secret contracts with British firms for, among other things, blockade runners. Sanford's nemesis was Bulloch, a man considered so worrisome that Sanford proposed to take extraordinary measures to neutralize him. In a letter to Seward, Sanford wrote:

> So dangerous do I consider this man that I feel disposed when he comes to the continent, to have him arrested on some charge or other and as he would have no papers, he would get no diplomatic protection & might be sent home for examination. . . . Of course no one official would appear in the matter. . . . This man if he gets away with his vessel, will do us an infinite deal of mischief.[5]

Sanford's agents penetrated the British postal service, along with telegraph offices and business firms. Postmen were paid £1 a week to supply information on correspondence delivered to known agents; telegraph offices were penetrated in order to intercept or, in some cases, tamper with messages from known enemy operatives. Clerks in the large business firms were offered bribes to hand over documents related to contracts negotiated with the Confederacy. Sanford proposed that all Confederate couriers bearing dispatches be followed back to the United States and their messages diverted to federal authorities. He also informed Seward that if he was provided with adequate funds, he could "arrange" to have Confederate vessels scuttled before they left the English Channel. Crew members of cargo ships could be bribed to divert ships to Union ports or to send them to the bottom. As Sanford told Seward, "£5000 would have sunk her [the cargo ship *Thomas Watson*]; accidents are so numerous in the channel you know."[6] Due to the erratic flow of funds from the United States, many of Sanford's propaganda activities were sustained through the use of private funds—in the first six months of 1863, he had spent $15,000 of his own money.

After a struggle with the American counsul in London for control of operations in England, Sanford shifted his efforts to the European mainland. Sanford's continental operations were similar to his efforts in Britain: monitoring and, whenever possible, disrupting the flow of supplies to the Confederacy. Strict secrecy was maintained throughout the organization. In one instance, Sanford was warned by a fellow operative, "Keep to verbals—and in a position to 'know nothing about it' in case of need. You can't . . . trust any of these people with a line of writing."[7] Sanford's network reached beyond Belguim and France into Spain, Italy, and Prussia. In many of these countries, Sanford and his agents sought to discover the amount of bids placed by Confederate agents for war matériel and offered to pay a slightly higher amount to cancel the contracts. Sanford once outbid the Confederates for a supply of guns they had ordered, noting to a fellow agent, "I have bought up the whole contract—60,000."[8]

The most ambitious operation run by Seward and Sanford involved a covert program to influence European public opinion to support the Union. Shortly after his arrival in Europe, Sanford recognized that there would be a struggle between North and South to win the support of both public and official opinion in Europe. Sanford recommended the adoption of a program of "subsidizing" key journals in Europe, along with the establishment of "cooperative" arrangements with political parties such as the Liberals in France. Sanford proposed an ambitious program of retaining the services of journalists or editors at newspapers all over Europe. He wrote to Seward, "We must have an organ of our own to repel the attacks of the hostile press of England and France and to give light upon our affairs."

Although Seward did discourage the more ambitious projects, primarily for budgetary reasons, he was thoroughly supportive of most of Sanford's propaganda campaign. One of the earliest and most successful efforts involved a Belgian newspaper, *L'Indépendance belge,* whose editor was paid 6,000 francs to tilt his coverage in favor of the Union. Sanford wrote to Seward regarding his arrangement with *L'Indépendance belge,* "We now have a pulpit to preach from which reaches a large audience and I consider it a very important gain." Sanford's greatest propaganda coup came when he successfully bribed a prominent Paris journalist, A. Malespine of the Paris *Opinion nationale.* Sanford believed that French public opinion could influence government policy toward the United States and noted on one occasion that "no man is more easily swayed by the sentiments of the masses" than Napoleon III. Malespine was placed on a retainer of 500 francs a month by the U.S. government for services rendered the northern cause. Malespine agreed to carry the fight "into the hostile camp" and leave no "article of import unanswered."

Sanford carried his campaign of media manipulation to Britain, hoping to cultivate an English version of Malespine. He arranged with a U.S. consul there to receive intelligence reports from the battle fronts, news that would be leaked to sympathetic reporters from friendly journals. He pleaded with Seward to send "somebody of mark here to take up & reply to

these abominable lies & misstatements, everyone of them as they appear."
He sought at one point to enlist the aid of a group of prominent northern
businessmen to purchase a Belgian newspaper as part of his campaign of
press manipulation. Testimony to Sanford's success in this area came
from no less an authority than one of his Confederate counterparts, who
wrote that *"L'Indépendance belge . . .* is under a peculiar influence in
its violent hostility to the Confederate States."[9]

To assist Sanford in molding European public opinion, Secretary of
State Seward sent a team of prominent Northerners to cultivate pro-
Union sentiment among political and religious leaders on the continent.
One of the secretary's agents, John Bigelow, was a former editor of the
New York Evening Post. As two historians of Civil War diplomacy have
noted, Seward sent Bigelow to Paris as a "propaganda agent in the guise
of consul general."[10] Bigelow's familiarity with the news business assisted
northern agents in their program of media manipulation. He took advantage of Sanford's secret service fund, in one instance paying 1,000 francs
to the financially strapped editor of *La Presse,* a leading French journal.[11] Manipulation of the European press was also the goal of another of
Seward's agents, prominent New York Republican Thurlow Weed. Weed
directed his most serious effort in England, where he sought to create a
sympathetic press. His main weapon in this campaign to gain access to
British journals was through the well-placed application of bribes. Money
for Weed's operation was provided by Henry Sanford, and with it he
gained access to several British journals. He also employed a writer to
generate material that would work its way into the British press.[12]

Churches were also targeted by the Lincoln administration as a source
of leverage over European governments. The administration enlisted the
support of major American religious figures to use their influence with
their European brethren. A key figure in this effort was Archbishop John
Hughes of New York, the Catholic cleric who had played a minor role in
Polk's decision to dispatch Moses Beach on his secret mission to Mexico.
Hughes was asked to use his influence within the Catholic Church in
Europe to win support for Lincoln's policies. Seward instructed the archbishop, "While in Paris, you will study how, in conjunction with Mr.
Dayton [the U.S. ambassador to France], you can promote healthful
opinions concerning the great cause in which our country is now engaged
in arms."[13] Among the tasks undertaken by the archbishop was a personal
appeal to Napoleon III of France and, according to Confederate agents, a
recruiting mission to lure Irish citizens to enlist in the Union army. The
archbishop was paid approximately $5,200 by the American government
for his expenses.[14] He received an additional reward for his services when
the Lincoln administration informed the Vatican that it would be most
pleased if Hughes were elevated to cardinal.[15] In addition to targeting the
European Catholic Church, Lincoln's agents sought to influence the Prot-
estant sects of Britain. This was the object of a mission undertaken by

American Episcopal bishop Charles McIlvaine. Bishop McIlvaine, according to one historian of Seward's diplomacy, "did good work with the English clergy and laity."[16]

Another target of Lincoln's covert propaganda campaign was the British working class and its trade unions. Union agents organized meetings of English workers to support Lincoln's policy and urge the government to assist the North; many "spontaneous" rallies were inspired and, in some cases, organized by northern agents. An American consul wrote to Secretary Seward in January 1863, "It has cost much labor & some money to get it [mass meetings] well started but I think both have been well spent & are producing results far better than [I] had any reason to hope."[17]

During Seward's tenure as secretary of state, the United States spent $41,000 on special agents, many of whom orchestrated the clandestine operations recounted in the preceding pages.[18] In addition to direct payments to his agents, Seward gave Sanford control of a $1 million fund to be used for "special activities" in Europe.[19] Seward allowed his agents direct access to his office and permitted them to engage in actions behind the backs of his ambassadors. This freewheeling approach generated a great amount of friction between his regular foreign service officers and the special agents. The support that the special agents received from both Seward and Lincoln in the face of protests from their own ambassadors is testimony to the importance both men placed on the work of these operatives.

Lincoln's Covert Operations in North America

President Lincoln also authorized a number of secret operations designed to shift sentiment within the United States, the Confederate states, and Canada against secession. No area of North America was exempt from this massive effort designed to lure major opinion leaders, particularly in the church and the press, to support the preservation of the Union. In addition, Lincoln authorized a mysterious mission that may have involved, for the second time in less than twenty-five years, a covert operation against American citizens.

Lincoln's efforts at secretly influencing Canadian public opinion was small in comparison with his efforts in Europe, apparently out of a belief that the ruling government in Britain was the appropriate place to exercise leverage. However, Canada was not entirely exempt from the administration's covert war. Two weeks before the start of the Civil War, Secretary Seward sent the president a memorandum outlining suggestions for the new administration's domestic and foreign policy. Seward suggested that Lincoln "send agents into Canada, Mexico, and Central America to rouse a vigorous continental spirit of independence on this continent against European intervention."[20]

The day Fort Sumter was fired on, the administration adopted part of

Seward's recommendation by dispatching a secret agent to Canada not only to monitor activities there, but also to steer public and official opinion in a favorable direction. President Lincoln presided over a cabinet meeting held as the Union began to dissolve and immediately signaled his willingness to fight a covert war beyond the battlefield. Attorney General Edward Bates recorded in his diary for April 12, 1861: "C.[abinet] C.[ouncil] S. ec. y [of] State. Proposes to send Geo. Ashmun to Canada as a special (secret) agent &c to keep political feelings right—as $10 a day and expen[se]s. Agreed."[21] Secretary Seward wrote to Ashmun that both government officials and the people of Canada held "erroneous views in regard to the states [sic] of affairs" in the United States and that action needed to be taken to "impart . . . correct information on the subject."[22]

Unfortunately for the Lincoln administration, any possible benefit from this operation was lost when word of it leaked to the press only four days after Ashmun's appointment. As a consequence, Seward informed the Canadian government that Ashmun would not proceed with his mission, though in fact the secretary hoped that Ashmun would act unofficially. The secretary did not request a return of $500 that had been advanced to Ashmun, and the letter of recall was dispatched in such a way as to reach Ashmun after his arrival in Canada, if at all. Ashmun acted as Seward hoped and remained in Quebec in an informal capacity.[23]

The Lincoln administration's effort at media manipulation was not limited to the foreign press. One newspaper, the *New York Herald,* had a large circulation both in the United States and in Europe, and the newspaper's attacks were hurting the administration both at home and abroad. The methods used by the administration to win the support of this journal involved the application of incentives bordering on bribery. Lincoln contacted one of his New York political operatives, the aforementioned Thurlow Weed, to apply pressure on the editor of the *Herald,* James Gordon Bennett, to shift the paper's position on the war. Weed noted in his autobiography that the *Herald* "by its large circulation in Europe, was creating a dangerous public sentiment abroad. Our representatives in England, France, Belgium, etc., regarded the influence of the '*Herald*' upon the public mind of Europe with apprehension." Weed went on to observe that "Mr. Lincoln deemed it more important to secure the 'Herald's' support than to obtain a victory in the field."[24] Bennett responded to Weed's overture by sending word to the president that the *Herald* would modify its position on the war in return for a commission for the editor's son in the revenue service. The editor's son received his commission, and the newspaper shifted its stance on the war (at least until the election of 1864 approached).[25] During the latter part of the conflict, Lincoln planned to nominate the editor as U.S. ambassador to France, though Bennett declined the offer.[26]

In addition to bribing newspapermen and editors, the tactics used in Lincoln's large-scale program of media manipulation also involved planting stories under false cover. As two historians of his patronage policies have noted, Lincoln appreciated the "power of the press and sought to engage the services of journalists and former journalists in federal posts at home and abroad. . . . Lincoln seems to have chosen more newspaper men for official positions than any of his predecessors."[27] His efforts at home were more subtle than those in Europe but nonetheless represented an attempt at government manipulation of the organs of information. An example of the Lincoln administration's thinking about the importance of propaganda can be seen in this quote from Attorney General Edward Bates: "Weak and hesitating men allow their bold and active enemies to make public opinion against them. Bold and active rulers make it on their side."[28]

In the fall of 1864 the president received a proposal to penetrate covertly all the newspapers in the Confederacy. A man named H. P. Livingston wrote on November 17, 1864:

> Allow me to present to you a plan, whearby the Union sentiment at the South, would be strengthened, The dissatisfaction of the people with their Government, increased and their Armey demoralized. Their are now but (36) newspapers printed in the Confederacy. they are poor few of them makeing money. I would suggest that the controle of many and nearley all of them may be had by purchase of the controleing interest. The amount of funds required would be small in comparison to the advantages that would result to our cause from the control of the Southern Press.

Lincoln forwarded the proposal to Secretary Seward with the notation "What says the Sec. of State to within?" Seward responded that the plan "seems to me very judicious and wise." He noted that he did not have the necessary funds at his disposal, but recommended that the president check with Secretary of War Stanton to see if he could finance the operation. Seward went on to recommend that if the secretary of war was unable to find the necessary funds, then the administration should turn to private sources. Seward wrote the president, "T. W. [Thurlow Weed]— might find money by contribution," a statement revealing once again the secretary of state's relish for "privatized" covert operations.[29]

Continuing a long-standing American tradition, Confederate clergymen were additional targets in Lincoln's covert war. One operation that occurred in 1863 involved an attempt to restore the allegiance of members of the Southern Methodist Church to the Union. Colonel James F. Jaquess, a Methodist minister serving in the Union army, volunteered to General James Garfield to travel into Confederate territory and seek out fellow Methodists there. His goal is not entirely clear, though the conventional interpretation is that an unofficial peace feeler was to be sent to the Confederate government through the Methodist Church. It is possible, however, that the mission was intended to drive a wedge between members of the Southern Methodist Church and the Confederate government. Lincoln viewed this undertaking as controversial enough to require him to be in a position to deny its existence. The president wrote to Jaquess's commander:

> Such a mission as he promises I think promises good, if it were free from difficulties, which I fear it can not be. First, he can not go with any government authority whatever. This is absolute and imperative. Secondly, if he goes without authority, he takes a great deal of personal risk—he may be condemned, and executed as a spy. If, for any reason, you think fit to give Col. Jaquess a Furlough, and any authority from me, for that object, is necessary, you hereby have it for any length of time you see fit.[30]

On at least two other occasions, Lincoln made it clear that he would have to maintain a discreet distance from Jaquess. On one, Lincoln wrote to Jacquess's commanding officer, "For certain reasons it is thought best for Rev. Dr. Jaques[s] not to come here [Washington]," and on another the president sent a coded communication: "Mr. Jaquess is a very worthy gentleman; but I can have nothing to do directly, or indirectly, with the matter he has in view."[31] Although Jaquess did cross southern lines for a brief period, his mission was a failure, neither causing any great shift of sentiment within the Southern Methodist Church nor developing any links with a peace faction in the Confederate government.

Perhaps the most controversial and intriguing operation of the Lincoln administration occurred in February 1863 and involved one of Lincoln's favorite covert agents, Thurlow Weed. Weed was the central player in a "privatized" secret mission shrouded in mystery to this day. The little-known event illuminates Lincoln's understanding of presidential power to authorize privately financed covert operations without the knowledge of Congress and—more broadly—to defend the nation's security. This understanding caused the president to interfere surreptitiously in the American electoral process so as to prevent the enemy from obtaining a victory behind the lines that it could not win on the battlefield.[32]

Although its purpose cannot be described with absolute certainty, the general outline of the operation is clear. The president appears to have decided to intervene covertly in elections in Connecticut and New Hampshire for the purpose of defeating "peace" Democrats critical of Lincoln's war policy. The operation began when President Lincoln summoned Thurlow Weed to Washington during the second week of February 1863. In a face-to-face meeting with his New York political operative in the White House, the president informed Weed, "We are in a tight place. Money for legitimate purposes is needed immediately; but there is no appropriation from which it can be lawfully taken. I didn't know how to raise it, and so I sent for you."[33] Lincoln asked Weed if he could raise the necessary funds from some of New York's major businessmen. He gave his operative a brief note to show potential contributors that Weed was on an authorized presidential mission. Lincoln wrote on the note, "The matters I spoke to you about are important, & I hope you will not neglect them." On the bottom of this page and over to the reverse side, Weed asked for the signatures of fifteen corporations and individuals who pledged $1,000 each to the president's effort.[34]

At this point, the trail becomes murky, with no conclusive evidence revealing how the money was spent. It appears that Secretaries Seward and Stanton had a hand in disbursing the funds, which were used to blunt the electoral prospects of anti-Lincoln Democrats in Connecticut and New Hampshire. Secretary of the Navy Gideon Welles's diary entry for February 10, 1863, noted that "Thurlow Weed is in town. He has been sent for, but my informant knows not for what purpose. It is, I learn, to consult in regard to a scheme of Seward to influence the New Hampshire and Connecticut elections."[35] Further evidence that the purpose of the funds was to influence the domestic electoral process can be seen in a note from Weed written to Lincoln on March 8, 1863: "The Secession 'Petard' in Connecticut, has probably 'hoisted' its own Engineers. Thank God for so much." Weed was referring to the narrow reelection victory (two thousand votes) of Republican governor William Buckingham over his Democratic opponents.[36]

Under Lincoln and Seward, the covert battlefield to control public opinion stretched from Europe to Canada and ultimately to the United States, as even states loyal to the Union were subjected to Lincoln's clandestine operations. To assist in this effort, President Lincoln enlisted the services of not only secret agents, but also members of the American clergy and the press. Lincoln would not agree with contemporary critics of covert operations who find a high wall of separation between those two vocations and their government. This new understanding, forcefully stated in 1976 by members of the Church Committee investigating the Central Intelligence Agency, represents a significant break with Lincoln's view of the propriety of employing clergymen and reporters to further American interests.

In many ways, "Mr. Lincoln's war" was a precursor to the ideological struggles of the twentieth century, where areas far from the front lines were considered part of the battle zone and the manipulation of public opinion was a legitimate government objective. Lincoln's conventional victory over the Confederacy has been long appreciated. We would do well to absorb the significance of his triumph in the covert arena as well.

One Hundred Years of Clandestine Activity

As the United States approached the centennial of its independence, a decision from the Supreme Court affirmed the concept of executive control of secret service operations, for the first time in its history. The case, *Totten, Administrator,* v. *United States* (1875), grew out of President Lincoln's wartime intelligence operations. The dispute centered on the clandestine services of William A. Lloyd, who had had a contract with the president to "ascertain the number of troops stationed . . . in the insurrectionary States, procure plans of forts and fortifications, and gain such other information as might be beneficial . . . and report to the President." Lincoln had agreed to pay Lloyd $200 a month for his services, but after the assassination Lloyd was unable to receive the full compensation promised by the president. Lloyd was reimbursed for his expenses only, and his estate brought suit requesting full compensation from the federal government.

The case reached the Supreme Court in the fall of 1875, and Justice Stephen Field delivered a brief but forceful opinion that rejected Lloyd's request but vigorously defended the authority of the president to contract for and dispatch secret operatives. The Court of Claims had rejected Lloyd's request in part because of a division within the court over the question of the authority of the president to bind the United States to a contract for secret services. As Justice Field's decision revealed, the Supreme Court had no doubt about this authority: "We have no difficulty as to the authority of the President in the matter. He was undoubtedly authorized during the war, as commander-in-chief of the armies of the United States, to employ secret agents."

Justice Field expressed his concern about the risks involved in exposing classified information if courts injected themselves into the highly secret realm of executive operations:

> The service stipulated by the contract was a secret service; the information sought was to be obtained clandestinely, and was to be communicated privately; the employment and the service were to be equally concealed. Both employer and agent must have understood that the lips of the other were to be for ever sealed. . . . This condition . . . is implied in all secret employments of the government in time of war, or upon matters affecting our foreign relations.

He observed that public disclosure of agents' activities might embarrass or compromise the American government and went on to note that a secret service "with liability to publicity in this way, would be impossible." Field wrote that an agent's only recourse was to look to the contingent fund of the department that had employed him and to make his case with those in the executive branch who controlled such funds. The courts were no place for such suits, as they would disclose matters of a confidential nature, of even greater confidence than that existing between a lawyer and client, a husband and wife, or a priest and confessor. Field concluded, "Much greater reason exists for the application of the principle to cases of contract for secret services with the government."[37] The Court's decision acknowledged the importance of strict standards of secrecy surrounding clandestine operations, and lodged in the executive branch wide discretion over the control of such operations. Such operations, as Justice Field further noted, were often necessary not only in times of war but in the normal course of foreign relations.

The Court's decision was a reflection of the prevailing sentiment within the American government over the need for conducting secret operations and for lodging the authority over them in the hands of the president. Within seven years of *Totten,* the United States would create its first bureaucratic establishment devoted to intelligence gathering, the ONI.[38] Nonetheless, covert operations would continue to be run from the State Department, as they had been since the creation of the Contingency Fund in 1790. This secret fund was still completely at the disposal of the president and would continue to provide for services too controversial to be handled through routine bureaucratic channels. The day was far off when all clandestine operations, routine intelligence missions as well as high-risk covert activities, would be merged under the control of one agency. Many historians of American clandestine activity erroneously conclude that the United States engaged in no such activity until the arrival of such an agency.

Covert Action in Hawaii

As it had since 1790, the State Department continued to maintain control over the most sensitive covert operations. One late-nineteenth-century example of this control can be seen in an effort to aid and abet a movement to acquire Hawaii that occurred during the administration of President Benjamin Harrison (1889–1893). The operation was conducted by the American ambassador, John Stevens, who received vague or open-ended instructions designed to keep the government in Washington discreetly distant from outright responsibility for the ambassador's actions. Additional precautions were taken to conceal any executive branch involvement by keeping sensitive dispatches out of the hands of Congress. President Harrison's secretary of state, John W. Foster, ordered Stevens to write two types of dispatches, one describing public affairs "in their open, historical aspect," and the other including comments on "matters of personal intrigue and the like."[39] Foster wrote to Stevens: "Many of your dispatches . . . combine these two modes of treatment to such a degree as to make their publication, in the event of a call from Congress or other occasion therefore inexpedient and, indeed, impracticable, without extended omissions." Congress was apparently unaware of the dual system of reporting and therefore any request for relevant State Department dispatches would have yielded an incomplete account of U.S. actions in Hawaii.[40]

Stevens, a firm believer in the movement to annex Hawaii, was given wide latitude by the administration in representing America's interests. He did receive "printed instructions" from the State Department, but they have never been found. On two occasions, Stevens wrote to the State

Department warning of political unrest in the islands that might provide an opening for Britain; he urged the adoption of "decisive" steps on the part of the United States. In both cases, the State Department did not reply to the ambassador's dispatches. In another case, Stevens asked for instructions on what he should do in case the Hawaiian government was toppled, but once again he apparently received no reply.[41] In one dispatch to the secretary of state, Stevens discussed the political differences between the two main groups advocating annexation by the United States. If the groups could unite, "they would carry all before them, providing the latter could get any encouragement that the United States would take these islands as a territory."[42]

In the spring of 1892, Lorrin Thurston, a representative of a secret Honolulu-based "annexation club," traveled to the mainland under the guise of visiting the Hawaiian exhibit at the Chicago World's Fair. In fact, Thurston was heading for Washington to "get into contact with the authorities, and ascertain their disposition" toward the annexation of Hawaii. While in Washington, the emissary met with Secretary of State Foster and Secretary of the Navy Benjamin Tracy, but "did not call upon the President, as both the President and Mr. Tracy thought it best that the President should not commit himself in the matter." Thurston later wrote in his memoirs that the president sent word through Tracy that the administration would be "exceedingly sympathetic" to a request for annexation.[43] Before his departure from the mainland, Thurston sent the secretary of state a memo outlining his "proposed line of action" to win annexation: the queen of Hawaii would be given the chance to step aside peacefully, but force would be used if she resisted; a provisional government would be established until Hawaii was incorporated into the United States.[44]

The administration began to prepare the American public for the eventual annexation of Hawaii by apparently planting stories in various journals decrying British intrigue in the islands and discussing their strategic value to the United States. The *Washington Post* carried a number of stories warning of British meddling and published excerpts from a "confidential" report concerning the importance of Pearl Harbor as a naval base.[45]

The uprising against Queen Liliuokalani finally took place on January 17, 1893, and was conducted by a number of Americans, including Sanford Dole. At the height of the uprising, Stevens ordered a detachment of 164 U.S. sailors and marines to come ashore and protect American property and lives. In a show of force designed to intimidate the monarchy, the servicemen were assigned to buildings near the queen's palace and other government offices. That strategy, coupled with Stevens's recognition of the provisional government, was instrumental in causing the queen to abdicate. President Harrison commended Stevens for his actions, denied to the Senate any American involvement in the insurrection, and authorized the ambassador to use his Marine Corps contingent to suppress any violence. Although incoming president Grover Cleveland withdrew the annexation treaty with Hawaii because of reports of U.S. complicity in the coup, Dole remained in power as leader of the new government. In any event, Cleveland's action only delayed the inevitable: the islands were formally annexed by the United States in 1898 during McKinley's presidency.[46]

The Bureaucratization of American Intelligence

President Cleveland's objections to his predecessor's actions in Hawaii did not lead him to reject the use of secret operations altogether. Cleveland, who had defeated Harrison in the election of 1892 to win a second term in office for himself, was an advocate of improved intelligence gathering. His terms in office enhanced the American military's efforts to activate bureaucratic organizations devoted to secret intelligence.[47] The U.S. Army had followed the navy's lead by setting up its own intelligence service in 1885, the Military Information Division (MID). The first signs of cooperation between the units were seen during the Spanish-American War, when the U.S. Secret Service, along with the ONI and the MID, combined forces to smash a Spanish spy ring operating in Montreal.[48] The Secret Service owed its existence to President Lincoln's decision at his last cabinet meeting in April 1865 to create an anticounterfeiting office in the Treasury Department. By the time of William McKinley's administration (1897–1901), the Secret Service's duties had evolved to include certain counterintelligence functions, including the successful effort in Montreal.[49]

During the Spanish-American War, the ONI's office in London spent over $27,000 on intelligence operations designed to monitor the activities of Spain's European diplomats (including penetration of its London embassy), track the movement of war matériel, and plant agents inside Spain itself. Additionally, the ONI's Paris operative hired the services of two Frenchmen who had numerous contacts in the Spanish government, while the Berlin office recruited an agent to observe the movement of Spanish ships in the Suez Canal. ONI achieved only mixed results, though its efforts were far more successful than those of its Spanish counterparts.[50]

In the aftermath of the Spanish-American War, the military scaled back its intelligence operations. The army's MID was all but scrapped, relegated to the Army War College as the caretaker of the library and map room. The few overseas intelligence operations that did take place were conducted on an improvised basis. One example occurred in 1909 when a navy officer and an army counterpart, using South African passports, traveled throughout Asia. In the guise of botanists, they mapped Japanese fortifications and naval ports throughout the Far East.[51]

In 1915, after the sinking of the *Lusitania,* President Woodrow Wilson had begun to shift toward preparedness for the world war raging in Europe. This policy provided the intelligence agencies with expanded resources and boosted agency morale. At this time, ONI and MID joined forces to conduct operations in the United States along with the newly created Bureau of Investigation of the Department of Justice. That agency, eventually renamed the Federal Bureau of Investigation, conducted overseas and domestic investigations of suspected spies and radicals opposed to the Allied war effort.[52]

As American involvement in the war drew closer, the Navy Department ordered the ONI to "arrange for securing information from abroad as to the strength and movements of enemy's forces. Plan for and prepare now a complete system of secret service, and cipher codes to be used."[53] ONI agents gathered intelligence at their stations in London, Paris, St. Petersburg, Rome, Vienna, Madrid, and The Hague. During the war, many of these operatives engaged in efforts to sway public opinion in favor of the Allies. Influential businessmen and government officials were encouraged to support the Western powers, and these efforts had some impact in diffusing pro-German sentiment in Spain and the Scandinavian countries. The naval attaché in Stockholm, who organized an office in Sweden to counteract German propaganda, created an "Allied News Agency" that received funding from British and American sources. Collaborative efforts were undertaken with President Wilson's Committee on Public Information to influence opinion through newspapers and movies.[54] The committee was actually the propaganda arm of the federal government. One of its most important endeavors was an initiative designed to keep Russia in the Allied camp after the fall of the czar. Over $1 million was spent on this campaign, which involved the use of movies, billboards, placards, and "every possible medium to answer lies against America."[55]

Throughout World War I, the primary covert battleground for America's secret operatives was Latin America. The ONI had a network of paid agents in the region who were expected to conduct a variety of functions. These included monitoring political developments in each nation, providing information on public opinion, observing the activities of Japanese and German visitors, and acquainting themselves with influential persons. One stunning success involved an ONI agent assigned to infiltrate the German community in Argentina and Brazil; he went on to become intimately familiar with German embassy personnel in Buenos Aires by joining their clubs and convincing them he was German. The ONI also utilized American business firms as cover for its intelligence operations, though it experienced difficulties with one large company, Vacuum Oil, which abused its access to ONI for its own profit.[56]

A controversial mission undertaken by the ONI was designed to influence Mexican internal affairs. A secret mission was ordered by ONI director Roger Welles to travel to Mexico, track down German communications outposts, and, most important, establish contacts with pro-American Mexicans who would accept assistance in overthrowing pro-German provincial governments. The ONI also attempted to have the State Department intervene to win the freedom of a Mexican leader who had been convicted of arms smuggling and was being held in a U.S. jail. The ONI hoped to return him to Mexico for use as a pro-American functionary. The State Department balked, perhaps out of bureaucratic resentment toward the ONI. Welles responded to the State Department's refusal by warning one of his field agents, "You must not become in the least discouraged and make any suggestions to this office abandoning any plans." The ONI director went on to lament, "You are suffering in a very small degree, comparatively, the same difficulty that this Office experiences constantly in a large degree . . . and that is the legal restrictions placed upon the carrying out of all matters of the kind in which you are engaged." Despite these "legal restrictions," ONI proceeded with its covert Mexican operation.[57]

Mexico was a key target of another secret undertaking of the Wilson administration, this one involving a propaganda battle between German and American operatives for the support of Mexican public opinion. His secretary of the navy stated that Wilson hated propaganda and quoted him as ordering the War Department to "call off" any agency of the army "attempting to organize propaganda of any sort."[58] Even so, various propaganda and counterpropaganda efforts were conducted with Wilson's approval. A concerted effort was directed by the administration at various Mexican newspapers deemed to be in the employ of German agents of influence. Although Wilson appears to have stopped short of authorizing the payment of bribes to counter this influence, he did not completely rule out clandestine means to influence the Mexican press.

The State Department considered a number of options. These included an embargo on shipping newsprint to Mexico and a proposal to have American, British, and French commercial interests increase their advertising so as to heighten the Allies' leverage over the papers. (These interests were to withdraw that support as a bloc if concessions to the Allied position were not forthcoming.) The American ambassador to Mexico supported the former and rejected the latter option, noting that the Germans had ample funds to cover any of the newspapers' revenue losses. Wilson endorsed the ambassador's proposals. He felt that they were "something more than interesting" and that "they ought to be acted on." [59] The paper embargo had a limited impact: the Mexican government resisted this external attempt to control the nation's press by providing those newspapers hit by the embargo with its own paper reserves and by seeking other sources of supply. It should also be said that the campaign to sway the content of the Mexican press involved the use of bribery by American agents. Although the State Department had an official policy of refusing to bribe newspaper personnel, it did not reprimand those operatives who resorted to such tactics and met with some success.[60]

Finally, Mexico was the scene of the first known American-sponsored assassination attempt. During Wilson's border war with Mexican bandits in 1916, the U.S. Army hired four Mexican citizens to poison revolutionary leader Francisco "Pancho" Villa. The operatives were instructed by a member of General John Pershing's staff to drop poison tablets into Villa's coffee, but the attempt failed. Pershing apparently hid news of this mission, a cover-up that persisted until the 1980s. There is no known evidence showing that President Wilson was aware of the operation.[61]

Yet Wilson, a symbol of open government and idealism in foreign policy, expressed his support for a clandestine arm of the executive branch. In a speech delivered in 1919 urging support for the League of Nations, Wilson discussed the president's unique role as defender of the nation's security:

> You have got to think of the President of the United States as the chief counsellor of the Nation, elected for a little while but as a man meant constantly and every day to be the Commander-in-Chief of the Army and Navy of the United States, ready to order them to any part of the world where the threat of war is a menace to his own people. And you cannot do that under free debate. You cannot do that under public counsel. Plans must be kept secret. Knowledge must by accumulated by a system which we have condemned, because it is a spying system. The more polite call it a system of intelligence. You cannot watch other nations with your unassisted eye. You have to watch them with secret agencies planted everywhere.[62]

One senses a certain reluctance on Wilson's part about the necessity of secret operations. The president who tried to avoid entangling the United States in the conventional war in Europe sought to keep his nation out of the covert war as well. Still, Wilson appears to have drawn a lesson from World War I about the new responsibilities of America as a world power, responsibilities that required "a system of intelligence."

The central coordination of America's intelligence agencies during World War I and in its aftermath was undertaken by an office in the State Department known as U-1, which performed these services until its elimination in 1927. Its demise came about in an atmosphere of State Department hostility toward spying that is best summed up by Secretary Henry Stimson's alleged comment in 1929: "Gentlemen do not read each others' mail."[63] This statement has been cited repeatedly by a generation of historians who view it as proof of America's pre–Cold War innocence, before the nation attained its superpower status and "lost its moral compass."[64]

By World War II, two of the "big three" of the American intelligence community—the ONI and the army's renamed Military Intelligence Division (or G-2)—had been badly weakened by budget and personnel cuts. Only the FBI, benefiting from the imaginative public-relations leadership of J. Edgar Hoover and some well-publicized victories against

Prohibition-era domestic criminals, had been spared the budget axe. As America approached its greatest test of arms, its foreign-intelligence capability would soon prove inadequate to the challenge that lay ahead.[65]

From the Office of Strategic Services
to the Central Intelligence Agency

A slow rebuilding came about in the aftermath of a fiasco involving the escape of fourteen members of a captured German spy ring in 1938. Embarrassment over this event led President Franklin Roosevelt to order improved coordination among his intelligence services. Shortly after this incident, the president enlisted the services of William J. Donovan, a Congressional Medal of Honor recipient from World War I, who had first met FDR at Columbia Law School. One of Donovan's first missions was a fact-finding tour of Britain, where members of the intelligence establishment were anxious to impress upon him the need for vigilance against German clandestine operations. President Roosevelt appointed Donovan coordinator of information (COI) on July 11, 1941, directing him "to carry out, when requested by the President, such supplementary activities as may facilitate the securing of information important for national security." From the very beginning, Donovan viewed his budding agency as more than a clearing house for intelligence. He sought to build an organization capable of conducting a wide variety of secret operations. Donovan had noted in a memo to Secretary of the Navy Frank Knox that "subversive operations in foreign countries" would have to be considered part of any new centralized intelligence authority.

Some of Donovan's proposals were enacted prior to the Japanese attack on Pearl Harbor, and numerous changes had been implemented by June 1942: the COI was renamed the Office of Strategic Services (OSS); the role of the OSS in domestic affairs was eliminated; and the OSS was subordinated to the Joint Chiefs of Staff, rather than reporting directly to the president. Donovan never achieved the level of coordinating authority he sought due to fierce resistance from bureaucratic rivals in the FBI, ONI, and G-2. In spite of this resistance, the president issued a military order creating the Office of Strategic Services on June 13, 1942, essentially restructuring the office of the COI and putting it under the direction of the Joint Chiefs of Staff. Part of the agency's mandate included the implementation of "special services" ordered by the Joint Chiefs of Staff. As Rhodri Jeffreys-Jones notes, important precedents were set in the establishment of the OSS that would have an impact on the design of the postwar Central Intelligence Agency. The most important concerned the denial of any authority to the OSS over domestic operations and the combining of intelligence-gathering functions with paramilitary covert operations.[66]

The OSS conducted clandestine activities around the world. Although many of its operations were on the periphery of the struggle, this organization did achieve some spectacular successes.[67] These included the surrender of Axis forces in Italy and the co-opting of the Thai prime minister, an appointee of the Japanese government who became an OSS operative. The OSS performed some important guerrilla operations behind enemy lines prior to D-Day and may have been involved in the assassination of Vichy French admiral Jean-François Darlan. OSS operative Allen Dulles developed high-level contacts with disgruntled members of the German general staff and the German intelligence services, including those involved in the assassination attempt on Hitler on July 20, 1944. Some OSS operations during the war foreshadowed the coming struggle with the Soviet Union, particularly when Donovan's men developed a relationship with a Romanian intelligence unit that provided information as early as 1944 on postwar Soviet designs on that nation.[68]

The OSS served as a hatchery for a score of future CIA figures—Dulles, Richard Helms, William Colby, and William Casey, all of whom later became directors of Central Intelligence. These men formed the core of an agency that came about after a reluctant President Harry Truman, fearing the creation of an American "Gestapo," nevertheless agreed to support the establishment of a centralized intelligence agency. Truman's abolition of the OSS was prompted by both an intense dislike of General Donovan and a desire to trim the size of the cumbersome wartime government.[69] The OSS was abolished by executive order effective October 1, 1945, and the Central Intelligence Group (CIG) was in turn established on January 22, 1946. This structure was replaced when the National Security Act of July 26, 1947, established the National Security Council (NSC), the office of secretary of defense, an independent air force, and the Central Intelligence Agency.

Congressional debate on the creation of the CIA focused primarily on the question of whether the agency should be under the direction of military or civilian overseers. It was ultimately agreed that the director of Central Intelligence could be a military man.[70] The act charged the CIA with five general tasks: advising the National Security Council on matters related to national security, proposing recommendations to the NSC regarding the coordination of intelligence activities, correlating and evaluating intelligence and providing for its appropriate dissemination, carrying out "services of common concern," and "perfrom[ing] such other functions and duties related to intelligence affecting the national security."[71]

The vaguely worded "such other functions" clause emerged as a critical component of the CIA's job description, as relations between the United States and the Soviet Union rapidly deteriorated. The CIA quickly became immersed in the type of operations with which it is now commonly associated. Elections in France and Italy saw the United States intervening through covert propaganda techniques and the application of large sums of money in an attempt to thwart the electoral prospects of the respective national Communist parties.

The success of pro-American parties in both of these countries led the administration to enlarge the agency's covert responsibilities. Two National Security Council directives, NSC-10/2 and NSC-68, called for the increased use of secret operations to counter Soviet-inspired machinations.[72] Congress pitched in with its passage, after closed hearings and very brief debate, of the Central Intelligence Act of 1949. The act included language remarkably similar to the language of the Contingency Fund legislation passed by the Congress in 1790. It read in part:

> The sums made available to the Agency may be expended without regard to the provisions of the law and regulations relating to the expenditure of Government funds; and for objects of a confidential, extraordinary or emergency nature, such expenditure to be accounted for solely on the certificate of the Director.

In sum, the act allowed the CIA director to conduct clandestine activities without specifically accounting for the expenditure of funds.[73] As the CIA's general counsel at the time, Lawrence Houston, noted, "Provisions of unvouchered funds and the inviolability of such funds from outside inspection is the heart and soul of covert operation."[74]

This new coordination between America's covert units was quickly put to use in two operations ordered by President Dwight Eisenhower. The targets were Iran and Guatemala, and in Eisenhower's opinion, both operations worked out quite well. The Eisenhower administration was convinced that the left-leaning government of Muhammad Mussadegh in Iran was slipping into the Soviet orbit. When Iran began talks with the Soviet Union over oil sales and a possible treaty of Cold War neutrality, U.S. concern grew. In 1952, the Iranian parliament requested that Mussadegh step down, a request that led to street violence involving the highly visible participation of the Iranian Communist party, the Tudeh. Parliament rescinded the order, but Mussadegh was becoming increasingly dependent on the support of the Tudeh. His decision to accept the support of the Communists in 1952 was a critical event in the drift toward American intervention. The British encouraged American fears of Soviet encroachment in this area, as they were anxious to preserve their control of the Iranian oil supply, which was in the process of being nationalized. British motives in wanting to preserve this access were not based entirely on mercenary considerations; the availability of Middle Eastern oil supplies had helped to overcome the Western European coal miners' unions, which were Communist-dominated.

In August 1953, CIA-sponsored riots in Tehran broke out, and by September, Mussadegh's government had been deposed. The ease with which this operation was conducted (for a cost of under $1 million) encouraged the Eisenhower administration to use the same techniques against the government of Jacobo Arbenz in Guatemala in 1954. Arbenz's nationalization of American business interests, particularly the United Fruit Company, had first brought him to the attention of the administration. His request for arms from the Soviet Union in March 1953 seemed ominous in Washington, as did his inclusion of the Communist party in the government and his association with figures such as Che Guevara. Those were the major reasons for the administration's campaign against Arbenz, not the preservation of American-owned banana plantations. Arbenz was toppled in June 1954 by a tiny guerrilla force trained and equipped by the CIA, which also provided critical propaganda support.

In the eyes of President Eisenhower, Iran and Guatemala appeared to be following a dangerous pattern that the United States had already witnessed in Eastern Europe, Korea, China, and Indochina. The perception in the White House was that Arbenz and Mussadegh, if not Communists, were at least dupes of the movement. The operations against them set the pattern for future American efforts against perceived Soviet allies.[75] The CIA was granted broad authority by the president and Congress to take whatever measures were necessary to protect the interests of the United States and the interests of the "Free World."

8 ■

The Distorted Legacy

The Rise of Congressional Control of Clandestine Operations

Covert action has been a tool of United States foreign policy for the past 28 years.

Final Report of the Church Committee, 1976[1]

■ From the time of the American Revolution until the creation of the Central Intelligence Agency in 1947, the prevailing opinion in the United States supported executive control of clandestine operations as an essential component of American foreign-policy making. The degree of executive authority appeared at times to be almost limitless, particularly when Congress ignored the use of secret service funds to manipulate political sentiment within the United States. There appears to have been a steady consensus within the legislative branch that the president was the appropriate administrator of the instruments of American foreign policy, especially those of a covert nature. The legislature limited its role to appropriating the funds necessary to sustain the president's capability to conduct clandestine operations.

After the creation of the Central Intelligence Agency, the House and Senate Armed Services and Appropriations committees were given limited oversight authority over the agency. In keeping with almost 160 years of American tradition, that authority was loosely constructed so as to give the president and his agency the discretion needed to conduct secret operations. Beginning in 1947, the oversight procedure involved "small ad hoc groups composed of a few senior committee members who reviewed the budget, appropriated funds, and received annual briefings on CIA activities. The DCIs [directors of Central Intelligence] kept senior committee members informed of large scale covert action projects at the approximate time of implementation."[2]

This adaptation of a clandestine capability to a formal bureaucracy, however, represented a significant concession to congressional interests on the part of the executive branch. Three of the more powerful members involved in the process from the beginning were Carl Vinson, chairman of the House Armed Services Committee; Clarence Cannon, chairman of the House Appropriations Committee; and Richard Russell, chairman of the Senate Armed Services Committee. Leverett Saltonstall, a member of both the Senate Armed Services and Appropriations committees, described the arrangement as follows: "Dominated by the Committee chairmen, members would ask few questions which dealt with internal agency matters or with specific operations. The most sensitive discussions were reserved for one-to-one sessions between [CIA Director Allen] Dulles and individual Committee chairmen."

Yet this loose control of the intelligence community reflected Congress's appreciation of the nature of the exceptional tasks assigned to the CIA. It was also a reflection of the congressional emphasis on seniority, the long-standing method of allocating power within the institution. Today most assessments of that oversight arrangement view it as deeply flawed; but as long as there was a prevailing foreign-policy consensus that viewed the Soviet Union as a threat to world peace, most members were satisfied with the mechanisms they had created. Indeed, real oversight did take place, as former CIA general counsel Lawrence Houston noted. The Senate Armed Services Committee under Chairman Russell was fiercely protective of the agency, but the House dealt with CIA appropriations, Houston recorded, "as thoroughly as any [other] appropriations. Cannon was chairman of the Appropriations Committee most of the time, and he established that we would bring to him any detail and he would question or have the committee question us. They knew our appropriations line by line."[3] In addition to this vigorous appropriations oversight, the House Armed Services staff maintained contact with officials in the Central Intelligence Agency.[4]

Senior members of Congress, at times numbering some twenty members, were given access to the agency's briefings and budget requests. The budget process generally worked as follows:

1. The director of Central Intelligence presented his estimate of the budget broken down into general categories.

2. Certification by committee chairmen constituted approval, with no authorization bill required.[5]

3. Appropriations for the CIA were concealed in the Department of Defense budget, exempt from floor debate and public disclosure.

4. The CIA accounted for specific expenditures except those made on the voucher of the director of Central Intelligence; vouchered funds would be accounted for, if such accounting was requested, in the hearings on the budget for the following year.[6]

The director was given further discretion with the establishment of the Contingency Reserve Fund for the CIA in 1952. This was a sum created for "unanticipated large projects" and was used to fund various covert operations.[7] An observer of this early period of interaction between the CIA and Congress has commented, "Congress deliberately handed to the director of Central Intelligence the authority to withhold information from the public, including Congress. . . . Efforts to regain a greater measure of congressional supervision of the intelligence establishment met with surprisingly little success in the first twenty years of CIA's existence."[8]

There was, however, one congressional activist who sought to put the CIA under a more intense spotlight. Joseph McCarthy, a junior senator from Wisconsin, chafed at the restraints imposed by the seniority system and came very close to applying his special brand of oversight to the intelligence community. McCarthy hoped to conduct the first major congressional investigation of the CIA and viewed that investigation as a top priority. McCarthy told his colleagues, "I have roughly a hundred pages of documentation covering incompetence, inefficiency, waste and Communist infiltration in the CIA, which I am holding in the hope that a committee will be established so that I can turn the information over to it."[9] He had in his sights certain individuals with Ivy League backgrounds employed by the agency. However, CIA Director Allen Dulles refused to cooperate with McCarthy, and the senator eventually backed down.

This event was fresh in the mind of President Eisenhower when he resisted Senator Mike Mansfield's proposal to reform the oversight process in 1955. Eisenhower vowed that Mansfield's resolution "would be passed over [his] dead body." Mansfield called for the creation of a Joint Committee on CIA Oversight, modeled after the Joint Committee on Atomic Energy, which also dealt with classified material. The fight to establish this committee was partly the result of a congressional turf struggle between those who had access to the agency and its secrets and those who did not. Mansfield, a member of the Senate Foreign Relations Committee, recognized the importance of intelligence matters in formulating American foreign policy and wanted a piece of the action. The Senate leadership and the Eisenhower administration's allies held firm, and the resolution was defeated by a vote of 59 to 27, with McCarthy's supporters backing Mansfield. Ironically, Mansfield had a chance to vote on a similar resolution sponsored by Senator Eugene McCarthy some ten years later. After the proposal was defeated, Senator Russell invited three members of the Foreign Relations Committee to sit on the Armed Services "Watchdog" Committee, and Mansfield was one of the three.[10]

Yet Mansfield's earlier effort was not completely in vain. In response to complaints from proponents of the joint committee proposal, Senator Russell created a formal CIA subcommittee of the Armed Services Committee. The Senate Appropriations Committee followed, establishing CIA subcommittees, an action also adopted in the House Armed Services and Appropriations committees. Russell and the other senior members of the oversight committees continued to dominate the process, but by the mid-1960s the CIA was increasingly called on to brief other committees and even individual members on a variety of topics. At this time, CIA Director Richard Helms increased the number of committee briefings; by 1967, seventeen committees received detailed information on the agency's activities. Generally, a junior member who sought access to operational details was privately briefed by the committee chairman or by the agency itself. One senior senator with broad access to the agency's inner workings was Henry Jackson of Washington, who developed a close relationship with the agency. Jackson often briefed junior members of the Armed Services Committee with the latest information from the intelligence community.[11]

Thus the popular view that Congress was kept in the dark by the agency and was unaware of its actions simply does not hold up under inspection. The truth was closer to what Senator Russell once told the CIA's congressional liaison: "There isn't a single member of this Senate that's so lowly that he can't make life unbearable for you fellows if he decides he wants to do it."[12] The fact that the senators rarely did "make life unbearable" was indicative of the bipartisan support for the Cold War foreign policy of American presidents from 1947 to 1974; it was not the result of any conspiracy to keep the members silent. Like the congressmen of old, America's Cold War legislators let the executive branch do its job. Nonetheless, significant concessions—commensurate with preserving secrecy—were made by the executive to allow for some level of congressional participation. The system of checks and balances was not disregarded, but rather an accommodation was reached between Congress and the executive that allowed for the dissemination of information from the CIA to senior members. The level of congressional oversight of Cold War–era clandestine operations far exceeded the level of any earlier period in the nation's history.

The Rise of Congressional Activism

By the mid-1970s, this system had collapsed. The prevailing sentiment of the day held that a series of imperial presidents had hijacked the Constitution and attempted to destroy the delicate system of checks and balances. Many critics took a different tack, seeing a runaway agency beyond the control of the executive branch. This line of attack had the advantage of protecting the memory of two popular presidents, Eisenhower and Kennedy, under whose administrations the CIA had conducted a variety of controversial covert operations. Both of these versions of history had the added benefit of allowing congress to deny any institutional acquiescence and preserve the myth of its ignorance of CIA "abuses."

In 1974, a new generation came to power in Congress, convinced that democratized, open policy making would prevent future Vietnams. These new members believed that the legislative branch possessed greater wisdom than the executive and that large groups of decision makers could avoid the flawed policies that were the "inevitable" result of decisions made behind closed doors. The president could no longer be trusted, so executive discretion would be curtailed henceforth.

The notion that senior members in Congress possessed a sense of institutional wisdom worthy of deference was also discarded. If anything, these senior members were viewed as co-conspirators with the executive in a scheme to create a "secret government." Congressman Robert Drinan of Massachusetts reflected the mood of the times: "The senior members of the House, and of the Senate, have conspired to prevent the younger members . . . from knowing anything about the CIA."[13] Junior members wanted to be power brokers themselves, and access to the world of secret operations was a major objective. Something of a revolution was under way, a war against the instruments of executive power, one that would overturn almost two hundred years of presidential control over clandestine operations. In this atmosphere, secrecy within the executive branch was viewed by Congress with great suspicion.

Nowhere was this secrecy more a fact of life than in the Central Intelligence Agency. One indicator of erosion of support for the agency and its activities could be seen in growing congressional and journalistic condemnation over CIA intervention in Salvador Allende's Chile. This condemnation, which reached its peak in the fall of 1974, led some members of Congress to seek a ban on all covert operations and to limit the CIA to collecting and analyzing intelligence. Senator James Abourezk of South Dakota proposed such a ban and garnered only seventeen votes (sixty-eight were opposed). All the same, many key leaders in the Democratic party supported the resolution, including Senate Majority Leader Mike Mansfield along with Senators Joseph Biden, Frank Church, George McGovern, Howard Metzenbaum, William Proxmire, Abraham Ribicoff, and Gaylord Nelson. In addition, three Republicans—Edward Brooke,

Mark Hatfield, and Richard Schweiker—voted to ban covert operations. The Senate floor debate on October 2, 1974, was brief but heated, with Abourezk plainly stating the intent of his legislation: "This amendment will . . . abolish all clandestine or covert operations by the Central Intelligence Agency . . . there is no justification in our legal, moral, or religious principles for operations of a U.S. agency which result in assassinations, sabotage, political disruptions, or other meddling in another country's internal affairs."

It was Abourezk's belief that strengthening the congressional oversight process was not enough, that the only way to avoid the kinds of operation run by the CIA in Chile was to "totally abolish this kind of reprehensible activity."[14] Another senator, Frank Church of Idaho, asserted that he was supporting his South Dakota colleague in order to register a protest against CIA abuses. Certain that the legislation would go down to defeat, Church viewed his vote as a symbolic gesture. Still, he hoped to prevent future use of covert operations that interfered with "the rights of other peoples" and were "contrary to the historic role played by the United States in world affairs."[15] Senator Metzenbaum of Ohio also supported the proposal because he believed that the CIA was bound not only by American law, but also by the laws of foreign nations in which the agency was operating.[16] Republican Senator Hatfield of Oregon expressed his concern that the proposed ban did not go far enough and wanted to prohibit all forms of clandestine activity, including the secret acquisition of intelligence.[17]

The opposition to Abourezk's proposal was led by Senators Hubert Humphrey, John Stennis, and Barry Goldwater, who argued that the proposal was hastily conceived and potentially dangerous to American security. In addition, Senator Humphrey held out the prospect for improved congressional oversight of the intelligence community. Although Abourezk's proposal went down to defeat, new allegations of CIA misconduct ensured that Congress would adopt a more vigorous program of oversight, if not outright veto power, over clandestine operations.[18]

On December 22, 1974, the *New York Times*, anxious to restore its image after being scooped by the *Washington Post* on Watergate, published a story with the headline "Huge CIA Operation Reported in U.S. Against Anti-War Forces, Other Dissidents in Nixon Years." Actually, this allegation turned out to be vastly overstated, a fact lost in the hysteria of the times.[19]

Both presidents Johnson and Nixon had been convinced that Communist nations were bankrolling or directing the antiwar movement and had ordered investigations into this possibility. The CIA's investigations, which included Operation Chaos, found no evidence of external control or funding of the antiwar movement, the Black Panthers, or the Students for a Democratic Society. The CIA generally kept its investigation within the confines of its charter—though it was clearly pushing the outer edge and occasionally crossed the line—by examining the foreign contacts of those domestic groups.[20] In three instances, the agency reported on the activities of American dissidents inside the United States, an action outside the CIA's charter.[21] The revelations came at a particularly vulnerable time for the agency and its overseers, barely a month after the election of the post-Watergate class of 1974 reformers who had campaigned "against the imperial presidency of Richard Nixon and promis[ed] a new morality in government."[22]

On December 30, 1974, Congress passed the Hughes-Ryan amendment, aimed at granting the legislature broadened oversight responsibility for covert operations. Hughes-Ryan effectively sought to eliminate the use of plausible deniability by the executive, a concept with a venerable tradition. The amendment read in part:

> No funds appropriated under the authority of this or any other Act may be expended by or on behalf of the [CIA] for operations in foreign countries, other than activities intended solely for obtaining necessary intelligence, unless and until the President finds that each such operation is important to the national security of the United States and reports, in a timely fashion, a description and scope of such operation to the appropriate committtees of Congress.[23]

The "appropriate committees of Congress" included the Foreign Relations, Armed Services, and Appropriations committees and five subcommittees—a total of 163 senators and congressmen plus top staffers. Writing in his memoirs five years after passage of the amendment, President Ford stated, "That amendment . . . effectively shut down covert operations anywhere in the world."[24] The amendment's cosponsor, Senator Harold Hughes of Iowa, saw in his effort a rebirth of appropriate democratic oversight of foreign policy. It was only the beginning of an attempt to restore to the American people, through their elected representatives, "control over the cloak-and-dagger operations." Hughes added, "I would admit that circumstances might develop in which covert action would be justified in time of war. I find it impossible, however, to envisage any circumstances in time of peace that would justify them."[25]

The revelations of the CIA's intervention in Chile and the exposure of Operation Chaos were pivotal events in the passage of Hughes-Ryan, yet neither effort was unique in the annals of American history. As we have seen, President Madison dispatched Joel Poinsett to Argentina and Chile in 1810, and he blatantly intervened in the internal politics of both nations. Covert assistance to pro-American political parties in Latin America has roots going back to the early nineteenth century. The effort to block Salvador Allende from coming to power in Chile actually had begun in the Kennedy administration, which hoped to make the country the showplace of its Alliance for Progress by providing both covert and overt support for the Christian Democratic party.[26]

It frequently has been suggested that measures directed against domestic dissent in the pre–Cold War period were perhaps questionable but always conducted openly. Yet, perhaps, Daniel Webster and Abraham Lincoln had utilized secret funds to counteract the efforts of their political opponents. Both of those earlier secret operations had a greater impact on the sanctity of the American political process than did Operation Chaos. The concept of national security having been loosely defined by American presidents throughout our history, the issue became whether Cold War–era presidents had twisted the concept into something alien to the American political tradition. The answer in Congress and in most academic circles was an unequivocal yes.

The Church Committee's Distorted Perspective

Both the House of Representatives and the Senate began major investigations into the activities of the intelligence community in early 1975. These investigations marked the beginning of a concerted congressional effort to do to presidential control of intelligence what the War Powers Act attempted to do to executive control of conventional military operations. The House investigation, conducted under the direction of Congressman Otis Pike of New York, was characterized by leaks and partisan bickering. The Senate investigation, chaired by Frank Church of Idaho, was conducted in such a way as to merit serious scrutiny. The Church Committee led the way in staking out the path for reform in the management of the nation's intelligence community. The investigation was a broad inquiry examining whether the intelligence community had engaged in "illegal, improper or unethical activities."[27] The committee examined assassination plots, covert operation in Chile, domestic intelligence operations, mail openings, and the use of clergy and the media for intelligence purposes. The committee also requested the preparation of a supplementary report on the history of American intelligence operations, *The Evolution and Organization of the Federal Intelligence Function: A Brief Overview (1776–1975)*.[28]

The report was prepared by Harold C. Relyea of the Congressional Research Service and was an adequate account of some early intelligence precedents, primarily military-intelligence operations. Nevertheless, it appears that very few members read the study, as the committee's final report all but ignored any of these historical precedents. The committee noted in its final report that "programs were examined from Franklin Roosevelt's administration to the present. This was done in order to present the historical context within which intelligence activities have developed."[29] A broader understanding of the historical context of the alleged "illegal, improper or unethical" activities could have been achieved by tracing the evolution of clandestine operations back to the founding of the nation.

The Church Committee's final report rightly noted the "significant new facets of the postwar system" as being the "great size, technological capacity and bureaucratic momentum" of the Cold War intelligence community. To be sure, these were significant changes, though Congress did adapt to them by establishing an oversight process for clandestine operations. In addition, the bureaucratization of intelligence arguably brought a sense of organization and control to an activity that had been conducted largely by "free-lancers" operating entirely at the discretion of individual presidents and their secretaries of state. The other significant change noted by the Church Committee in its final report was "the public's acceptance of the necessity for a substantial permanent intelligence system"; the report added that prior to 1947 a formal system of intelligence was only sporadically adopted by the government, generally in times of war or national emergency.[30]

The committee's statement is somewhat misleading, however, for the Contingency Fund had been a part of American government since 1790, and some military intelligence units had been functioning continually since 1882. The fund had been used to launch covert operations in times of war and peace; and although the earlier operations were undoubtedly ad hoc efforts, there was consistent congressional support for providing clandestine funds over which the president exercised total control. At no point during the period from 1790 to 1947 did Congress curtail the president's authority over secret service funds, even after revelations of possible domestic abuse.

The committee's final report thus basically ignores the Contingency Fund as a source of executive control of clandestine operations. It devotes only a few sentences to this critical resource for secret operations. After briefly acknowledging the use of operatives paid by the Contingency Fund to conduct "missions similar to modern-day political covert action," the report also gives a misleading interpretation of the first mission of this sort. It states that President Washington dispatched an agent, Gouverneur Morris, to Britain "because Washington's Secretary of State, Jefferson, was not yet functioning"—as if a bureaucratic snafu was the reason Washington sent a secret envoy to Britain and delayed informing Congress for over a year.[31] A footnote points readers seeking further information to Henry M. Wriston's *Executive Agents in American Foreign Policy*.[32]

Furthermore, in the body of the report's text, the committee delicately obfuscated the fact that since 1790 the president had been allowed freedom to withhold from Congress information regarding secret service expenditures: "Congress, with its own constitutional powers in foreign affairs, its power of the purse . . . had the option of regulating the practice of using executive agents on foreign intelligence missions." The fact that every Congress since 1790 had chosen not to do so is relegated to a footnote with the wrong date for the beginning of this practice.[33]

Most important, the Church Committee report misses the wider historical legacy altogether. It boldly states, "There were no precedents for the peacetime use of covert action involving the use of armed force of the type conducted after 1947."[34] Yet on the contrary, we have already seen several examples: Secretary of State Jefferson's peacetime effort to assist insurgents attempting to remove British and Spanish forces from the Louisiana Territory, or Madison's role in the overthrow of Spanish authority in West Florida and the establishment of a secret army in East Florida. In the Floridas, American operatives fomented violent revolution against the possessions of a nation with which the United States was at peace. Joel Poinsett's covert military activities in Chile would seem to be a precedent, as would the Harrison administration's complicity in the overthrow of the Hawaiian monarchy.

At another point, the report drops the "peacetime" qualification and boldly claims that "covert action has been a tool of United States foreign policy for the past twenty-eight years."[35] In fact, covert operations of both a military and a diplomatic nature have been part of American foreign policy since the founding. The report also slights the important question of whether the United States was truly at peace in the period between 1947 and 1974 when this "new" covert action came into vogue.

The Church Committee final report makes reference to the courts' reluctance to deal with covert presidential prerogative. It expresses a hope that increased judicial activism will confront certain unaddressed constitutional questions. In a footnote, the report does recognize a Supreme Court case that affirmed the concept of presidential control of clandestine operations, *Totten, Administrator,* v. *United States* (1875). As noted in Chapter 7, Justice Field's decision appears to recognize broad executive authority; it refers to the importance of executive secrecy in wartime activity as well as in matters "affecting our foreign relations."[36] Yet the Church Committee interpreted the decision in a very narrow manner, stating that the Court acknowledged the authority of the president to conduct only "wartime" covert action.

The historical myopia of the committee had a direct impact on its recommendations for reform. This was plainly visible in its criticism of CIA use of clergymen, the media, and academics for intelligence purposes. As has been shown, this practice has roots in American history that extend to the American Revolution. The Continental Congress dispatched an American journalist to Montreal to establish a pro-American newspaper to win sympathy for the American cause during the Revolution and sent a Catholic priest to propagandize in Quebec on behalf of the United States. General Washington used a clergyman to extract intelligence from captured British spies before their execution. Various administrations co-opted foreign journalists to propagandize on behalf of American interests, often through outright bribery. American newspaper editor Moses Beach ran a covert operation for President Polk, while editor James Gordon Bennett slanted his journal's coverage at the request of President Lincoln. Lincoln employed clerics to pressure their brethren across the Atlantic, and Daniel Webster employed secret funds in hiring a Harvard historian to win American support for a boundary treaty with Britain.

Nonetheless, a new understanding was emerging of the distinctive role these groups play in a democratic society and of the need to "protect" them from engaging in suspect activities on behalf of the government. The committee's final report states:

> [R]eligious groups—like academia and the press—[are considered] to be among the most important of our society's institutions. As such, any covert relationship that might either influence them or jeopardize their reputation is extremely sensitive. . . . Making operational use of U.S. religious groups for national purposes both violates their nature and undermines their bonds with kindred groups around the world.[37]

The committee endorsed a new CIA policy announced in February 1976 that prohibited "any operational use of Americans following a religious vocation."[38] Although the committee stopped short of recommending an outright ban on "covert relationships" between the government and academics and the media, its report was highly critical of such contacts. Of course, if this standard had been followed by General Washington during the American Revolution, Nathan Hale would have been prevented from using the cover of a schoolmaster to conduct his intelligence operation in 1776.[39] For some members of the Church Committee staff, the very idea of contacts between the CIA and the media or academic community made their "blood boil."[40] The "dilution" of certain information in the committee's report on these contacts was requested by the executive branch and agreed to by Chairman Church, though this agreement "most annoyed" Senators Gary Hart, Walter Mondale, and Philip Hart.[41]

The most sensational secret activity examined by the Church Committee was Operation Mongoose, the code name for the covert campaign against Fidel Castro. One aspect of this involved the CIA in plans to assassinate Castro. Planning for such an operation began late in the Eisenhower administration and was apparently discussed at the highest levels of the government. During the early 1960s, the pressure to remove Castro was unwavering, with one former agency official likening it to "white heat."[42] This imperative led the agency to pursue a variety of schemes to eliminate Castro involving poisons and exploding sea shells; by far, the most newsworthy involved an alliance with organized-crime elements. None of the attempts succeeded, and the assassination effort against Castro was canceled in the aftermath of President Kennedy's assassination.[43]

Along with Castro, other potential targets were Patrice Lumumba in the Congo, Colonel Abdul Kassem in Iraq (who may have been the target of an effort temporarily to disable him through mind-altering drugs rather than assassination), and Rafael Trujillo in the Dominican Republic. The lack of written evidence and failing memories of key players prevented the Church Committee from establishing conclusively that Eisenhower or Kennedy ordered the assassination of any foreign leader.[44] The committee's inability to firmly establish the chain of command in the various assassination plots led Senator Church to suggest at one point that "the CIA may have been behaving like a rogue elephant on a rampage."[45] Although no foreign leaders were killed by CIA operatives, "It wasn't for want of trying," as former CIA director William Colby remarked.[46]

On February 18, 1976, President Gerald Ford issued an executive order prohibiting agencies of the U.S. government from participating in assassination plots. This order was welcomed by the Church Committee, which had directed a significant amount of its investigative resources at piecing together the details of the Castro assassination plots. Senator Church expressed the prevailing sentiment of the day: "It is simply intolerable that any agency of the government of the United States may engage in murder."[47] Both Chairman Church and one of his key investigators implied that race may have been a factor behind the plots, the latter noting that "in each instance, the object of our machinations had been the nonwhite leader of a small, poor country."[48] The staff director of the committee's assassination inquiry concluded that the investigation revealed the "immorality and brutality of mind" behind the plots.[49]

The committee's report condemned assassination as a practice at odds with traditional American standards of decency. And in fact, assassination as a foreign-policy weapon was apparently not utilized by American presidents in the nation's early history. Thomas Jefferson once wrote, "Assassination, poison, perjury. . . . All of these were legitimate principles in the dark ages which intervened between ancient and modern civilization, but exploded and held in just horror in the 18th century."[50]

By the twentieth century, however, there appears to have been an acceptance in some quarters of the use of assassination as a wartime option. The American military's effort to dispose of Pancho Villa in 1916 was the first example of official U.S. government involvement in this practice. Other examples include the assassination of Japanese admiral Isoroku Yamamoto, mastermind of the Pearl Harbor attack.[51]

The acceptance of assassination as an appropriate wartime tool raises the question of whether the Kennedy administration's Operation Mongoose, particularly its assassination component, violated accepted American standards of conduct. As already noted, whether the United States was at peace during this time is an open question, as is the question of whether an opponent of assassination such as Jefferson would have tolerated a Soviet-dominated Cuba. In the early nineteenth century, Jefferson viewed Cuba's possession by Great Britain as a potential "great calamity" and saw the island as the strategic linchpin of the Caribbean.[52]

The Church Committtee's majority report can thus be regarded as a disturbing mixture of historical ignorance and moral fastidiousness. There is something to the criticism made by committee vice chairman John Tower, who noted the futility of designing an intelligence community fit for employment "in an ideal world."[53] Throughout the Cold War, the CIA was locked in a struggle in "the back alleys of the world," as it was aptly described by former secretary of state Dean Rusk.[54] These were alleys where standards of decency were seldom observed. Former secretary of state Henry Kissinger had the Church Committee in mind when he criticized the "illusion that tranquility can be achieved by an abstract purity of motive for which history offers no example."[55]

The Church Committee seems to have been caught up in the heady atmosphere of détente, where warming relations with the Soviet Union in the mid-1970s replaced the sense of confrontation that had dominated U.S.–Soviet relations for over twenty-five years. There was also an underlying sense that American foreign policy had been based on false assumptions about the Soviet Union and the threat of Communism, assumptions that for many had been shattered in Vietnam. The United States was no longer seen as a force for good in the world. As a result, efforts were made to restrain the instruments of American foreign policy, particularly those of a covert nature.

In the wake of congressional and media investigations of the intelligence community, a tidal wave of condemnation was directed against America's Cold War presidents and the agency that did their bidding. One candidate for president in 1976, Senator Fred Harris of Oklahoma, stated in regard to the CIA, "We've got to dismantle the monster!"[56] Other critics were less strident, but still convinced that the clandestine operations approved by these presidents represented a significant break with traditional standards of American conduct. The prevailing sentiment within Congress was that the American system of government had been torn from its moorings, having all but discarded the teachings of Washington, Jefferson, and Madison. Within both scholarly and political circles, the message was clear: efforts to curtail executive discretion over secret operations were designed to restore the nation to the Founders' understanding of the limits of executive power and the importance of decency in American foreign policy.

Senator Church noted at the beginning of his investigation, "I believe that we can find a formula that will bring covert activity into line with our traditional principles. For example, there must be a way to require an oversight committee's consent for certain kinds of covert operations."[57]

Church stated on another occasion how far the United States had drifted from the Founders' legacy since the 1940s:

> Since World War II, with steadily escalating consequences, many decisions of national importance have been made in secrecy, often by the executive branch alone. These decisions are frequently based on information obtained by clandestine means and available only to the executive branch. . . . The cautions expressed by the Founding Fathers and the constitutional checks designed to assure that policy making not become the province of a few men have been circumvented through the use of secrecy.[58]

Senator Church was convinced that something had changed drastically since the late eighteenth century. Church remarked, "Above all, we have lost . . . the good name and reputation of the United States from which we once drew a unique capacity to exercise moral leadership."[59]

The spirit of the Founders was frequently invoked by Church and others favoring tightened congressional restrictions on executive use of covert operations. Senator Charles Mathias of Maryland, a supporter of the proposal to create permanent intelligence oversight committees in Congress, proclaimed in 1976, "In this, our Bicentennial Year, the Senate has a special opportunity to renew the values of those who founded this country . . ." and "restor[e] the Framers' plan" (by creating the new oversight structure).[60] Senator Walter Mondale of Minnesota echoed a similar theme: the creation of strengthened congressional oversight would bring the United States "back to the genius of the Founding Fathers." Mondale urged that the most important way the nation could celebrate the Bicentennial was to make certain that the intelligence agencies "report their activities to this Congress, all of them."[61] Senator Edmund Muskie of Maine declared that Congress was simply seeking a "restoration" of powers over intelligence matters apparently lost in the distorted atmosphere of the Cold War. "By controlling the purse strings [of the intelligence agencies], the select committee and Congress will have restored its rightful role in directing America's future intelligence activities."[62]

Senator Church argued for overt intervention when any involvement was necessary. He invoked the lessons of "history," referring to efforts "in the 1840s and 1850s [when the United States] openly supported resistance movements in Latin America." Church did leave the door open for covert operations in times of national emergency or in cases "where intervention is clearly in tune with our traditional principles."[63] Yet for the senator, secrecy and the preservation of freedom were often seen as irreconcilable. He noted in frustration that criticism of congressional leaks of classified information had shifted the issue from "how to preserve freedom" to "how to keep secrets."[64] In a speech announcing his candidacy for president in 1976, Church restated the myth of pre–Cold War American innocence. The senator believed that the actions of America's Cold War presidents were outside the mainstream of acceptable standards of conduct laid down by the Founders: "In stark contrast with contemporary presidents, our founding fathers were a different breed. They acted on their faith, not their fear. They did not believe in fighting fire with fire . . . evil with evil."[65] More than once, Church invoked the specter of evil in his discussion of the CIA and executive branch abuses: "Ours is not a wicked country and we cannot abide a wicked government."[66]

Although Church failed in his White House bid, his triumphant Democratic opponent shared the Idaho senator's perspective on the importance of obedience to law and morality in the implementation of American foreign policy. Jimmy Carter considered awarding the Idaho senator the vice-presidential nomination but gave it instead to a follow member of the Church Committee, Walter Mondale. Both men made a major campaign issue out of CIA and executive branch "excesses." To Mondale, the CIA had a record "which is completely beyond understanding."[67] He stated that "almost anything bad that happens in this world is attributed to the CIA," but found himself "in the unhappy position of not being able to take the stand that U.S. covert action should be banned."[68] Jimmy Carter went even further; responding to a question from the press in 1976, he declared that he would not use the CIA to overthrow a Communist government at odds with the United States. He added, "I don't see any reason for the CIA through covert means to try to overthrow governments."[69] He expanded on this point on another occasion, ruling out attempts not only to overthrow foreign governments, but even to "modify the character" of those governments.[70] Such efforts were not in the interest of "world peace" and ran counter to the American practice of conducting its foreign policy in the open.[71] America's foreign-policy setbacks were the result of the government's forging ahead without consulting the American people and doing things "contrary to our basic character."[72] Revelations of CIA activities had also contributed to America's increased crime rate, Carter believed.[73] After his election as president, Carter modified his stance somewhat, expressing "shock" at the number of people the CIA had to brief on its operations.[74] Comments such as this led Senator Daniel Patrick Moynihan of New York to state, "He's just discovered it's *his* CIA."[75]

President Carter sought to shift CIA resources away from clandestine activities by agents in the field and toward the use of technical means to gather intelligence. This decision seems to have been partly the result of his misgivings about covert operations in general. The administration cut personnel from the clandestine division, apparently out of a desire to steer the agency away from "the dirty stuff." By 1979, covert manpower in the CIA had dropped to 40 percent of its 1950s level.[76] Many observers of the American intelligence community believe the president's disregard for human intelligence assets weakened his ability to make informed judgments about Iran, where his own National Security Council adviser noted "the astonishing lack of information" in the wake of the shah's collapse and the seizure of the U.S. embassy.[77]

The New Oversight: The Struggle for Control of American Clandestine Activity

In response to proposals from the Church and Pike committees, the Senate created the Select Committee on Intelligence in May 1976, and the House established the Permanent Select Committee on Intelligence in July 1977. With their creation, the United States granted its legislative branch the greatest amount of control of any Western democracy over intelligence matters. In contrast, Britain and France continued to shield their intelligence services from media and parliamentary inquests. Perhaps only Canada comes closest to regulating its intelligence community in as stringent a manner.[78]

This regulation is especially rigorous in regard to budget. The CIA's budget is reviewed item by item by the House and Senate intelligence committees along with the intelligence subcommittees of both appropriations committees. Hearings are held on any aspect of the budget that members decide to probe, including withdrawals from the Contingency Reserve Fund for unanticipated expenditures.[79] Through their formal oversight of the budget process, the committees have established themselves as a significant force in the direction of the American intelligence community.

The committees also have developed informal methods that effectively curtail executive discretion, such as threatening to reveal publicly covert plans under consideration. These developments have ensured that covert activities are no longer the unique preserve of the executive branch, as they were for almost two hundred years. In essence, the president must clear his actions with a congressional board of overseers because defiance of these formal and informal arrangements can have great legal and political costs. Thus within the intelligence agencies of the executive branch, secrecy, speed, and dispatch have been replaced by hesitation and risk avoidance. The Central Intelligence Agency has become in many ways "just another bureaucracy."[80] Nominees for high-level CIA positions are now expected to please "constituencies": those in the White House, within the agency itself, and on Capitol Hill.[81] Congress no longer defers to the executive branch on CIA personnel matters. Deputy Director (later director) of Central Intelligence Robert Gates also noted that Congress has "far greater knowledge of and influence over the way the CIA and other intelligence agencies spend their money than anyone in the executive branch would dream of exercising," and added that Congress may exert more influence over CIA priorities and allocation of resources than the executive. He observed further that the CIA finds itself "in a remarkable position, involuntarily poised nearly equidistant between the executive and legislative branches."[82]

Most important, these committees have contributed to the vacillation that often marks American foreign policy. This vacillation is seen not only in the articulation of appropriate policy goals, but also in the tactics needed to implement them. The execution of policy is no longer an executive function, as Congress micromanages the details of covert policies it has approved. For example, Congress authorized clandestine support for an insurgent army harassing the Nicaraguan government, but then objected to the placement of mines in Nicaraguan ports and the distribution of a guerrilla warfare manual discussing the "neutralization" of Sandinista officials. This operation, one of the largest covert efforts of the 1980s, demonstrated that both policy and tactical consensus can be achieved only by patching together temporary alliances between Congress and the executive, subject to revisions at Congress's—or an individual legislator's—whim.

As the situation now stands, one committee, in one branch of Congress, or even one committee member, can veto a secret presidential initiative. An example of the use of intelligence-committee veto power occurred with a Reagan administration proposal to assist a coup in the former Dutch colony of Surinam. The CIA had been approached by a group of exiles who were concerned about the pro-Communist leanings of their government. The agency began a feasibility study for such an operation, but even that was too much for the committees. Resistance to the plan first surfaced in the House Intelligence Committee and was eventually echoed in the Senate. It appears that the administration considered going forward with the plan until the Senate Intelligence Committee opposed it. A *New York Times* account stated that the plan "fed concerns in Congress about covert CIA activities in general." It was dropped because the informal legislative veto power of the two committees guaranteed its demise.[83]

As previously noted, the threat to "go public" has been made by individual legislators determined to halt a covert operation that offends their sensibilities. The late Leo Ryan, coauthor of the Hughes-Ryan amendment, defended the practice of individual members blowing the whistle on covert operations if that was the only way to block an operation the member disliked. The tactic knows no ideological bounds. Senator Jesse Helms of North Carolina is said to have expressed his displeasure over a CIA program to aid covertly the election campaign of El Salvador's president José Napoleón Duarte by allegedly leaking this story to the media.[84] One member of Congress, Senator Joseph Biden of Delaware, has boasted of being "the single most active Democrat on the Intelligence Committee." He noted with pride in 1986 that he "twice threatened to go public with covert action plans by the Reagan administration that were harebrained," causing the administration to cancel the operations.[85]

The increased involvement of the House of Representatives in overseeing clandestine operations represents a particularly sharp break with the past. The access now enjoyed by the House can have disastrous consequences. This was evident in a 1981 incident, almost comical in nature, involving a CIA covert operation to assist Chad in its struggle against a Libyan invasion force. The Reagan administration had opted to covertly assist Chadian forces in the hope of "bleeding" the regime of Colonel Muammar al-Qaddafi. It was the first such operation authorized by Reagan, and it got off to an awkward start. House committee members were leery of it and sent a "secret" letter to the president voicing their concerns. One committee member, Congressman Clement Zablocki of Wisconsin, leaked to *Newsweek* that the letter was a response to an administration plan to "topple" Qaddafi. The story was blown out of proportion by the magazine; the administration took the unusual step of publicly denying it, while trying to conceal the fact that the United States was secretly assisting Libya's Chadian enemies.

A scramble then ensued in the press to find out which country was the target of an operation that generated this congressional protest, and a number of completely inaccurate stories began to circulate. Mauritania emerged as the leading candidate, allegedly because of an erroneous statement made by a White House source who meant to say Mauritius (where a covert operation was under consideration). Mauritania reacted with horror to these reports and vigorously demanded an explanation from the State Department, which went to great lengths to reassure this country of American friendship. Congressman Zablocki was eventually briefed by committee staff and given a more accurate picture of the Chadian operation but was never disciplined for his actions by committee chairman Edward Boland, perhaps because of a grudging acceptance by the chairman that leaks were "epidemic."[86]

Committee members are not the only source of leaks that have canceled or compromised certain operations. Prominent television journalist Jim Lehrer has noted the temptations that committee staffers experience with their access to some of the nation's deepest secrets:

> I think the House and Senate Intelligence Committees are colanders of leaks, and it comes from the staff. It doesn't come from the principals. . . . Let me tell you, when you're thirty years old or thirty-four and you're carrying all that wisdom and heavy stuff in your head, they are going to tell it.[87]

Former CBS correspondent Daniel Schorr, hardly an admirer of presidential use of covert operations, has noted that CIA covert operations in five different countries all became public after congressional committees were briefed.[88] Leaks are a continuing problem that the committees have had a tendency to dismiss as something "everybody does." It was revealed during the Reagan years that even when a committee majority supports a covert operation, a determined minority can disrupt it. An administration plan for covert action against Libya in 1985 garnered the support of a narrow margin in both intelligence committees. Nonetheless, the plan was leaked to the *Washington Post* (Congress cleared itself of responsibility after conducting its own investigation).[89] In another instance, revelations of covert assistance to the UNITA rebels in Angola reached the press thirty-six hours after it was revealed to the committees.[90] In 1987, Senator Patrick Leahy of Vermont was forced to resign from the Senate Intelligence Committee after he allowed a reporter access to a report that the committee had voted not to release.[91] In 1988, former Speaker of the House Jim Wright, an opponent of the Reagan administration's Nicaragua policy, revealed to the press that the CIA had briefed members of Congress about its role in organizing opposition rallies in Nicaragua. This information had apparently been provided in confidence; yet the Speaker decided on his own to release the information. Many House Democrats defended Wright's actions, one congressman noting that "the issue today is Republican administrations overthrowing governments."[92]

Although the practice is not limited to Congress, one has to appreciate the difference between a leak from the executive branch designed to enhance the implementation of policy (perhaps by sending a signal to a foreign government) and a leak from the legislative branch intended to veto or cripple a policy that a determined minority could not defeat through the formal processes of government.

Leaks have been part of the American political landscape from the beginning, as a letter from Benjamin Franklin and Robert Morris written in 1776 indicates. Upon learning that France would provide covert assistance to the Americans, these two men wrote, "We agree in opinion that it is our indispensable duty to keep it a secret, even from Congress. . . . We find, by fatal experience, the Congress consists of too many members to keep secrets." Aware of this perennial danger, the Continental Congress adopted an oath of allegiance binding its members to a strict code of secrecy and guaranteeing expulsion for any member who violated the oath.[93]

One of the most disturbing questions to emerge from this new method of oversight is whether Congress, our most democratic institution, is capable of making those tough and often distasteful decisions that are required of nations competing in the international arena. Coupled with this problem is the issue of whether individual legislators serving on the intelligence committees can resist shifts in public opinion and stay on course should those tough decisions be exposed. For example, when it was publicly revealed in the early 1970s that the CIA had been conducting a "secret war" in Laos, Senator Stuart Symington of Missouri expressed surprise and indignation at the revelation, despite the fact that he had first been briefed on the matter in 1966.[94]

A more recent case occurred in the spring of 1984 when a political firestorm erupted over the aforementioned mining of Nicaraguan harbors. The original CIA proposal submitted to Congress on covert activities against Nicaragua had referred to mining as a possible component of the operation, and President Reagan approved such a plan in December 1983. CIA Director Casey had briefed the House Intelligence Committee as early as January 31, 1984, about the mining, approximately three weeks after the operation began. It is possible that some senators and staff members were also told around this time, while the full Senate Intelligence Committee was informed on March 8, 1984, and then again on March 13, 1984.[95]

When the story broke in the press on April 6, 1984, however, many congressmen would not support the mining publicly: they acted as if they were hearing about it for the first time and demanded that it stop.[96] Although false, many news accounts at the time also played up the fact that the CIA had not informed the Congress about the mining. Senator Patrick Leahy of Vermont, a vocal opponent of the Reagan administration's foreign policy, declared, "There were senators who voted one way the week before and a different way the following week who knew about the mining in both instances and I think were influenced by public opinion, and I think that's wrong and that it is a lousy job of legislative action."[97]

For Leahy and others, the mining flap was an embarrassment to Congress. Despite his own objections to the policy, Leahy knew that Congress had been informed of the mining.[98] The whole mining controversy certainly raises serious questions about Congress's ability to avoid public posturing and to take responsibility when controversial operations are exposed.

Planning for the covert operation directed against Panamanian strongman Manuel Noriega provides another example of the ill effects of democratized decision making on clandestine operations. Congress lambasted both the Reagan and Bush administrations in public for failing to remove General Noriega, while in private they refused to approve any effort that might involve violence. Stung by its experience with the mining controversy, the Reagan administration bluntly informed the committees that any effort to remove General Noriega could conceivably involve violence. In one instance, the Reagan administration proposed to support a coup led by Panamanians but could not give a 100 percent guarantee that the general would not be harmed. Should Noriega have been killed in the attempt, the United States would have been in violation of the ban on participation in assassinations. The committees rejected the administration's plan for a coup and instead supported an ineffective program that included clandestine radio broadcasts into Panama.[99] A committee spokesman admitted that the upcoming American election was a factor in the reluctance to endorse the Reagan coup plan: "No matter what side you're on, you probably don't want to let a U.S. election turn on that kind of crap shoot, especially if there's no reason it has to be done right then."[100]

The Bush administration inherited the Noriega problem and immediately ran into the same congressional roadblocks. In early 1989, the Senate Intelligence Committee cut Bush's request for $20 million in covert aid to Panamanian opposition parties because a Panamanian who was helping the CIA was involved in corrupt activities.[101] Throughout this time, Congress continued its criticism of the White House for its inability to remove Noriega from power. When Noriega was briefly detained in October 1989 by rebel Panamanian army officers in a failed coup attempt, the administration responded in a halting manner, in part because of the steadfast Senate opposition to U.S. involvement in such a potentially violent situation. In the wake of this failure, the fifth attempted coup against Noriega, the Bush administration began to push for greater latitude in providing assistance to coups that might lead to violence. However, Congress still was (and is) somewhat leery of granting any such latitude.[102] In December 1989, the U.S. government, which had engaged for a year and a half in an internal debate over the propriety of harming Manuel Noriega, invaded Panama with 22,500 troops. At least 220 Panamanians as well as 23 Americans died in the process—but Noriega was taken alive.[103]

Still another instance of the constricting effect of congressional oversight occurred in July 1989, at the time of the murder of Marine Lieutenant Colonel William Higgins in Lebanon. Former Central Intelligence Agency Director James Schlesinger admitted that the United States did not know where the other hostages were or who was holding them. Schlesinger said in a television interview:

> We've suffered some blows in our intelligence capability, we lost assets in the embassy bombing and the present set of circumstances makes penetration of these organizations difficult. . . . [P]enetration can only be achieved by having an individual prove his bona fides . . . the individual may need to knock off a bank or some such thing. . . . This wouldn't sit well with congressional overseers and the *Washington Post*.[104]

In seeking at least a full partnership, if not more, in the world of clandestine operations, Congress has put itself in the uncomfortable position of having to approve unpleasant deeds. Many members of Congress would prefer to avoid such a responsibility, for their office does not provide the protections afforded a president in case of embarrassing disclosures. Congressional committees are thus no place to make such high-risk decisions. Either for political reasons or from a genuine concern that America abide by certain moral precepts, many in Congress lean toward risk-free options. This tendency has had a ripple effect through the intelligence community; for every abuse that may have been prevented by the new restraint, the national interest has been harmed by fragmented policy making. This situation makes clear the benefits of decisions adopted within a limited circle. There are judgments that the president of the United States is in the best position to make—and plausibly to deny.

The Iran-Contra Affair and Prospects for the Future

The Iran-Contra affair generated renewed calls for restraints on America's "secret government." It is difficult to state with any certainty whether the affair represents a new twist in the long history of American secret operations. On the one hand, it may well be the first covert operation in the nation's history where it is plausible to believe that the president was unaware of the undertaking, that staff members conducted their own "off-the-shelf" operation. On the other, it may be the epitome of a classic covert operation, where a president directed his operatives to fulfill an objective but remained intentionally distant from the details of the undertaking.

The latter interpretation would put the Iran-Contra affair somewhat within the bounds of American tradition. The Iranian aspect of the operation—the ransoming of American hostages—is somewhat comparable to an initiative taken by the Washington administration in 1793. President Washington paid ransom for American hostages held by Algerian pirates and adopted a policy of bribery to prevent further hostage taking. When Congress demanded that Washington turn over information related to his secret diplomacy, the president reluctantly complied, but protested that it would be improper for some details to be revealed to the public.[105] Washington's secretary of state, Thomas Jefferson, recorded a conversation he had had with the president about payment of an annual bribe to the pirates; the president had expressed his reluctance to consult with the House in advance, "for he did not like throwing too much into democratic hands."[106]

The Nicaraguan end of the operation is somewhat comparable to Madison's effort in East Florida, in which that president manipulated Congress and then briefly ignored its rejection of his policies. It is difficult to point to examples of a chief executive defying explicit congressional restrictions on clandestine activities, primarily because no president before Gerald Ford was required to inform Congress about such operations. Even if it had prior knowledge, the Congress of old would probably have deferred to the judgment of the executive and refused to prohibit a covert mission.

The vehicle Congress used to prohibit covert assistance to the contras was the Boland amendment of 1985, which had been tacked onto an appropriations bill whose veto would have shut down the government. It sought to prevent the CIA or "any other agency or entity of the United States involved in intelligence activities" from spending funds in support of the contras. President Reagan has stated that he instructed his staff to assist the contras where possible but to stay within the law. Therefore, the question of whether the Boland amendment applied to the NSC is critical to any examination of whether Reagan's operatives broke the law. It appears that the operatives did break the "spirit" of the Boland amendment, but perhaps not its "letter." Congress seems to have granted the administration some room to maneuver, perhaps to avoid the accusation of "losing" Nicaragua.

One can appreciate the frustration of the administration in trying to conduct a coherent policy toward Nicaragua while dealing with a hesitant Congress. The United States gave aid to the Sandinistas in 1980, took it away for fiscal 1981, granted covert support for the contras in 1981 and 1982, denied any aid for "the purpose of overthrowing the government" in 1983, and in 1984 removed the language about overthrowing the government but provided a limited amount of funding that was guaranteed to run out before the end of the fiscal year.[107]

For a good part of Ronald Reagan's first term in office, the Senate supported the president's policy, while a narrow margin in the House gave the administration much of what it wanted. Support for the administration's policy began to dissipate in the latter half of the first term, particularly after the controversies previously discussed in this chapter— the mining and the revelation of a CIA manual that included references to "neutralizing" Sandinista officials. For many congressional Democrats, the administration's policy toward Nicaragua was an example of superpower abusiveness and was often described as "another Vietnam." For the White House, Nicaragua was "another Cuba," a Soviet foothold in Central America that needed to be excised.

In the final analysis, the Iran-Contra affair was a struggle for the control over both American policy toward Nicaragua and the covert instruments of that policy. Those seeking evidence of the radical shift in the balance of power away from the executive branch need look no further than the repeated clashes between CIA Director William Casey and members of the intelligence oversight committees in the 1980s. Throughout Reagan's tenure, the president and Casey attempted to wrest control over clandestine operations from Congress. They tried to play by the old rules, and they lost.

The Iran-Contra revelations once again generated widespread shock and indignation against the "secret government." Many of the myths that had emerged from the Church Committee were handed down to the Iran-Contra Committee, repeating the theme of the pernicious effects of the Cold War in warping the American system of government. The historical record was again distorted to suit contemporary purposes, as when the majority report of the committee noted that "peacetime covert action became an instrument of U.S. foreign-policy in response to the expansion of Soviet political and military influence following World War II."[108] During the committee's hearings, the chief architect of the prohibition on funding for the contras, Congressman Edward Boland of Massachusetts, quoted Virginia's George Mason to bolster his case that Congress should play a role in the oversight of covert operations, apparently unaware that Mason had refused to sign the Constitution.[109] The media echoed with a drumbeat of accusations repeating variations on the theme that "for forty years a secret government has been . . . growing like a cancer on the Constitution."[110]

Proposals for further restrictions on executive use of covert operations met with great enthusiasm and included legislation that would have mandated that all covert actions be reported to Congress within forty-eight hours. Another proposal sought to establish an independent inspector general's office in the CIA. The forty-eight-hour notification passed in the Senate, but was withdrawn by the House after the controversy erupted over Speaker Wright's public remarks about CIA operations in Nicaragua.[111] President Bush agreed to give Congress notice within "a few days" of nearly all clandestine operations and would hold back for longer periods only in the most extreme cases. Intelligence Committee vice chairman Senator William Cohen of Maine noted that the committees "would take a dim view" toward any such withholding.[112]

The inspector general proposal was signed into law by President Bush on November 30, 1989, despite the president's complaint the the bill "could impair the ability of the CIA to collect vitally needed intelligence information."[113] The CIA already had an inspector general, but Congress wanted one more responsive to legislators' interests. The creation of this position represents the most significant reform of the post–Iran-Contra period. The inspector general must now be nominated by the president and is subject to confirmation by the Senate and required to make regular reports to Congress. The inspector general is now the third Central Intelligence Agency official subject to Senate confirmation. This development furthers the process of binding the CIA to the Congress and will ensure a more cautious agency response to executive proposals for high-risk operations. As Senator Ernest Hollings of South Carolina put it, "A presidentially appointed inspector general at CIA will be another link in the chains that tie down our government and render it passive."[114] In the Senate floor debate, Senator Hollings put his finger on the consequences of these additional restrictions on the agency; he stated that the CIA was in danger of becoming just another agency staffed by "cautious bureaucrats who avoid the risks that come with taking action, who fill out every form in triplicate" and put "the emphasis on audit rather than action." He noted the broad powers that would be given the independent inspector general, including a requirement that the CIA director must report to Congress within seven days whenever he asks the inspector general to halt an investigation. The net result of the new position is, as Hollings put it, congressional micromanagement of an agency that "ought to be under strong centralized executive branch management."[115]

One positive proposal for reform recently debated grew out of the Noriega fiasco: a reexamination of the outright ban on U.S. participation in plots that could lead to violence against a foreign leader. As noted earlier, this ban eliminated certain options for President Bush in Panama and may well have tied President Reagan's hands in formulating a response to the terrorist activities of Libyan leader Muammar al-Qaddafi.[116] In both cases, the president had to resort to using conventional forces to achieve an objective that could well have been realized through a U.S.-supported coup. A coup would have had the added benefit of sparing the lives of American servicemen as well as of innocent civilians and might have diminished the type of diplomatic repercussions that both conventional military strikes produced.[117]

As previously stated, the executive order that prohibited government employees from "engag[ing] in, or conspir[ing] to engage in assassination" was issued by President Ford in 1976. The United States thus became the only nation that explicitly prohibits its intelligence agencies from participating in assassinations.[118] The order's ludicrousness is best summed up by Senator Cohen, who remarked that it appears to ban "placing a poison pen in one of Col. Muammar Qaddafi's jump suits, but permits the release of a gravity bomb."[119] Undoubtedly, assassination is an option that should be used with great restraint, especially in view of possible retribution. Yet a unilateral and unconditional prohibition of this alternative may well reduce the resolve necessary to fend off acts of violence against the United States.[120]

The Bush administration attempted to reinterpret this prohibition in a less restrictive manner that essentially would have prevented CIA operatives from being disciplined if unanticipated violence occurred during a coup attempt, but there had been "no specific intent to assassinate."[121] This effort, needless to say, did not win accolades on Capitol Hill. For instance, Senator Daniel Patrick Moynihan believed that "the issue is intervention. Intervention in the internal affairs of another nation is a violation of the U.N. Charter and the Charter of the Organization of American States. It is a violation of law." According to Moynihan, then CIA director William Webster was a man of "peace and law" who would not issue such an order, but someone else in that role might.[122] Besides raising once again the old canard about the the CIA as a rogue killing machine, Senator Moynihan's position avoided the issue of what the appropriate American response should be in a hypothetical situation such as the return to power of a Pol Pot. If the United States had access to an individual who offered to overthrow such a genocidal leader, would it have to refuse on the grounds that he might be harmed? Would the dictates of international law proscribe any intervention? Would the only recourse to an American president be an invasion in which noncombatants would no doubt die, all to spare the life of Pol Pot? The president of the United States needs options beyond sending in the marines or asking the United Nations to issue a proclamation condemning genocide.

The most important reform that should be made to the current system would be the elimination of the intelligence committees and the restoration of the system that existed from 1947 to 1974. By returning to the old system, senior members of Congress would retain access to the intelligence community while a greater degree of executive discretion and confidentiality of operations would be restored. It is highly unlikely that Congress will reinstate this method of oversight, nor is it likely that Congress will adopt the reasonable half-measure of establishing a joint committee on intelligence to reduce leaks, eliminate duplication, and dampen institutional rivalries. The Iran-Contra Committee rejected a minority report proposal for a joint committee and a change allowing the president to notify the "gang of four" (the Speaker of the House, House minority leader, Senate majority leader, and Senate minority leader) in special circumstances instead of the current "gang of eight" (the aforementioned plus the chairmen and ranking minority members of both intelligence committees).[123] Instead, recent developments in Congress have served to increase congressional control of clandestine operations, including the gentlemen's agreement on the forty-eight-hour notification and installation of an independent CIA inspector general—independent of everyone but Congress.

Restoring a Sense of Perspective

The end of the Cold War has removed for the moment any sense of urgency surrounding intelligence issues. We would, however, be deluding ourselves to think that clandestine operations are a thing of the past. Presidents will always resort to such activities when they believe that the national interest requires it. There are those who see an active role for the CIA in conducting covert operations against drug traffickers and terrorist organizations. A presidential commission appointed to investigate the bombing of Pan Am Flight 103 recommended "confronting terrorism at its source" through covert actions designed to prevent, disrupt, or respond to terrorist attacks.[124] When these operations are undertaken, the difficulties described here will resurface, as Congress attempts to play a role it was not designed to play. The executive branch should not be constrained from moving with what Alexander Hamilton called secrecy and dispatch. Congressional reforms of the past twenty years threaten to replace this understanding of executive power with one based on a disdain for executive secrecy and a desire to shackle executive discretion.

To some extent, the old system was based on an unwritten understanding that the president would conduct covert operations with a prudential concern for the interests of the country. A republican form of government depends on a certain amount of deference to the judgment of elected officials, a faith in the integrity of those elevated to positions of high responsibility. Executive discretionary power can be abused, but removing that authority can have even greater consequences. Suspicion of both presidential and congressional leadership has led to the current state of government by congressional committee, a prescription for inaction and indecision.

In the post-Watergate atmosphere of American politics, secret operations abroad have been viewed in the same light as abuses of power at home. They all have been seen as symptoms of the imperial presidency. In many quarters, it became accepted that covert actions represented a betrayal of traditional standards of American conduct and a pernicious expansion of executive power. The perpetuation of this myth has served the cause of those in Congress and elsewhere who have the most to gain by a shift in power away from the executive. This myth has also served the purposes of those who believe that American power has to be restrained in the interests of world peace.

Distorted accounts of the actions of the Cold War presidents continue to dominate contemporary discussion of intelligence matters in academic, political, and media circles and show little signs of abating. A review of the practices of these administrations reveals that they authorized operations that were commensurate with the level of threat at the time. As previously noted, the contemporary presidents who authorized the actions faced greater dangers than did many of their predecessors, during a time when American responsibilities in the international arena exceeded those of any previous era. The major Cold War alteration in regard to clandestine operations occurred in Congress, where a tradition of deference to the executive was discarded.

Between 1776 and 1882, some of America's most prominent presidents authorized covert activities that seem repugnant to some of us today. The operations were conducted by agents hired by presidents who understood that men are not angels and that international politics is an arena of high-stakes competition marked by treachery and deceit. Those presidents took comfort in the fact that the goal of their actions was to assist America's security interests or, in some instances, to help individuals or groups committed to the democratic cause. Contemporary critics of covert activity view this latter objective with particular disdain. This zeal for democracy is viewed as highly dangerous in a world of nuclear weapons. It is also seen as an antiquated notion in certain circles where the very idea of assuming that one's political order is superior is viewed as a sign of ignorance.

The main vehicle for American covert operations in modern times has been the Central Intelligence Agency; since 1947, this agency has been involved in what, to borrow a phrase, intelligence historian Edward Jay Epstein has called "the invisible war."[125] Critics of American covert operations talk about their unprecedented peacetime use in our time. Yet the overwhelming majority of those conducted by the CIA were directed against the Soviet Union, its client states, or Soviet-sponsored insurgencies.[126] This period has been aptly described by one observer as an "era of violent peace." It has been marked by countless episodes of hostility between Soviet and American operatives, who recognized no distinction between zones of war and peace.[127] This was a war against a regime that frequently proclaimed its desire to attack Western interests through a variety of options, including clandestine support for "wars of liberation" around the globe. Paying tribute to the more than fifty CIA officers who have died in the line of duty since 1950, a display of stars on a wall in the Central Intelligence Agency headquarters serves as a stark reminder to the brutal nature of this conflict.

This "peacetime" era witnessed the deaths of over 100,000 other Americans killed in hostilities with Soviet allies in Korea, Southeast Asia, Grenada, Libya, and El Salvador. President Kennedy aptly described the awkward position of the CIA by noting, "Your successes are unheralded—your failures are trumpeted."[128] The CIA's role in the West's Cold War victory will become clear as the passage of time allows for the release of information chronicling the agency's successful efforts in the years since its inception.

The day will also come when the covert operations of America's presidents from Truman to Bush will be seen as reasonable actions well within the bounds of traditional American practice. This understanding can occur only when political figures and academics discard notions of America's pre–Cold War innocence and acknowledge the unpleasant fact that such operations have been with us from the start. Many of the early presidents reviewed in this study were great men, and their stature will not be diminished by an honest assessment of their clandestine undertakings. The destruction of the myth of innocence will not lower the reputations of these individuals, but should serve to elevate those of many of their successors.

Myths are important to a nation in any number of ways, not the least of which is serving as a source of inspiration for its citizens. Yet they can also distort a nation's thinking and preclude its making sound decisions grounded in a clear understanding of the lessons of history. A politicized myth should be replaced by an accurate accounting of America's clandestine past. In the entrance to the CIA headquarters in Langley, Virginia, the words from John 8:32 are inscribed on the wall: "And ye shall know the truth, and the truth shall make you free." The truth is that from Truman to Bush, America's presidents conducted their clandestine foreign policy in a manner that remained faithful to the practices and beliefs of their revered predecessors.

Appendix

Presidents and
Secretaries of State
Cited in This Work

President	Secretary of State
George Washington (1789–1797)	Thomas Jefferson (appointed 1789)
John Adams (1797–1801)	
Thomas Jefferson (1801–1809)	James Madison (appointed 1801)
James Madison (1809–1817)	Robert Smith (appointed 1809)
	James Monroe (appointed 1811)
James Monroe (1817–1825)	John Q. Adams (appointed 1817)
John Quincy Adams (1825–1829)	Henry Clay (appointed 1825)
Andrew Jackson (1829–1837)	Martin Van Buren (appointed 1829)
	John Forsyth (appointed 1834)
William Henry Harrison (1841)	Daniel Webster (appointed 1841)
Martin Van Buren (1837–1841)	
John Tyler (1841–1845)	Daniel Webster (appointed 1841)
James K. Polk (1845–1849)	James Buchanan (appointed 1845)
Abraham Lincoln (1861–1865)	William H. Seward (appointed 1861)
Grover Cleveland (1885–1889) (1893–1897)	
Benjamin Harrison (1889–1893)	John W. Foster (appointed 1892)
William McKinley (1897–1901)	
Woodrow Wilson (1913–1921)	Robert Lansing (appointed 1915)
Herbert Hoover (1929–1933)	Henry Stimson (appointed 1929)
Franklin D. Roosevelt (1933–1945)	

President	Secretary of State
Harry S Truman (1945–1953)	
Dwight D. Eisenhower (1953–1961)	
John F. Kennedy (1961–1963)	Dean Rusk (appointed 1961)
Lyndon B. Johnson (1963–1969)	
Richard M. Nixon (1969–1974)	Henry Kissinger (appointed 1973)
Gerald R. Ford (1974–1977)	
Jimmy Carter (1977–1981)	
Ronald Reagan (1981–1989)	
George Bush (1989–1993)	

Notes

Introduction

1. William S. Cohen, "Congressional Oversight of Covert Actions: The Public's Stake in the Forty-Eight Hour Rule," *Harvard Journal of Law and Public Policy* 12, no. 2 (Spring 1989): 285.

2. See, for example, Arthur Schlesinger, Jr., who observed that "secret operations had started in his [Truman's] administration" (*The Imperial Presidency* [Boston: Houghton Mifflin, 1973], 317). See also Thomas Powers, who wrote that he longs "for the old-fashioned seriousness, civility and rectitude" of American leaders such as Henry Stimson, who allegedly shut down a State Department code-breaking operation because "gentlemen do not read each others' mail." Powers added, "Incredibly, that was then true. It was not until World War II that the United States plunged into its romance with the clandestine" ("Panama: Our Dangerous Liaison," *New York Times Book Review,* February 18, 1990, 27). Finally, see Rhodri Jeffreys-Jones, who mistakenly asserts that "peacetime covert operations had not been undertaken in the first century-and-a-half of the nation's life, so their inherent advantages and disadvantages were not appreciated" (*The CIA and American Democracy* [New Haven: Yale University Press, 1980], 21).

3. U.S. Congress, Senate, *Final Report of the Select Committee to Study Governmental Operations with Respect to Intelligence Activities, Foreign and Military Intelligence,* S. Rept. 94–755, 94th Cong., 2d sess., 1976, bk. 1, 152.

4. U.S. Congress, *Report of the Congressional Committees Investigating the Iran-Contra Affair with Supplemental, Minority, and Additional Views,* H. Rept. 100–433 and S. Rept. 100–216, 100th Congress, 1st sess., 1987, 375. (Hereafter cited as Iran-Contra Report)

5. Bill Moyers, *The Secret Government: The Constitution in Crisis* (Cabin John, Md.: Seven Locks Press, 1988), 55.

6. "Mitchell: Kerry Is GOP 'Smear' Target," *Boston Globe,* undated wire report.

7. "U.S. Officials Clash at Hearing on Power to Seize Fugitives," *New York Times,* November 9, 1989, A-10.

8. "Assassinations: Can't We Learn," *New York Times,* October 20, 1989, A-35.

9. "Wright on Hot Seat over CIA Remarks," *Boston Globe,* September 23, 1988, 6.

10. "Damned If You Coup . . . ," *Newsweek,* October 16, 1989, 34.

11. U.S. Congress, Senate, Senator Robert Byrd Speaking on "Opportunity in Cambodia," *Congressional Record,* 101st Cong., 1st sess., June 2, 1989, S 6090.

12. *The Presidential Campaign, 1976, Volume One, Part One, Jimmy Carter* (Washington, D.C.: Government Printing Office, 1978), 44.

13. "Cuomo Raps Bush for CIA Connection," *Boston Globe,* September 21, 1988, 14.

14. See *Taking the Stand: The Testimony of Lieutenant Colonel Oliver L. North* (New York: Pocket Books, 1987), 12.

15. Hamilton to Oliver Wolcott, Jr., June 5, 1798, in *The Papers of Alexander Hamilton,* ed. Harold C. Syrett, 27 vols. (New York: Columbia University Press, 1961), 21:487. (Hereafter cited as *Hamilton's Papers*)

16. Iran-Contra Report, 383.

17. "Bush Agrees to Notify Congress on Covert Actions," *New York Times,* October 27, 1989, A-9.

18. See Richard Shultz, Jr., "Covert Action and Executive–Legislative Relations: The Iran-Contra Crisis and Its Aftermath," *Harvard Journal of Law and Public Policy* 12, no. 2 (Spring 1989): 475, and Iran-Contra Report, 545.

19. Message of President James K. Polk to the House of Representatives, April 20, 1846, in *A Compilation of the Messages and Papers of the Presidents, 1798–1908,* ed. James D. Richardson (Washington, D.C.: Bureau of National Literature and Art, 1908), 4:435.

20. Robert Cecil, "The Thinking Behind Intelligence," *Times Literary Supplement,* November 10–16, 1989, 1232.

Chapter 1

1. *The Writings of George Washington from the Original Manuscript Sources, 1745–1799,* ed. John C. Fitzpatrick, 39 vols. (Washington, D.C.: Government Printing Office, 1931–1944), 7:199–200, (Hereafter cited as *Washington's Writings*)

2. James Thomas Flexner, *George Washington in the American Revolution (1775–1783)* (Boston: Little, Brown, 1967), 44.

3. Bruce W. Bidwell, *History of the Military Intelligence Division, Department of the Army General Staff: 1775–1941* (Frederick, Md.: University Publications of America, 1986), 2.

4. Richard W. Rowan, *The Story of Secret Service* (New York: Literary Guild of America, 1938), 157, 682n.12.

5. Worthington Ford, ed., *Journals of the Continental Congress, 1774–1789* (Washington, D.C.: Government Printing Office, 1906), 6:985.

6. See Robert Middlekauff, *The Glorious Cause: The American Revolution, 1763–1789* (New York: Oxford University Press, 1982), 234–52; Jerrilyn Marston, *King and Congress: The Transfer of Political Legitimacy, 1774–1776* (Princeton, N.J.: Princeton University Press, 1987), chap. 5; and Martin Diamond, Winston Mills Fisk, and Herbert Garfinkel, *The Democratic Republic: An Introduction to American National Government* (Chicago: Rand McNally, 1970), 26–27.

7. See Marston, *King and Congress,* 220, 220nn.61, 62.

8. See Ford, ed., *Journals of the Continental Congress,* June 5, 1776, 5:417.

9. Washington's intimate involvement in creating and directing American intelligence operations is reflected in his ownership of the horse used by the New York City spy ring and in other instances of personal payments to assist his agents' operations. See John Bakeless, *Turncoats, Traitors, and Heroes* (Philadelphia: Lippincott, 1959), 227.

10. I focus on this particular spy ring in part because of the volume of correspondence it generated. This ring also appears to have been uppermost in Washington's mind, meriting more entries in his wartime diary than any other spying organization. See *The Diaries of George Washington, 1748–1799*, ed. John C. Fitzpatrick, 4 vols. (Boston: Houghton Mifflin, 1925), 2:208, 214, 221. Other spy rings worthy of mention include Major John Clark's, which operated in Philadelphia and reported to Washington through General Thomas Mifflin; the Mersereau ring, which operated on Staten Island throughout the war and was led by two brothers named John and Joshua Mersereau; and a loose-knit group run by Colonel Elias Dayton and Colonel Mathias Ogden that gathered intelligence in the New York and New Jersey areas. Individual efforts deserve mention as well, including those of John Honeyman, whose secret reports contributed to the successful attack against Hessian troops in Trenton in December 1776, and Philadelphia socialite Lydia Darragh, who reported to Washington on British movements in Philadelphia. Additionally, three American captains—Caleb Bruen, David Gray, and Elijah Hunter—all managed at different points during the war to penetrate the British intelligence service. See John Bakeless, "General Washington's Spy System," *Manuscripts,* 12, no. 2 (Spring 1960): 28–37.

11. See *Washington's Writings*, 14:277.

12. Charles Swain Hall, *Benjamin Tallmadge: Revolutionary Soldier and American Businessman* (New York: Columbia University Press, 1943), 45.

13. Ibid.

14. After the Hale fiasco, Washington gave the appearance of abandoning the use of secret agents. Many historians accepted this as a fact until the publication of Morton Pennypacker's *The Two Spies: Nathan Hale and Robert Townsend* (Boston: Houghton Mifflin, 1930) and his follow-up study, *General Washington's Spies on Long Island and in New York* (Brooklyn, N.Y.: Long Island Historical Society, 1939). Through meticulous research, Pennypacker was able to identify the agents who went on to fulfill Washington's desire to penetrate British headquarters. The true identity of the individuals had been known only to Washington, Benjamin Tallmadge, and General Charles Scott, who helped create the ring. This concealment of the names of the individuals involved in the Culper Ring for 150 years has to rank as one of America's best-kept secrets. (The identity of one member of the ring was not proved conclusively until 1959.)

15. Tallmadge was a classmate of Hale at Yale College (class of 1773) along with Robert Townsend, the chief American operative in New York City. Rowan suggests that sentimental considerations may have driven Hale's successors to pursue their risky undertaking (*Secret Service,* 151).

16. George C. Constantinides, *Intelligence and Espionage: An Analytical Bibliography* (Boulder, Colo.: Westview Press, 1983), 222.

17. Benjamin Tallmadge, *Memoir of Colonel Benjamin Tallmadge* (New York: Society of Sons of the Revolution in the State of New York, 1904), 42–43.

18. Bakeless, *Turncoats*, 227–28.

19. See Pennypacker, *General Washington's Spies*, passim, and Washington to Brigadier General James Clinton, November 8, 1778, *Washington's Writings*, 13:216.

20. Allison Ind, *A Short History of Espionage* (New York: McKay, 1963), 64.

21. The invisible ink had been developed in England by Sir James Jay, brother of John Jay. In a letter written to Thomas Jefferson, Sir James recounted that

when relations between Britain and the United States began to deteriorate, he set out to develop an ink that "would elude the generally known means of detection" and provide "great advantages both in a political and military line, which we might derive from such a mode of procuring and transmitting intelligence." Sir James utilized his own invention to provide Benjamin Franklin and Silas Deane with the plan of General Burgoyne's march from Canada to the United States, which ended with the American victory at the battles of Saratoga. See David Kahn, *The Codebreakers: The Story of Secret Writing* (New York: Macmillan, 1967), 179.

22. Corey Ford, *A Peculiar Service: A Narrative of Espionage in and Around New York During the American Revolution* (Boston: Little, Brown, 1965), 192–93.

23. Bakeless, *Turncoats*, 231. Bakeless notes that Alexander Hamilton was the only staff member known to have handled intelligence reports delivered to Washington, though he probably did not know the identity of the sources. A more complete discussion of Hamilton's involvement in intelligence matters can be found in Chapter 2.

24. Washington to Rev. Alexander McWhorter, October 12, 1778, *Washington's Writings*, 13:71–72.

25. See, for instance, Washington to Brigadier General Edward Hand, March 24, 1779, ibid., 14:288.

26. Bakeless, *Turncoats*, 292. Only the return of Arnold by the British could have saved André. Washington desperately wanted to hang Arnold and authorized several special operations designed to kidnap Arnold and return him for trial (ibid., 302). See also CIA, *Intelligence in the War of Independence* (Washington, D.C.: Central Intelligence Agency, 1976), 18.

27. Washington to Governor Robert Dinwiddie, November 9, 1756, *Washington's Writings*, 1:498–99.

28. Washington to Brigadier General Charles Scott, September 25, 1778, ibid., 12:498.

29. Washington to Elias Boudinot, May 3, 1779, ibid., 14:478; to Major Alexander Clough, August 25, 1778, ibid., 12:355.

30. Washington to Major Benjamin Tallmadge, April 30, 1781, ibid., 22:11.

31. Washington to Nathaniel Sackett (intelligence operative), April 8, 1777, ibid., 7:372.

32. Elias Boudinot was Washington's commissary of prisoners and one of his trusted intelligence managers. Boudinot was responsible for interrogating British prisoners and also ran Lydia Darragh, whose home was used by the adjutant general of the British Army. See Rowan, *Secret Service*, 682n.14.

33. Washington to Boudinot, May 3, 1779, *Washington's Writings*, 14:478.

34. Washington to Colonel Elias Dayton, July 26, 1777, ibid., 8:479. From the original letter in the Walter L. Pforzheimer Collection on Intelligence Service, Washington, D.C.

35. Ibid.

36. Washington to Scott, November 8, 1778, ibid., 13:217.

37. See Washington to Lord Stirling, January 2, 1779, ibid., 13:476n.

38. Washington to Major General Thomas Mifflin, April 10, 1777, ibid., 7:385.

39. Washington to Tallmadge, September 24, 1779, ibid., 16:330–31. See also Washington to Major Alexander Clough, August 25, 1778, ibid., 12:356.

40. Washington to the president of Congress, May 11, 1779, ibid., 15:45.

41. See Bakeless, *Turncoats,* chap. 1, and Carl Van Doren, *Secret History of the American Revolution* (New York: Viking Press, 1941), 18–23.

42. Washington to Major General Alexander McDougall, March 28, 1779, *Washington's Writings,* 14:304.

43. Washington to Scott, October 31, 1778, ibid., 13:187–88.

44. Washington to Josiah Quincy, March 24, 1776, ibid., 4:422.

45. Washington to Daniel Clymer (deputy commissary general of prisoners), November 11, 1777, ibid., 10:40.

46. For one of many examples, see Washington to Major General Israel Putnam, July 25, 1777 (ibid., 8:468), in which he discusses a high-level British military communication apparently intended to fall into American hands.

47. Bidwell, *History of MID,* 4.

48. See Washington to Putnam, November 4, 1777; to Major General Philemon Dickinson, November 4, 1777; and to Major John Clark, Jr. (intelligence manager for Philadelphia spy network), November 4, 1777, *Washington's Writings,* 10:2, 4, 8, 8n.11.

49. See former CIA director William J. Casey's *Where and How the War Was Fought: An Armchair Tour of the American Revolution* (New York: Morrow, 1976), 101, 135–36.

50. One critical instance where Washington's use of deception saved his army occurred after the American triumph at the Battle of Trenton. A British force under the command of General Cornwallis let Washington slip away when they assumed he was still trapped against a river bank. The escape was accomplished by several hundred men left behind who burned fires throughout the night and appeared to be digging entrenchments while the main force actually evacuated the area. See Middlekauff, *Glorious Cause,* 362.

51. The title of this section heading is taken from Rowan, *Secret Service,* 149.

52. Much of the material in this section is derived from CIA, *Intelligence in the War of Independence,* and Edward F. Sayle, "The Historical Underpinnings of the U.S. Intelligence Community," *International Journal of Intelligence and Counterintelligence* 1, no. 1 (Spring 1986): 1–27.

53. Bakeless notes that the Revolutionary War saw "an interminable series of kidnapping plots . . . a few of which were successful" (*Turncoats,* 85).

54. Washington received intelligence in March 1778 regarding the location of General Henry Clinton's personal quarters. He authorized Brigadier General Samuel Parsons to seize Clinton (and his official papers) and offered advice as to how this secret mission might be accomplished (i.e., suggesting that the participants wear British uniforms). See Washington to Brigadier General Samuel Holden Parsons, March 5 and 8, 1778, *Washington's Writings,* 11:29–30, 51.

55. Washington to Colonel Mathias Ogden, March 28, 1782, ibid., 24:91.

56. See Philip Ziegler, *King William IV* (London: Collins, 1971), 39.

57. See, for instance, Washington to Major Philip Schuyler, November 16, 1778, *Washington's Writings,* 13:264; to Major General Horatio Gates, November 14, 1778, ibid., 13:268; to Brigadier General Jacob Bayley, November 25, 1778, ibid., 13:326.

58. See Gustave Lanctot, *Canada and the American Revolution, 1774–1783* (Cambridge, Mass.: Harvard University Press, 1967), 119, 183, 188.

59. Ford, ed., *Journals of the Continental Congress,* February 26, 1776, 4:173.

60. Annabelle M. Melville, *John Carroll of Baltimore: Founder of the American Catholic Hierarchy* (New York: Scribner's, 1955), 44; Peter Guilday, *The Life and Times of John Carroll, Archbishop of Baltimore (1735–1815)* (Westminster, Md.: Newman Press, 1954), 94. Another instance of American use of clerical "cover" for intelligence purposes occurred during the attempt to capture Quebec in 1775 and 1776, when Aaron Burr disguised himself as a priest and hid in monasteries while crossing British lines seeking American reinforcements. See CIA, *Intelligence in the War of Independence,* 28.

61. Sayle, "Historical Underpinnings," 8.

62. See Ralph E. Weber, "As Others Saw Us," *Studies in Intelligence* (September 1987): 34.

63. See *The Papers of Henry Laurens,* ed. David Chesnutt (Columbia: University of South Carolina Press, 1985), 10:220n.8.

64. See CIA, *Intelligence in the War of Independence,* 30, and Sayle, "Historical Underpinnings," 6.

65. Ford, ed., *Journals of the Continental Congress,* November 20, 1775, 3:361; CIA, *Intelligence in the War of Independence,* 30.

66. Lyman H. Butterfield, "Psychological Warfare in 1776: The Jefferson–Franklin Plan to Cause Hessian Desertions," *Proceedings of the American Philosophical Society* 94, no. 3 (June 1950): 233–41.

67. The letter was so craftily written it has continued to deceive twentieth-century readers. See ibid., 234. In the letter, the "count" (Franklin) writes to the Hessian commander, "I am about to send you some new recruits. Don't economize them. . . . It is true, grown men are becoming scarce there [in Germany], but I will send you boys. . . . Finally, let it be your principal object to prolong the war . . ." (*The Writings of Benjamin Franklin,* ed. Albert H. Smyth [London: Macmillan, 1906], 7:27–29).

68. Butterfield, "Psychological Warfare," 236, 240–41.

69. See William B. Clark, "John the Painter," *Pennsylvania Magazine of History and Biography* 63, no. 1 (January 1939): 1–23.

70. Sayle, "Historical Underpinnings," 7; CIA, *Intelligence in the War of Independence,* 9. See William B. Clark, *Ben Franklin's Privateers: A Naval Epic of the American Revolution* (Baton Rouge: Louisiana State University Press, 1956).

71. Washington to Henry Laurens, August 25, 1778, *Washington's Writings,* 12:356. Washington pressed the Congress for gold instead of paper money, in part because it carried more weight with potential sources than Continental currency.

72. Ibid., 356n.89.

73. Washington to Robert Morris, December 30, 1776, ibid., 6:457n.17.

74. See, for instance, Washington's private letter to Laurens, president of the Continental Congress, in which he appears to promise a detailed accounting of a particular intelligence expenditure in the future but gives his word as justification for the time being (September 4, 1778, ibid., 12:397). Another example of congressional reliance on Washington's discretion can be found in Congress's refusal to compensate a former intelligence agent without first obtaining Washington's approval. See Ford, ed., *Journals of the Continental Congress,* April 21, 1786, 30:208.

75. Washington to the president of Congress, September 4, 1778, *Washington's Writings,* 12:400.

76. *Secret Journals of the Acts and Proceedings of Congress* (Boston: Wait, 1821), April 27, 1779, 1:112.

77. Ibid.

78. See Washington to Brigadier General Samuel Holden Parsons, December 18, 1779, *Washington's Writings*, 17:285. It is important to note that the small amount of hard currency in Washington's possession was almost exclusively reserved for intelligence purposes. See Washington to Colonel Stephen Moylan, August 1, 1799, ibid., 16:34.

79. Washington to the president of Congress, September 4, 1778, ibid., 12:400.

80. Washington to the superintendent of finance [Robert Morris], January 8, 1783, ibid., 26:20.

81. Washington to Tallmadge, September 11, 1783, ibid., 27:149. Bakeless notes that American spies were not as pleased with this arrangement as one might presume; the prospect of being caught by the British with French gold in their pockets was not at all comforting (*Turncoats*, 237).

82. Washington to Tallmadge, September 11, 1783, *Washington's Writings*, 27:149: "The Intelligence received by the Count . . . was precisely the same as that which was transmitted to me at the same periods."

83. See, for instance, Tallmadge's plea to Washington to be allowed to enter New York City first in order to save members of the Culper Ring "who served us very essentially, and who may otherways be treated amiss" (Washington to Tallmadge, April 4, 1783, ibid., 26:284n.1).

84. Bakeless, "General Washington's Spy System," 32.

85. Washington to Noah Webster, July 31, 1788, *Washington's Writings*, 30:26–27.

86. Ibid.

87. Bakeless, "General Washington's Spy System," 36.

88. See Edmund R. Thompson, "Intelligence at Yorktown," *Defense/81* (October 1981): 25–28.

89. Bakeless, "General Washington's Spy System," 34.

90. See Jefferson to John Colvin, September 20, 1810, in *The Life and Selected Writings of Thomas Jefferson,* ed. Adrienne Koch and William Peden (New York: Modern Library, 1944), 606.

91. Washington to Noah Webster, July 31, 1788, *Washington's Writings*, 30:28.

Chapter 2

1. *Hamilton's Papers*, 21:487.

2. *John Jay, the Making of a Revolutionary: Unpublished Papers, 1745–1780,* ed. Richard Morris (New York: Harper & Row, 1975), 13, 331–59.

3. U.S. Congress, Senate, *Final Report of the Select Committee to Study Governmental Operations with Respect to Intelligence Activities*, S. Rept. 94–755, 94th Cong., 2d sess., 1976, Supplementary Reports on Intelligence Activities, bk. 6, 14.

4. Alexander Hamilton, John Jay, and James Madison, *The Federalist Papers,* ed. Jacob Cooke (Middletown, Conn.: Wesleyan University Press, 1961), No. 70, 472. The quotation introducing this section is from *The Federalist*, No. 15, 96.

5. Secret Journals of Congress, November 29, 1775, in *The Revolutionary Diplomatic Correspondence of the United States,* ed. Francis Wharton (Washington, D.C.: Government Printing Office, 1889), 2:61–62. (Hereafter cited as *Diplomatic Correspondence*)

6. *John Jay, Revolutionary,* ed. Morris, 197n.3. The other "great secret committee" Jay was referring to was the Commerce Committee, known for a while as the Secret Committee, which negotiated foreign supply contracts. See H. James Henderson, *Party Politics in the Continental Congress* (New York: McGraw-Hill, 1974), 170, and Edmund C. Burnett, ed., *Letters of Members of the Continental Congress* (Washington, D.C.: Carnegie Institution, 1921), 1:372n.2.

7. *Diplomatic Correspondence,* 2:61.

8. Committee of Secret Correspondence to Arthur Lee, November 30, 1775, in *Letters of Delegates to Congress, 1774–1789,* ed. Paul H. Smith (Washington, D.C.: Library of Congress, 1977), 2:410.

9. Richard Henry Lee, *Life of Arthur Lee, LL.D., Joint Commissioner of the United States to the Court of France, and Sole Commissioner to the Court of Spain and Prussia During the Revolutionary War* (Boston: Wells and Lilly, 1829), 1:53.

10. Central Intelligence Agency, *Intelligence in the War of Independence* (Washington, D.C.: CIA, 1976), 9.

11. Ibid.

12. William Jay, *The Life of John Jay with Selections from His Correspondence and Miscellaneous Papers* (New York: Harper, 1833), 1:64.

13. *Diplomatic Correspondence,* 462. William Jay states that "Mr. Jay appears to have been its chief organ of correspondence" (*Life of John Jay,* 64).

14. *John Jay, Revolutionary,* ed. Morris, 195. In Jay's own words, "When Mr. Deane went to France I communicated to him a Mode of invisible writing unknown to any but the Inventor and myself" (Jay to Morris, September 15, 1776, ibid., 315). Deane's secret correspondence to Jay was mailed under the pseudonym "Timothy Jones" (ibid., 371n.2).

15. Ibid., 316n.1.

16. See the cover letter in Jay, *Life of John Jay,* 1:67, and the concealed letter as developed by Jay in *Diplomatic Correspondence,* 2:148. The "cold insipid letter" remark is from Robert Morris to Jay, February 4, 1777, in Jay, *Life of John Jay,* 1:66.

17. *Diplomatic Correspondence,* 1:462.

18. Jay believed the letter to be genuine; Wharton states that the letter was probably a forgery that achieved its intended effect (*Diplomatic Correspondence,* 1:462, 5:238–242). Richard Morris states categorically that the letter was genuine (*The Peacemakers: The Great Powers and American Independence* [New York: Harper & Row, 1965], 325).

19. *John Jay, Revolutionary,* ed. Morris, 270n.2.

20. Ibid., 330n.4. Jay eventually came to believe that Carmichael was a British spy. See ibid., 769–71.

21. CIA, *Intelligence in the War of Independence,* 14.

22. Blanche E. Hazard, *Beaumarchais and the American Revolution* (Boston: Slocomb, 1910), 13.

23. Beaumarchais to Arthur Lee, June 12, 1776, *Diplomatic Correspondence,* 1:373.

24. Hazard, *Beaumarchais,* 19.

25. Silas Deane to Jay, December 3, 1776, in *John Jay, Revolutionary,* ed. Morris, 325–26.

26. Ibid., 329n.1.

27. Jay to Beaumarchais, January 15, 1779, ibid., 531–32.

28. John Bakeless, *Turncoats, Traitors, and Heroes* (Philadelphia: Lippincott, 1959), 136; *John Jay, Revolutionary,* ed. Morris, 333–36.

29. Jay to Alexander McDougall, March 21, 1776, in *John Jay, Revolutionary,* ed. Morris, 241.

30. Washington to the Secret Committee of the New York Legislature, July 13, 1776, *Washington's Writings,* 5:266n.23.

31. See Bakeless, *Turncoats,* chap. 7, and *John Jay, Revolutionary,* ed. Morris, 277, 278.

32. Washington to the Secret Committee of the New York Legislature, July 13, 1776, *Washington's Writings,* 5:267.

33. Bernard Mason, *The Road to Independence: The Revolutionary Movement in New York, 1773–1777* (Lexington: University of Kentucky Press, 1966), 202.

34. Frank Monaghan, *John Jay* (New York: Bobbs-Merrill, 1935), 91.

35. Mason, *Road to Independence,* 202. See also Alexander Flick, *Loyalism in New York During the American Revolution* (New York: Columbia University Press, 1901), 120.

36. See *John Jay, Revolutionary,* ed. Morris, 333–37.

37. See Bakeless, *Turncoats,* 171–74.

38. Jay to Edward Rutledge, July 6, 1776, in *The Correspondence and Public Papers of John Jay, 1763–1826,* ed. Henry Johnston (New York: Da Capo Press, 1971), 1:68.

39. Monaghan, *John Jay,* 91.

40. *John Jay, Revolutionary,* ed. Morris, 331.

41. Jay to Robert Livingston, July 1, 1776, ibid., 281–82, 282n.2.

42. See ibid., 288, and Jay's Motion for an Instruction to the Delegates, July 9, 1776, ibid.

43. Ibid., 508.

44. See ibid., 507'–32, and Jay to Gerard, French minister to the United States, January 13, 1779, ibid., 530. See also Worthington Ford, ed., *Journals of the Continental Congress, 1774–1789* (Washington, D.C.: Government Printing Office, 1906), January 6, 1779, 13:30.

45. Washington to Jay, April 23, 1779, *Washington's Writings,* 14:435–37.

46. Jay to Washington, April 26, 1779, *Diplomatic Correspondence,* 3:137.

47. Ibid.

48. Washington to the president of Congress, February 19, 1779, *Washington's Writings,* 14:134; Bakeless, *Turncoats,* 239.

49. See Jay to Washington, August 24, 1779, in *John Jay, Revolutionary,* ed. Morris, 627; Washington to Jay, September 7, 1779, *Washington's Writings,* 16:248–49; McDougall to Jay, March 21, 1779, in *John Jay, Revolutionary,* ed. Morris, 578–79; and Bakeless, *Turncoats,* 241–43.

50. Washington to the president of Congress, May 11, 1779, *Washington's Writings,* 15: 44–45.

51. Jay to Washington, August 24, 1779, in *John Jay, Revolutionary,* ed. Morris, 627.

52. Washington to the president of Congress, March 1, 1779, *Washington's Writings,* 14:165–66.

53. Ibid., 14:165n.94. Washington was referring to rumors he had heard from American agents in Europe that France had agreed to a joint U.S.–French expedition to remove British forces from Georgia.

54. Jay to McDougall, March 28, 1779, in *John Jay, Revolutionary,* ed. Morris, 581.

55. For a discussion of the fluctuating policies of Congress regarding foreign affairs, see *Diplomatic Correspondence,* 1:460–61.

56. Jay to Livingston, February 6, 1782, ibid., 5:149.

57. Jay to James Lovell, October 27, 1780, ibid., 4:105.

58. Action of Congress as to Special Agency for Correspondence with Jay, March 24, 1781, ibid., 4:324.

59. Jay to Livingston, September 18, 1782, ibid., 5:740.

60. Ibid., 1:252, 555–56.

61. William M. Goldsmith, *The Growth of Presidential Power: A Documented History* (New York: Chelsea House, 1974), 1:16–19.

62. Donald L. Smith, *John Jay: Founder of a State and Nation* (New York: Teachers College Press, 1968), 133.

63. The quotation heading this section is from *The Federalist,* No. 72, 489.

64. Broadus Mitchell, *Alexander Hamilton: Youth to Maturity, 1755–1788* (New York: Macmillan, 1957), 110.

65. Ibid., 105.

66. Ibid., 110.

67. Bakeless, *Turncoats,* 228. Intelligence historian Edward F. Sayle places Hamilton even closer to the center of Washington's intelligence network, crediting him with developing a method of "secret writing for agents" ("The Framers on the Realities," *Studies in Intelligence* [September 1987]: 2).

68. For a description of these events, see Bakeless, *Turncoats,* 236–37; Morton Pennypacker, *General Washington's Spies on Long Island and in New York* (Brooklyn, N.Y.: Long Island Historical Society, 1939), 84–85; and Hamilton to the Marquis de Lafayette, July 21, 1780, *Hamilton's Papers,* 2:362–63.

69. Hamilton to Colonel Stephen Moylan, April 3, 1778, *Hamilton's Papers,* 1:452–53.

70. *Washington's Writings,* 13:355.

71. *Hamilton's Papers,* 2:10.

72. *Washington's Writings,* 14:165–66.

73. *Hamilton's Papers,* 2:14.

74. *Washington's Writings,* 14:291–92.

75. Ibid., 15:42–45.

76. Ibid., 222–23.

77. Ibid., 302.

78. Ibid., 374.

79. Pennypacker, *General Washington's Spies,* 54.

80. *Hamilton's Papers,* 2:216–18.

81. Certificate for Lieutenant Thomas Pool, September 30, 1785, ibid., 3:623.

82. Michael J. O'Brien, *Hercules Mulligan: Confidential Correspondent of General Washington* (New York: Kennedy, 1937), 41.

83. See "Certificate on John Hanson" by Anthony L. Bleecker, Peter S. Curentius, Alexander Hamilton, John Lamb, and Hercules Mulligan, January 24, 1796, *Hamilton's Papers,* 20:49–50.

Some historians have questioned the existence of a close relationship between Hamilton and Mulligan, but the existence of this certificate would seem to verify that the two shared a very early baptism of fire. Mulligan also wrote a brief account of this encounter and other incidents in Hamilton's life, a copy of which can be found in *William and Mary Quarterly* 4, no. 2 (April 1947): 209–11.

84. Corey Ford, *A Peculiar Service: A Narrative of Espionage in and Around New York During the American Revolution* (Boston: Little, Brown, 1965), 316. Ford places the four men together in New York's Fraunces Tavern when word arrived that Congress had declared independence.

85. A full account of Mulligan's activities as an American agent can be found in O'Brien, *Hercules Mulligan,* chaps. 7–9.

86. Ford, *Peculiar Service,* 164.

87. O'Brien, *Hercules Mulligan,* 100–102.

88. An alternative interpretation, offered by Walter L. Pforzheimer, is that as the British left New York, the patriots were prepared to take measures against Mulligan as a result of his close relationship with the British. Upon being informed of this possibility, Washington breakfasted with Mulligan, and the situation was stabilized. Interview with Walter L. Pforzheimer, former CIA legislative liaison officer, May 1991.

89. Bakeless, *Turncoats,* 240.

90. Ford, *Peculiar Service,* 323.

91. Hamilton to Lieutenant Colonel John Laurens, October 11, 1780, *Hamilton's Papers,* 2:467–68.

92. Hamilton to Major General Henry Knox, June 7, 1782, ibid., 3:92. The idea of a retaliatory execution was eventually rejected by Washington.

93. Mitchell, *Hamilton,* 105.

94. Hamilton to James Duane, September 3, 1780, *Hamilton's Papers,* 2:404.

95. Hamilton to Oliver Wolcott, Jr., June 5, 1798, ibid., 21:487.

96. See Sayle, "Framers on the Realities," 2–3, and CIA, *Intelligence in the War of Independence,* 8–11.

97. See Marvin Meyers, *The Mind of the Founder: Sources of the Political Thought of James Madison* (Hanover, N.H.: University Press of New England, 1981), 16, 47, and Forrest McDonald, *E Pluribus Unum: The Formation of the American Republic, 1776–1790* (Indianapolis: Liberty Press, 1979), 36–40.

98. James Madison, *Notes of Debates in the Federal Convention of 1787 Reported by James Madison* (New York: Norton, 1987), 373. The "moderate" expenditures refer to Washington's use of his personal expense account to fund part but not all of his secret service activities.

99. Ibid., 145.

100. Ibid., 216.

101. Ibid., 241.

102. Ibid., 255.

103. Ibid., 136.

104. Ibid., 364.
105. Ibid., 366.
106. Ibid., 367–68.
107. *The Federalist,* No. 68, 459.
108. Madison, *Notes of Debates,* 418–19.
109. Ibid., 437.
110. *The Federalist,* No. 15, 95.
111. Ibid., No. 60, 403. Toward the end of his life, Hamilton repeated his concern over the potential for foreign disruption of American society through the activity of agents and private citizens of foreign birth. See "Lucius Crassius (or "The Examination")," no. 8, January 12, 1802, *Hamilton's Papers,* 25:495–97.
112. *The Federalist,* No. 43, 294.
113. Ibid., 292.
114. Ibid., No. 62, 416.
115. Ibid., No. 70, 476.
116. Ibid., 472.
117. Ibid., No. 75, 507.
118. Ibid., No. 64, 434–36.
119. Ibid., No. 43, 293.
120. Washington to Patrick Henry, February 24, 1777, *Washington's Writings,* 7:199–200.
121. Morris, *Peacemakers,* 459. The comment was made by Napoleon to American diplomat Robert Livingston.

Chapter 3

1. *Register of Debates,* 21st Cong., 2d sess., 294.
2. Edward S. Corwin, *The President's Control of Foreign Relations* (Princeton, N.J.: Princeton University Press, 1917), 65–66.
3. Henry Merritt Wriston, *Executive Agents in American Foreign Relations* (Baltimore: Johns Hopkins University Press, 1929), 122; Edward F. Sayle, "The Framers on the Realities," *Studies in Intelligence* (September 1987): 7.
4. Edward F. Sayle, "The Historical Underpinnings of the U.S. Intelligence Community," *International Journal of Intelligence and Counterintelligence* 1, no. 1 (Spring 1986): 9. Sayle notes that the sharp rise in the Contingency Fund budget was due in part to the cost of ransoming American captives held in Algiers.
5. Abraham D. Sofaer, *War, Foreign Affairs, and Constitutional Power: The Origens* (Cambridge, Mass.: Ballinger, 1976), 80.
6. See *Washington's Writings,* 30:492.
7. Wriston's *Executive Agents* is generally regarded as the foremost scholarly work on executive agents and the Contingency Fund. Wriston's description of these early congressional debates is confined to a two-paragraph summation. This lack of detail is puzzling in a book that is so utterly comprehensive in its discussion of a variety of issues related to executive agents. Furthermore, Wriston's summation is also inaccurate. Wriston states that it was "assumed" throughout the discussions in the House that every agent would be nominated to the Senate; a close examination of the debate reveals that no such assumption existed for many members, perhaps not even a majority. He goes on to state that

there was no hint of anticipation that the Contingency Fund certificate would be used by the president to pay salaries and expenses for diplomatic agents not nominated to the Senate. But again, a close reading of the actual debate reveals that this use was very much expected and generated sharp exchanges on the floor of the House. See Wriston, *Executive Agents*, 208–12. In light of these inadequacies, I believe it important to summarize the House debate in the following pages.

8. John Jay of New York was secretary for foreign affairs under the Articles of Confederation and continued to act in that capacity at the request of Washington until Thomas Jefferson took office as secretary of state on March 22, 1790.

9. Congressman Alexander White of Virginia. The complete name of and the state represented by this individual and those listed hereafter are taken from the *Biographical Directory of the American Congress, 1774–1927* (Washington, D.C.: Government Printing Office, 1928).

10. *Annals of Congress*, 1st Cong., 1st sess., 1790, 1102. (Hereafter cited as *Annals*)

11. Congressman William L. Smith of South Carolina. Smith went on to become an American envoy to Spain and Portugal.

12. *Annals*, 1102–3.

13. Congressman Roger Sherman of Connecticut, member of the Constitutional Convention.

14. Congressman James Jackson of Georgia.

15. Congressman Richard B. Lee of Virginia.

16. *Annals*, 1104.

17. Ibid., 1119.

18. Congressman Michael Jenifer Stone of Maryland.

19. Congressman Benjamin Huntington of Connecticut.

20. *Annals*, 1120.

21. There is no listing of a Congressman Lawrence in Congress during this period, according to the *Biographical Directory of the American Congress*.

22. *Annals*, 1122.

23. Ibid., 1122–23.

24. Ibid., 1123.

25. Ibid., 1123–24.

26. Ibid., 1124.

27. Congressman Egbert Benson of New York.

28. *Annals*, 1124–25.

29. Congressman James Jackson of Georgia.

30. Congressman Elias Boudinot of New Jersey. Boudinot's role in this debate is intriguing. Boudinot was a former president of the Continental Congress and, as mentioned, played a prominent role in the Revolutionary War as commissary of prisoners (the American general in charge of British prisoners of war). Washington viewed the post as affording "better opportunities than most other officers in the army, to obtain knowledge of the Enemy's Situation, motions and . . . designs." One can safely assume that Boudinot's war experience (as well as his work in the Continental Congress) led him to support a wide grant of executive discretion in the appointment and control of executive agents.

See Richard W. Rowan, *The Story of Secret Service* (New York: Literary

Guild of America, 1938), 682–83n.14, and CIA, *Intelligence in the War of Independence* (Washington, D.C.: CIA, 1976), 35. For a more complete account of Boudinot's career as Washington's "procurer of intelligence," see George Adams Boyd, *Elias Boudinot: Patriot and Statesman, 1740–1821* (Princeton, N.J.: Princeton University Press, 1952).

31. *Annals,* 1127.

32. Ibid., 1128.

33. Wriston, *Executive Agents,* 211.

34. *Annals,* 1130.

35. Ibid., 1004.

36. Ibid., 1005, 1015.

37. Senator Caleb Strong of Massachusetts, former member of the Constitutional Convention and member of the Committee of Correspondence and Safety during the American Revolution. It is unclear which committee Strong chaired in the Senate; in all probability, it was the foreign relations or appropriations committee.

38. *Annals,* 1014, 1015.

39. Ibid., 1016, 1017. The three Senate conference committee managers were Senator Rufus King of New York, former member of the Constitutional Convention; Senator George Read of Delaware, a signer of the Declaration of Independence and member of the Constitutional Convention; and Senator Ralph Izard of South Carolina, a former American envoy to the Court of Tuscany under the Articles of Confederation and member of the Committee of Secret Correspondence, America's first foreign intelligence directorate. See CIA, *Intelligence in the War of Independence,* 9, 17.

40. *Annals,* 1030.

41. William Maclay, *The Journal of William Maclay, United States Senator from Pennsylvania, 1789–1791* (New York: Boni, 1927), 296. The Maclay journal is a rare look inside the Senate at a time when it met behind closed doors.

42. *Annals,* 1st Cong., 2d sess., 2292.

43. *Annals,* 2d Cong., February 9, 1793, 1411–12.

44. Lawrence S. Kaplan, *Colonies into Nation: American Diplomacy, 1763–1801* (New York: Macmillan, 1972), 193.

45. Washington to Gouverneur Morris, October 13, 1789, *Washington's Writings,* 30:439–40.

46. Ibid., 440.

47. Ibid., 445.

48. Wriston, *Executive Agents,* 211.

49. Washington's message to Congress on this day read in part: "Soon after I was called to the administration of the Government, I found it important to come to an understanding with the Court of London. . . . For this purpose I authorized informal conferences with their Ministers. . . . I have thought it proper to give you this information, as it might, at some time, have influence on matters under your consideration" (*Annals,* 1st Cong., 2d sess., 1962–63). The message was referred to a seven-member House committee that included James Madison. I was unable to find any report from this committee in the *Annals,* though Wriston notes the existence of such a report that "did not deny the right of the President to act as he had done" (*Executive Agents,* 210).

50. Maclay, *Journal,* 389. One Morris biographer refers to additional evidence

of congressional discontent over his appointment as an executive agent, though it appears that the discontent was related more to Morris's personality than to a dispute over the propriety of his appointment. According to Daniel Walther, "Morris's appointment was not endorsed without difficulty in Congress. He enjoyed the esteem and confidence of Washington, which was much, but the members of Congress had little liking for him" (*Gouverneur Morris: Witness of Two Revolutions* [New York: Funk and Wagnalls, 1934], 152).

51. Sofaer, *War, Foreign Affairs, and Constitutional Power,* 78.

52. Washington to Lieutenant Colonel David Humphreys, December 23, 1780, *Washington's Writings,* 21:6–7.

53. Ibid., 102.

54. Jefferson to David Humphreys, August 11, 1790, in *The Papers of Thomas Jefferson,* ed. Julian P. Boyd, 28 vols. (Princeton, N.J.: Princeton University Press, 1950–), 17:125. (Hereafter cited as *Jefferson's Papers*)

55. Ibid.

56. Ibid., 125–26.

57. Ibid., 126.

58. Edward M. Cifelli, *David Humphreys* (Boston: Twayne, 1982), 81.

59. Ibid.

60. Ibid., 83.

61. Wriston, *Executive Agents,* 210; Maclay, *Journal,* 296, 385.

62. Richard B. Morris, ed., *Alexander Hamilton and the Founding of the Nation* (New York: Dial Press, 1957), 437–47.

63. *Hamilton's Papers,* 21:487.

64. Wriston, *Executive Agents,* 212. In February 1814, Senator Christopher Gore introduced a resolution attempting to restrict the power of the president in sending treaty negotiators abroad without senatorial consent. The debate did touch on the question of "public" versus "private" ministers but made little reference to the functions of those private emissaries. I have therefore chosen not to review this debate. For a full discussion, see Wriston, *Executive Agents,* 212–19.

65. Unlike that concerning the first debate on the establishment of the Contingency Fund, Wriston's description of these two debates is a comprehensive one. However, his focus was different from mine. This study is concerned with the use of executive agents as intelligence gatherers and meddlers in the internal affairs of other nations. Wriston's is essentially a diplomatic history concerned with the legal status of those agents involved in treaty making. Wriston's primary focus is examining how these "near" diplomats fit into our constitutional scheme, although the closing chapter of Wriston's book does review examples of agents operating in secret to gather intelligence or disseminate propaganda.

66. Wriston, *Executive Agents,* 219–22.

67. *Annals,* 15th Cong., 1st sess., 1465.

68. Ibid.

69. Ibid.

70. Ibid., 1466.

71. Congressman John Forsyth of Georgia, secretary of state under Andrew Jackson from 1834 to 1837.

72. *Annals,* 1467.

73. Ibid.

74. *Register of Debates,* 21st Cong., 2d sess., 293.

75. Ibid., 294.

76. Wriston seems to imply that the use of the word *spy* was unintentionally assimilated with "secret agents" (*Executive Agents*, 241).

77. *Register of Debates*, 295.

Chapter 4

1. *The Writings of Thomas Jefferson,* ed. H. A. Washington, 9 vols. (Washington, D.C.: Taylor and Maury, 1853), 5:97. (Hereafter cited as *Jefferson's Writings*)

2. See Edward F. Sayle, "The Historical Underpinnings of the U.S. Intelligence Community," *International Journal of Intelligence and Counterintelligence* 1, no. 1 (Spring 1986): 6, and Lyman H. Butterfield, "Psychological Warfare in 1776: The Jefferson–Franklin Plan to Cause Hessian Desertions," *Proceedings of the American Philosophical Society* 94, no. 3 (June 1950): 234.

3. Worthington Ford, ed., *Journals of the Continental Congress, 1774–1789* (Washington, D.C.: Government Printing Office, 1906), June 5, 1776, and August 21, 1776, 5:417, 693.

4. Jefferson to William S. Smith, August 10, 1786, *Jefferson's Papers,* 10:212. The map bearer avoided "the searches that travellers are submitted to" through the cover provided by a diplomatic passport (ibid., 213n).

5. Jefferson to William Carmichael, June 3, 1788, ibid., 13:230–31, 235. The source Jefferson refers to was the Chevalier de Bourgoing, secretary of the French legation in Madrid. Bourgoing was a major intelligence source for American diplomats in Europe. See ibid., 12:178n.

6. Jefferson to James Monroe, November 11, 1784, in *The Works of Thomas Jefferson,* ed. Paul L. Ford, 12 vols. (New York: Knickerbocker Press, 1905), 4:374. (Hereafter cited as *Jefferson's Works*) For a brief discussion of Dumas's efforts to "cultivate" the Dutch press, see Ralph E. Weber, "As Others Saw Us," *Studies in Intelligence* (September 1987): 34.

7. Jefferson to John Jay, May 4, 1787, *Jefferson's Papers,* 11:341–42.

8. Jefferson to the U.S. minister to Portugal, David Humphreys, April 11, 1791, *Jefferson's Works,* 6:240–41. This segment of the letter was written in code.

9. Jefferson to Jay, August 14, 1785, *Jefferson's Papers,* 8:373–74. Jefferson would tap John Paul Jones for another secret mission in 1792, this time to engage in negotiations with the bey of Algiers. Jefferson's written instructions to Jones demonstrate his belief in the utility of secret diplomacy: "Entire secrecy is recommended to you, and that you so cover from the public your departure and destination, as that they may not be conjectured or noticed" (Jefferson to John Paul Jones, June 1, 1792, *Jefferson's Writings,* 431). Jones died before the mission could take place.

10. For a discussion of the Ledyard expedition and other secret initiatives undertaken during Jefferson's tenure as minister to France, see R. W. Van Alstyne, *The Rising American Empire* (New York: Oxford University Press, 1960), 78–80.

11. Amendments to Foreign Intercourse Bill, December 1, 1792, *Jefferson's Works,* 7:187–88.

12. Quoted in *Encyclopaedia Britannica,* 1954 ed., s.v. "Jefferson, Thomas."

13. Jefferson to Washington, April 2, 1791, *Jefferson's Papers,* 20:97.

14. Jefferson to Carmichael and William Short, April 24, 1792, *Jefferson's Writings*, 3:353.

15. See Isaac J. Cox, "The New Invasion of the Goths and Vandals," *Proceedings of the Mississippi Valley Historical Association for the Year 1914–15* 3 (1916):184–85.

16. The two generals, George Rogers Clark and Benjamin Logan, were well known on the American frontier for their battlefield exploits against the Indians and the British. In addition to his status as an American military officer, Clark had been commissioned a major general in the Franch army. See Dumas Malone, *Jefferson and the Ordeal of Liberty* (Boston: Little, Brown, 1962), 105; John Bakeless, *Lewis and Clark, Partners in Discovery* (New York: Morrow, 1947), 86; and André Michaux, "Journal of André Michaux," in *Early Western Travels*, ed. R. G. Thwaites (Cleveland: Clark, 1904), 3:39–42.

17. Cabinet Opinion on Filibusters, March 10, 1793, *Jefferson's Works*, 7:257.

18. See Frederick J. Turner, "Genet's Attack on Louisiana and Florida," *American Historical Review* 3 (1898): 650–71, and Samuel Flagg Bemis, ed., *The American Secretaries of State and Their Diplomacy* (New York: Knopf, 1927), 2:82. For a sympathetic account of Jefferson's actions in this matter, see Malone, *Jefferson and the Ordeal of Liberty*, 104–9.

19. Bakeless, *Lewis and Clark*, 41, 86.

20. Ibid., 85. The mission was a failure.

21. David Lavender, *The American Heritage History of the Great West* (New York: American Heritage, 1965), 62.

22. See Bakeless, *Lewis and Clark*, 60–66.

23. Ibid., 98.

24. Francis Prucha, *The United States Army on the Frontier, 1783–1846* (Lincoln: University of Nebraska Press, 1969), 84–85.

25. Jefferson to Madison, May 27, 1793, *Jefferson's Works*, 7:346.

26. Jefferson to Madison, September 14, 1803, ibid., 10:31.

27. Jefferson to Albert Gallatin, October 29, 1803, ibid., 10:45–46. American concerns over Spanish resistance to the transfer proved unfounded, as France regained possession of the territory on November 30, 1803, and handed it over to U.S. control on December 20, 1803. Jefferson realized that the transfer of territory between Spain and France was essentially a matter between those two nations, hence his desire to portray any attack as a French action. Undoubtedly, he also sought to avoid both wider hostilities with Spain and the appearance of an overly aggressive appetite for land.

28. John Randolph, quoted in Alexander DeConde, *A History of American Foreign Policy* (New York: Scribner's, 1971), 120–21.

29. Henry Adams, *History of the United States of America During the Administrations of Thomas Jefferson* (New York: Library of America, 1986), 699.

30. It is important to note that the American government viewed the Indian tribes as occupying a unique status. This status was below that accorded foreign nations in Europe and elsewhere but above that of other domestic groups. I have therefore decided to include those of Jefferson's dealings with the Indians that demonstrate a willingness to employ covert means to further American interests.

31. Jefferson to Charles Carroll, April 15, 1791, *Jefferson's Writings*, 3:246–47.

32. Jefferson to Monroe, April 17, 1791, *Jefferson's Works*, 6:242.

33. Jefferson to Washington, April 17, 1791, ibid., 6:245.

34. Cabinet Opinion on Secret Indian Agent, June 1, 1793, ibid., 7:353–55. Secretary of the Treasury Alexander Hamilton opposed the plan as poor policy and contrary to the nation's sense of honor. Ibid., 356.

35. It should be noted that Jefferson was convinced throughout the confrontation with the Creeks that Spanish agents were secretly arming and inciting them to attack American settlements. See Jefferson to Carmichael and Short, November 3, 1792 and May 31, 1793, ibid., 7:173, 348–49.

36. See Reginald Horsman, *Expansion and American Indian Policy, 1783–1812* (East Lansing: Michigan State University Press, 1967), 125.

37. Ibid., 137.

38. Ibid., 147.

39. See Reginald Horsman, "American Indian Policy in the Old Northwest, 1783–1812," *William and Mary Quarterly* 18, no. 1 (January 1961): 49.

40. Jefferson to Gallatin, January 7, 1808, *Jefferson's Writings*, 5:227–28.

41. See Jefferson to Monroe, November 11, 1784, *Jefferson's Papers*, 7:512, and February 6, 1785, 640.

42. Jefferson to Carmichael, January 30, 1785, ibid., 7:630.

43. *Annals*, 9th Cong., 2d sess., 704. The correspondence related to the overthrow operation was given to Congress by the Jefferson administration in four installments: December 11, 1805; January 13, 1806; February 4, 1806; and November 1807.

It should be noted that there is no historical consensus as to the true source of the idea to overthrow the pasha; Cathcart's letter is the first written record of the operation, though the plan has all the hallmarks of Eaton's flair for the dramatic.

44. Ibid.

45. See Samuel Edwards, *Barbary General: The Life of William H. Eaton* (Englewood Cliffs, N.J.: Prentice-Hall, 1968).

46. William Eaton to Madison, September 5, 1801, *Annals*, 704.

47. Eaton to Madison, December 13, 1801, ibid., 705–6.

48. James Cathcart to Madison, August 25, 1802, ibid., 706–9.

49. Madison to Cathcart, August 22, 1802, ibid., 709.

50. Eaton was aware of the administration's concern about the cost of the overthrow effort and sought to finance the operation by having Hamet sign an agreement stating that upon his return to the throne a percentage of the tribute he extorted from other nations would be used to reimburse the United States for the costs of restoring him to power. See Eaton to the secretary of the navy, February 13, 1805, ibid., 716.

51. See Edwards, *Barbary General*, 132–35, and Glenn Tucker, *Dawn Like Thunder: The Barbary Wars and the Birth of the U.S. Navy* (Indianapolis: Bobbs-Merrill, 1963), 350. See also Louis B. Wright and Julia Macleod, *The First Americans in North Africa: William Eaton's Struggle for a Vigorous Policy Against the Barbary Pirates, 1799–1805* (Princeton, N.J.: Princeton University Press, 1945), 148.

52. Jefferson's *Anas*, May 26, 1804, in *Jefferson's Works*, 1:382. Henry Adams states that Jefferson was put off by Eaton's proposal, that Eaton returned to the Mediterranean and "chose to act without authority rather than not act at all." This statement is patently untrue, as can be seen in documentary evidence and in a review of the events that occurred before and after the White House meeting.

See Adams, *United States During Jefferson,* 594–95. This version of Eaton as a rogue agent was accepted by Jefferson's biographer Dumas Malone and Madison's biographer Irving Brant.

53. Edwards, *Barbary General,* 133–34. Edwards states that placing Eaton on the Navy payroll introduced a level of ambiguity that allowed him a greater degree of latitude in making preparations for the operation: Eaton's "lack of a precise status suited his own purposes. The State Department assumed he was working for the Navy, and the uniformed officers of the Navy considered him a State Department man."

54. Secretary of the Navy Robert Smith to Eaton, May 30, 1804, *Annals,* 712.

55. Madison to Tobias Lear, June 6, 1804, ibid., 711.

56. Smith to Commodore Samuel Barron, June 6, 1804, ibid., 712–13.

57. Verbal orders from Barron to Captain Hull [attested to by Isaac Hull and William Eaton], September 15, 1804, ibid., 714.

58. Eaton to Smith, February 13, 1805, ibid., 716.

59. For a description of the march across the desert, see Wright and Macleod, *Eaton's Struggle,* chap. 7, and Tucker, *Barbary Wars and U.S. Navy,* chap. 22.

60. Barron to Eaton, May 19, 1805, *Annals,* 737–39.

61. Lear to Eaton, June 6, 1805, ibid., 746.

62. Eaton to Commodore John Rodgers, June 30, 1805, ibid., 748–50.

63. Abraham D. Sofaer, *War, Foreign Affairs, and Constitutional Power: The Origins* (Cambridge, Mass.: Ballinger, 1976), 221.

64. Jefferson to the Senate and House of Representatives of the United States, February 4, 1806, *Annals,* 694.

65. Ibid., 695.

66. Ibid., 696.

67. Madison to Eaton, May 20, 1801, ibid., 703.

68. Cathcart to Madison, July 2, 1801, ibid., 704.

69. Ibid.

70. Eaton to Madison, September 5, 1801, ibid.

71. Madison to Cathcart, August 22, 1802, ibid., 709.

72. Smith to Barron, June 6, 1804, ibid., 712–13.

73. The administration considered Eaton such an indispensable resource in the area that in at least one instance Jefferson rejected his request for a leave of absence: "The President has taken into consideration your request of leave of absence, and thinks it might be too injurious to the affairs of the United States, especially during the present critical state of the Mediterranean" (Madison to Eaton, May 20, 1801, ibid., 703–4).

74. The best account of this entire affair is found in Sofaer, *War, Foreign Affairs, and Constitutional Power,* and yet even here the crucial White House meeting between Jefferson and Eaton is not mentioned. This omission appears to be the result of Sofaer's reliance on the *Annals* as the main source of his account. The material found in the *Annals* was provided to Congress by the Jefferson administration and did not make any mention of the White House meeting or the subsequent transfer of arms and supplies to Eaton.

Eaton received additional financial support for his activities from the Contingency Fund. See Madison to Richard Harrison, auditor of the Treasury, February 11, 1804, in *Naval Documents Related to the United States Wars with the*

Barbary Powers, vol. 3, *Naval Operations* (Washington, D.C.: Government Printing Office, 1941), 402–3.

75. Madison to Cathcart, August 22, 1802, ibid., 709. Glenn Tucker provides additional evidence of the extent to which Jefferson and Madison were willing to back this operation, when they in effect overrode the objections made by the American naval commanders on the scene (*Barbary Wars and U.S. Navy,* 229–30).

76. Eaton to the secretary of the navy, December 5, 1805, *Annals,* 760.

77. See Tucker, *Barbary Wars and U.S. Navy,* 436.

78. Jefferson's opinion on the powers of the Senate respecting diplomatic appointments, April 24, 1790, *Jefferson's Papers,* 16:379.

79. Jefferson to Benjamin Vaughan, July 2, 1787, *Jefferson's Writings,* 2:167.

80. Jefferson to Madison, December 20, 1787, *Jefferson's Papers,* 12:440–41.

81. Jefferson to Elbridge Gerry, May 13, 1797, *Jefferson's Works,* 8:285.

82. Monroe to Jefferson, March 9, 1812, in *The Writings of James Monroe,* ed. Stanislaus M. Hamilton (New York: Putnam, 1901), 5:199. Monroe is referring to the activities of British secret agent John Henry, who was dispatched to New England at the height of Jefferson's unpopular embargo.

83. Jefferson to the commissioners of Spain, July 9, 1792, *Jefferson's Works,* 7:134.

84. Jefferson to Thomas Cooper, Esq., September 10, 1814, *Jefferson's Writings,* 6:380–81. Two years prior to the assault on Washington, Jefferson predicted that the British might burn a major American city, though he assumed the target would be New York or Boston. He mentioned this concern in two separate letters written in the summer of 1812, urging retaliation against London "not by expensive fleets" but by "hired incendiaries" whose hunger "will make them brave every risk for bread" (Jefferson to General Thaddeus Kosciusko, June 28, 1812, *Jefferson's Works,* 11:259; Jefferson to William Duane, August 4, 1812, ibid., 265).

85. Jefferson to Monroe, January 1, 1815, *Jefferson's Works,* 11:445.

86. Jefferson skillfully used congressional surrogates to enact his legislative program. In one instance, he instructed a senator not to reveal Jefferson's authorship of a constitution for the Louisiana territory: "In communicating it to you I must do it in confidence that you will never let any person know that I have put pen to paper on the subject and if you think the enclosed can be of any aid to you you will take the trouble to copy it and return me the original." In another case, a congressman for whom the administration had drafted a bill was instructed, "Be so good as to copy the within and burn this original, as he [Jefferson] is very unwilling to meddle personally with the details of the preceedings of the legislature" (William Goldsmith, *The Growth of Presidential Power: A Documented History,* 3 vols. [New York: Chelsea House, 1974], 1:357–58).

87. Adams, *United States During Jefferson,* 467.

88. Jefferson to Monroe, January 8, 1804, *Jefferson's Works,* 10:61. Jefferson began his practice of using private citizens to undertake secret initiatives early in his diplomatic career. One example was the mission of Thomas Barclay to Morocco in 1785. See Henry M. Wriston, *Executive Agents in American Foreign Relations* (Baltimore: Johns Hopkins University Press, 1929), 25, 104.

89. Jefferson to Robert Livingston, April 18, 1802, *Jefferson's Works,* 9: 363–64. Jefferson appears to have had a lifelong fascination with codes and cyphers,

leading one historian to dub him the "father of American cyptography." See David Kahn, *The Codebreakers: The Story of Secret Writing* (New York: Macmillan, 1967), 192–95.

90. Jefferson to Gallatin, August 30, 1808, *Jefferson's Works*, 11:48 n.1.

91. Opinion on the powers of the Senate respecting diplomatic appointments, April 24, 1790, *Jefferson's Papers*, 16:379.

92. Jefferson to George Hay, June 17, 1807, *Jefferson's Writings*, 5:97.

93. Jefferson to the secretary of war, Henry Dearborn, July 18, 1808, ibid., 5:322.

94. The phrase "empire for liberty" is taken from Jefferson to Madison, April 27, 1809, ibid., 5:444.

Chapter 5

1. *The Writings of James Madison,* ed. Gaillard Hunt (New York: Putnam, 1908), 8:105–6.

2. Charles C. Tansill, "Robert Smith," in *The American Secretaries of State and Their Diplomacy,* ed. Samuel Flagg Bemis (New York: Knopf, 1927), 3:185–86.

3. See Alexander DeConde, *A History of American Foreign Policy* (New York: Scribner's, 1971), 129, and Rufus K. Wyllys, "The East Florida Revolution of 1812–1814," *Hispanic American Historical Review* 9, no. 4 (November 1929): 417.

4. See Julius W. Pratt, *Expansionists of 1812* (Gloucester, Mass.: Smith, 1957), 67–69.

5. Jefferson to Senator John Breckinridge, August 12, 1803, *Jefferson's Writings*, 4:499.

6. Jefferson to President Monroe, October 24, 1823, *Jefferson's Works*, 12: 320.

7. Irving Brant, *James Madison: The President, 1809–1812* (Indianapolis: Bobbs-Merrill, 1956), 173.

8. See DeConde, *American Foreign Policy,* 119–20, and Pratt, *Expansionists,* 69–70. Henry Adams states that "to the territory of West Florida the United States had no right" (*History of the United States During the Administrations of James Madison* [New York: Library of America, 1986], 456).

9. Quoted in DeConde, *American Foreign Policy,* 121.

10. The material in this section is derived primarily from Isaac J. Cox, *The West Florida Controversy, 1798–1813: A Study in American Diplomacy* (Baltimore: Johns Hopkins University Press, 1918), and Brant, *Madison, 1809–1812.* Brant's account is very helpful, but one senses at times an attempt to portray Madison's role in this affair in a most favorable light. He places great emphasis on efforts by "lawless" American renegades to seize the territory in contrast to Madison's effort to "promote a peaceable and orderly revolution" (178).

11. Tansill, "Robert Smith," 182.

12. Cox, *West Florida Controversy,* 297.

13. Ibid., 330.

14. Brant, *Madison, 1809–1812,* 175.

15. Tansill, "Robert Smith," 183.

16. Cox, *West Florida Controversy,* 330–31.

17. Holmes's activities in this affair are detailed at length in Isaac J. Cox, "The American Intervention in West Florida," *American Historical Review* 17, no. 2 (January 1912): 294–311 passim.

18. Brant, *Madison, 1809–1812,* 176.

19. Cox, *West Florida Controversy,* 331.

20. Madison to Robert Smith, July 17, 1810, in *Madison's Writings,* ed. Hunt, 8:105–6.

21. Brant, *Madison, 1809–1812,* 176.

22. Ibid., 175–76.

23. Charlton W. Tebeau, *A History of Florida* (Coral Gables, Fla.: University of Miami Press, 1971), 104.

24. Brant, *Madison, 1809–1812,* 184.

25. Ibid., 182.

26. Tansill, "Robert Smith," 185–86.

27. Ibid. Cox suggests that Madison might have kept his own secretary of state in the dark regarding some aspects of the West Florida affair (*West Florida Controversy,* 537).

28. Brant, *Madison, 1809–1812,* chap. 12.

29. Madison to Jefferson, October 19, 1810, in *Letters and Other Writings of James Madison, Fourth President of the United States* (Philadelphia: Lippincott, 1865), 2:484–85. Jefferson apparently did not reply to this letter.

30. See Nelson S. Dearmont, "Federalist Attitudes Toward Governmental Secrecy in the Age of Jefferson," *The Historian* 37, no. 2 (February 1975): 231–32. Dearmont notes, "Madison was well aware his authority was doubtful and that Congress might obstruct his action, so he successfully suppressed news of the proclamation as well as of the action it prescribed until he delivered his message to Congress in December."

31. Brant, *Madison, 1809–1812,* 189.

32. *Annals,* 11th Cong., 3d sess., December 27, 1810, 44–45.

33. Ibid., 40.

34. Ibid., 41–42.

35. See Pratt, *Expansionists,* 76. Crawford's assessment of the situation was subsequently echoed by Secretary of State Smith in a letter to Crawford, stating that the president wished him to select an agent to handle East Florida. The section heading is taken from this letter. See Brant, *Madison, 1809–1812,* 176, 231–32. See also Paul Kruse, "A Secret Agent in East Florida: General George Mathews and the Patriot War," *Journal of Southern History* 18, no. 2 (May 1952): 193, and Rembert W. Patrick, *Florida Fiasco: Rampant Rebels on the Georgia–Florida Border, 1810–1815* (Athens: University of Georgia Press, 1954), 7. Along with Kruse and Patrick, the main sources I have relied on for background information on the East Florida operation were Rufus K. Wyllys, "East Florida Revolution," 415–45; Isaac J. Cox, "The Border Missions of General George Mathews," *Mississippi Valley Historical Review* 12, no. 3 (December 1925): 309–33; and Pratt, *Expansionists.*

36. Cox, "Border Missions of Mathews," 310–13.

37. Wyllys, "East Florida Revolution," 419.

38. Cox, "Border Missions of Mathews," 313.

39. Ibid., 313–14.

40. See Pratt, *Expansionists,* 73–74, 79; David Hunter Miller, *Secret Statutes*

of the United States (Washington, D.C.: Government Printing Office, 1918), 4–6; and Kenneth W. Porter, "Negroes and the East Florida Annexation Plot, 1811–1813," *Journal of Negro History* 30, no. 1 (January 1945): 9.

41. Pratt, *Expansionists,* 77.

42. Ibid.; Kruse, "Secret Agent," 200; Cox, *West Florida Controversy,* 523. Cox states that Mathews's reports from Florida in the fall of 1810 "aroused the extravagant hopes of the president."

43. Patrick gives the date for the White House meeting as New Year's Day, 1811, though at other points in the book he suggests it may have been later in the month (*Florida Fiasco,* 175).

44. See Wyllys, "East Florida Revolution," 421.

45. Quoted in Kruse, "Secret Agent," 197.

46. Cox, "Border Missions of Mathews," 313–17.

47. George Mathews to Secretary of State Smith, February 25, 1811, in Kruse, "Secret Agent," 198–99. Although I have seen the original correspondence at the National Archives, I have chosen in this instance to follow Kruse's "translation" for this particular letter as Kruse seems to have deciphered words I was unable to comprehend. The description of Mathews from a contemporary says it all: "brave, honest, but extremely illiterate" (Cox, "Border Missions of Mathews," 310n.4).

48. Mathews and John McKee to Smith, April 24, 1811, in *State Department Territorial Papers, Florida Series, 1777–1824,* vol. 1, *October 13, 1777– December 1811* (National Archives Microfilm, M-116). (Hereafter cited as *State Department Territorial Papers*)

49. McKee to Monroe, June 26, 1811, ibid.

50. McKee to Smith, May 1, 1811, ibid.

51. McKee to Monroe, January 1, 1812, ibid.

52. McKee to Monroe, January 22, 1812, ibid.

53. McKee to Monroe, May 22, 1811, ibid.

54. McKee to Monroe, January 22, 1812, ibid.

55. Mathews to Monroe, May 14, 1811, ibid. Fortunately for future scholars, Mathews hired a secretary to write the remainder of his East Florida correspondence for him.

56. Monroe to Mathews, June 29, 1811, in Kruse, "Secret Agent," 204.

57. Mathews to Monroe, June 28, 1811, *State Department Territorial Papers.*

58. Cox, "Border Missions of Mathews," 319.

59. Mathews to Monroe, August 3, 1811, *State Department Territorial Papers.*

60. Kruse, "Secret Agent," 205.

61. Mathews to Monroe, October 14, 1811, *State Department Territorial Papers.*

62. Kruse, "Secret Agent," 206.

63. Mathews to Monroe, October 14, 1811, *State Department Territorial Papers.*

64. Wyllys, "East Florida Revolution," 425.

65. See Patrick, *Florida Fiasco,* 62–64, and Wyllys, "East Florida Revolution," 425. Patrick states that Mathews was aware, through newspaper reports, that Monroe ignored the British protest over his activities.

66. Pratt, *Expansionists,* 109.

67. Ibid., 203n.20.

68. See Patrick, *Florida Fiasco*, chaps. 7, 8.

69. Ibid., 64–66. See also Cox, "Border Missions of Mathews," 319, and Wyllys, "East Florida Revolution," 424. Brant estimates the invasion force consisted of approximately two hundred men of whom eight to ten were Spanish subjects (*Madison, 1809–1812*, 443).

70. Mathews to Monroe, March 14, 1812, *State Department Territorial Papers*.

71. The administration considered these papers so important it spent the entire budget of the secret service fund to obtain them. For an interesting account of the Henry affair, see Bradford Perkins, *Prologue to War: England and the United States, 1805–1812* (Berkeley: University of California Press, 1963), 369–72, and Samuel Eliot Morison, *By Land and by Sea* (New York: Knopf, 1953), chap. 12.

72. See Pratt, *Expansionists*, 109–10, 114–15.

73. Monroe to Mathews, April 4, 1812, *State Department Territorial Papers*.

74. See Pratt, *Expansionists*, 113n.104.

75. Governor David Mitchell to the governor of East Florida, May 4, 1812, *State Department Territorial Papers*.

76. See Patrick, *Florida Fiasco*, 151.

77. See Wyllys, "East Florida Revolution," 440.

78. Patrick, *Florida Fiasco*, 122–23.

79. Ibid., 251–52. The speech was delivered in secret session.

80. Adams, *United States During Madison*, 216–17.

81. See Kruse, "Secret Agent," 215–16, and Pratt, *Expansionists*, 114–15.

82. See Reginald Horsman, *Expansion and American Indian Policy, 1783–1812* (East Lansing: Michigan State University Press, 1967), 164. In discussing American policy toward the Indians during 1811 to 1812, Horsman states that it was standard practice to pressure the Indians through a "constant reiteration of requests, arguments or bribery."

83. See Irving Brant, *James Madison: Secretary of State* (Indianapolis: Bobbs-Merrill, 1953), 305–6. The prostitute was procured for Ambassador Sidi Suliman Mellimelli of Tunisia during the winter of 1805 and 1806.

84. See Edward F. Sayle, "The Historical Underpinnings of the U.S. Intelligence Community," *International Journal of Intelligence and Counterintelligence* 1, no. 1 (Spring 1986): 10–11.

85. Ibid., 11. See also Irving Brant, *James Madison: Commander in Chief* (Indianapolis: Bobbs-Merrill, 1961), 366, and Robert Remini, *Andrew Jackson and the Course of American Empire, 1767–1821* (New York: Harper & Row, 1977), 251–53.

86. See Adams, *United States During Madison*, 767.

87. For a discussion of East Florida as a haven for former slaves and a source of resistance to the U.S.-sponsored revolt, see Porter, "Negroes and the East Florida Plot," 9–29. For mention of East Florida as a profitable center of illicit trade for Americans, see Patrick, *Florida Fiasco*, 46–47.

88. DeConde, *American Foreign Policy*, 119.

89. Cox, "Border Missions of Mathews," 314.

90. It should be noted that the administration never accused Mathews of doctoring his intelligence reports in order to generate support for his actions in East Florida. This conceivably would have given the administration a more credible cover story.

91. See Ralph Ketchum, "James Madison and the Presidency," in *Inventing the American Presidency,* ed. Thomas E. Cronin (Lawrence: University of Kansas Press, 1989), chap. 14.

92. See J. Fred Rippy, *Joel R. Poinsett: Versatile American* (Durham, N.C.: Duke University Press, 1935), chap. 4.

93. See Dorothy M. Parton, "The Diplomatic Career of Joel Roberts Poinsett" (Ph.D. diss., Catholic University, 1934), 3–4, and Rippy, *Joel Poinsett,* 35–37.

94. Henry M. Wriston, *Executive Agents in American Foreign Relations* (Baltimore: Johns Hopkins University Press, 1929), 408–9.

95. See Rippy, *Joel Poinsett,* 37–38.

96. Quoted in Parton, "Poinsett Diplomatic Career," 10n.16.

97. Joel R. Poinsett, "State of Parties and Characters of the Revolution," Undated. Records of the Department of State, Communications from Special Agents, 1794–1906 (National Archives Microfilm, M-37, roll 2, vol. 3).

98. Quoted in Parton, "Poinsett Diplomatic Career," 25.

99. Ibid., 20–21.

100. Rippy, *Joel Poinsett,* 40.

101. Thomas E. Weil et al., *Area Handbook for Chile* (Washington, D.C.: Government Printing Office, 1969), 29.

102. See Parton, "Poinsett Diplomatic Career," 16–17.

103. See ibid., 27–28, and Rippy, *Joel Poinsett,* 43–47.

104. Joel Poinsett to Monroe[?], undated report (National Archives Microfilm, M-37, roll 2, vol. 3).

105. Rippy, *Joel Poinsett,* 43. Poinsett referred in one letter to Secretary Monroe of the "numerous letters" he had sent him from Chile. It is possible that some of his correspondence never reached Washington due to British interception of American communications during the War of 1812. Diplomatic historian William Manning has noted that this is somewhat improbable due to the standard practice of sending duplicates by different conveyances (*Diplomatic Correspondence of the United States Concerning the Independence of the Latin-American Nations* [New York: Oxford University Press, 1925] 2:896n.1).

106. Parton, "Poinsett Diplomatic Career," 33; William L. Neumann, "United States Aid to the Chilean Wars of Independence," *Hispanic American Historical Review* 27, no. 2 (May 1947): 210.

107. Rippy, *Joel Poinsett,* 53.

108. Ibid., 50–56.

109. Ibid., 57.

110. See Manning, ed., *U.S. Diplomatic Correspondence,* 896n.1. Monroe issued the order on September 26, 1818, while serving as president. Monroe was not one to quibble when it came to altering the historical record. In an attempt to quell the furor surrounding Andrew Jackson's aggressive actions in Florida in 1818, President Monroe proposed to "correct those passages" in some of Jackson's letters that threatened to embarrass his administration. See Remini, *Andrew Jackson,* 368.

111. *The Papers of Andrew Jackson,* ed. Harold D. Moser (Knoxville: University of Tennessee Press, 1991), 3:96n.4.

112. See Harry Ammon, *James Monroe: The Quest for National Identity* (New York: McGraw-Hill, 1971), 410–11.

113. See Henry B. Cox, "Reasons for Joel Poinsett's Refusal of a Second Mis-

sion to South America," *Hispanic American Historical Review* 43, no. 3 (August 1963): 405–8.

114. Parton, "Poinsett Diplomatic Career," chap. 3; Rippy, *Joel Poinsett,* chap. 7.

115. See Rippy, *Joel Poinsett,* 131n.1.

116. Quoted in J. Fred Rippy, "Britain's Role in the Early Relations of the United States and Mexico," *Hispanic American Historical Review* 7, no. 1 (February 1927): 5.

117. Ibid., 7; Rippy, *Joel Poinsett,* 122. It should be noted that the two major biographers of Poinsett, Rippy and Parton, disagree as to the extent of his meddling in Mexican politics. Their differences are most pronounced regarding Poinsett's involvement in organizing the York Rite Masons as part of the machinery of a pro-American political party. Parton sees Poinsett playing a more passive role in Mexican politics. She accepts some of Poinsett's denials of intermeddling at face value—despite reports from outside observers at the time, including at least two Americans, that he was deeply involved in Mexican party politics. Parton also appears to have overlooked some important correspondence regarding Poinsett's activities that Rippy includes in his study. Rippy's version of events is shared by diplomatic historian Samuel Flagg Bemis in *John Quincy Adams and the Foundations of American Foreign Policy* (Westport, Conn.: Greenwood Press, 1949), 562–63, and Mary W. M. Hargreaves, *The Presidency of John Quincy Adams* (Lawrence: University Press of Kansas, 1985), 80.

118. Joel Poinsett to Henry Clay, October 12, 1825, in *The Papers of Henry Clay,* ed. James F. Hopkins (Lexington: University Press of Kentucky, 1972), 4:733. The letter was written in code. (Hereafter cited as *Clay's Papers*)

119. For a discussion of Clay's ties to the Masons and that organization's rebellious activities in Latin America, see Hargreaves, *Presidency of J. Q. Adams,* 141. For a reference to the Spanish government's belief in American approval of Masonic-inspired insurrections, see also Manning, ed., *U.S. Diplomatic Correspondence,* 3:2025.

120. Rippy, "Britain's Role," 9.

121. Poinsett to Clay, January 4, 1826, *Clay's Papers,* 5:10. Clay wrote on the letter, "To be submitted to the President."

122. Poinsett to Clay, January 7, 1826, ibid., 5:14. The letter was marked private.

123. *Memoirs of John Quincy Adams, Comprising Portions of His Diary from 1795 to 1848,* ed. Charles Francis Adams (Philadelphia: Lippincott, 1875), 7:277.

124. Rippy, *Joel Poinsett,* 122. The letter to King was written in October 1825 (ibid., 131n.3); the letter to Van Buren was written in March 1829 (ibid., 131n.4).

125. Ibid., 123.

126. *J. Q. Adams and American Foreign Policy,* 563. The two private letters were written on April 26 and July 18, 1827.

127. Rippy, *Joel Poinsett,* 126. The letter from Clay was sent on November 19, 1827.

128. Parton, "Poinsett Diplomatic Career," 129.

129. Poinsett to Clay, January 7, 1826, *Clay's Papers,* 5:14.

130. Poinsett to Clay, May 10, 1827, ibid., 6:753.

Chapter 6

1. Message of President James K. Polk to the House of Representatives, April 20, 1846, in *A Compilation of the Messages and Papers of the Presidents, 1798–1908*, ed. James D. Richardson (Washington, D.C.: Bureau of National Literature and Art, 1908) 4:435.

2. Anthony Butler to Secretary of State Martin Van Buren, in Glenn W. Price, *Origins of the War with Mexico: The Polk–Stockton Intrigue* (Austin: University of Texas Press, 1967), 19.

3. Quoted in Robert Remini, *Andrew Jackson and the Course of American Freedom, 1822–1832* (New York: Harper & Row, 1981), 218.

4. Ibid., 220.

5. Quoted in Price, *Origins of War with Mexico*, 20.

6. See Eugene C. Barker, "President Jackson and the Texas Revolution," *American Historical Review* 12, no. 4 (July 1907): 791.

7. Ibid., 792.

8. Anthony Butler to President Andrew Jackson, January 2, 1833, in *Correspondence of Andrew Jackson*, ed. John Spencer Bassett (Washington, D.C.: Carnegie Institution, 1931) 5:2. (Hereafter cited as *Jackson's Correspondence*)

9. See Butler to Jackson, February 10, 1833, in *Diplomatic Correspondence of the United States: Inter-American Affairs, 1831–1860*, ed. William Manning (Washington, D.C.: Carnegie Endowment, 1937) 8:258–60, and Price, *Origins of War with Mexico*, 21.

10. Jackson to Butler, October 30, 1833, *Jackson's Correspondence*, 5:221–22.

11. Butler to Jackson, October 28, 1833, ibid., 5:219–20.

12. Jackson to Butler, November 27, 1833, ibid., 5:228–30.

13. Butler to Jackson, February 6, 1834, ibid., 5:244–47.

14. Butler to Jackson, May 25, 1831, in *U.S. Diplomatic Correspondence*, ed. Manning, 8:242–44.

15. See, for instance, Robert Remini, *Andrew Jackson and the Course of American Democracy, 1833–1845* (New York: Harper & Row, 1984), 354.

16. See Richard Stenberg, "President Jackson and Anthony Butler," *Southwest Review* 22 (July 1937):391–404.

17. See Barker, "Jackson and Texas Revolution," 803.

18. See Richard N. Current, "Webster's Propaganda and the Ashburton Treaty," *Mississippi Valley Historical Review* 34, no. 2 (September 1947):188, and Norma L. Peterson, *The Presidencies of William Henry Harrison and John Tyler* (Lawrence: University Press of Kansas, 1989), 118–19.

19. Francis O. J. Smith to Secretary of State Daniel Webster, June 7, 1841, in *The Papers of Daniel Webster: Diplomatic Papers, 1841–1843*, ed. Kenneth Shewmaker (Hanover, N.H.: University Press of New England, 1983), 1:94–96. (Hereafter cited as *Webster's Papers*)

20. See Frederick Merk, *Fruits of Propaganda in the Tyler Administration* (Cambridge, Mass.: Harvard University Press, 1971), 63–64.

21. Smith to Webster, July 2, 1841, *Webster's Papers*, 1:96–98.

22. See Smith to Webster, November 20, 1841, ibid., 1:161–62. See also Current, "Webster's Propaganda," 190–91, and Merk, *Fruits of Propaganda*, 64.

23. Smith to Webster, November 20, 1841, *Webster's Papers*, 1:161–62.

24. Peterson, *Harrison and Tyler*, 120.

25. See Merk, *Fruits of Propaganda*, 89.

26. Smith to Webster, November 20, 1841, *Webster's Papers*, 1:161–62.

27. Webster to Smith, April 10, 1842, ibid., 1:533–34.

28. Webster to Jared Sparks, May 16, 1842, ibid., 1:562.

29. Merk, *Fruits of Propaganda*, 65–67; Maurice G. Baxter, *One and Insepa-rable: Daniel Webster and the Union* (Cambridge, Mass.: Belknap Press, 1984), 341–42.

30. An example of Tyler's desire to restrain expenses can be seen in his com-ment regarding a $250 payment to Sparks for his map mission: "I can only say that I should regard $250 to Mr. Sparks for the map fully enough. I do not doubt but that it will satisfy him. If otherwise we can see more about it" (Merk, *Fruits of Propaganda*, 65n.51).

Baxter believes that Ashburton's money was used to supplement Sparks's Con-tingency Fund payment of $250. He raises the possibility that some of the money may have been used to bribe state officials (*Webster and the Union*, 343). Others have suggested that Webster himself received some of the money. Merk states that the identity of the person who distributed the British money and who received payments simply cannot be determined (*Fruits of Propaganda*, 71).

31. Merk, *Fruits of Propaganda*, 71.

32. Current, "Webster's Propaganda," 193–94; Merk, *Fruits of Propaganda*, 78, 85–86.

33. Smith to Webster, August 12, 1842, *Webster's Papers*, 1:681–83.

34. See Merk, *Fruits of Propaganda*, 88.

35. Ibid.

36. Ibid., 188.

37. Ibid., 88–89.

38. Message of President James K. Polk to the House of Representatives, April 20, 1846, in *Compilation of Presidents' Messages and Papers*, ed. Richardson, 4:433–34.

39. Ibid., 435.

40. Webster to Robert Charles Winthrop, May 2, 1846, in *The Papers of Daniel Webster: Correspondence, 1844–1849*, ed. Charles M. Wiltse (Hanover, N.H.: University Press of New England, 1984), 6:148–49.

41. See Merk, *Fruits of Propaganda*, 89.

42. Webster to Sparks, March 11, 1843, *Webster's Papers*, 1:786.

43. See Henry M. Wriston, *Executive Agents in American Foreign Relations* (Baltimore: Johns Hopkins University Press, 1929), 267.

44. See Anna K. Nelson, "Secret Agents and Security Leaks: President Polk and the Mexican War," *Journalism Quarterly* 52 (Spring 1975):9–10.

45. Stockton was a naval officer of some consequence; he was offered (but declined) a cabinet position as secretary of the navy by President John Tyler. See Peterson, *Harrison and Tyler*, 183.

Circumstantial evidence such as this makes it difficult to accept Stockton as a rogue agent. At the very least, this theory makes Stockton more than "a minor flamboyant figure," as one historian of the Polk presidency describes him. See Paul H. Bergeron, *The Presidency of James K. Polk* (Lawrence: University Press of Kansas, 1987), 58. Stockton eventually wound up in California, scheming with other agents to acquire that region for the United States.

46. Quoted in R. W. Van Alstyne, *The Rising American Empire* (New York: Oxford University Press, 1960), 138. Bancroft appears to have been the point man in Polk's cabinet for handling his secret efforts at territorial acquisition.

47. Ibid. For a helpful but somewhat polemical account of Stockton's intrigue in Texas, see Price, *Origins of War with Mexico*. See also Richard Stenberg, "The Failure of Polk's Mexican War Intrigue of 1845," *Pacific Historical Review* 4, no. 1 (March 1935): 39–68.

48. See Nelson, "Secret Agents," 10–13. See also Bergeron, *Polk Presidency*, 83–84; David M. Pletcher, *The Diplomacy of Annexation: Texas, Oregon, and the Mexican War* (Columbia: University of Missouri Press, 1973), 366–67, 444–49; and William Goldsmith, *The Growth of Presidential Power: A Documented History,* (New York: Chelsea House, 1974), 2:846–47.

49. See Nelson, "Secret Agents," 11–12.

50. *The Diary of James K. Polk During His Presidency, 1845–1849*, ed. Milo M. Quaife (Chicago: McClurg, 1910), 3:290–92.

51. Secretary of the Navy George Bancroft, quoted in Nelson, "Secret Agents," 9.

52. See Richard R. Stenberg, "President Polk and California: Additional Documents," *Pacific Historical Review* 10, no. 2 (June 1941): 219.

53. Nelson, "Secret Agents," 10.

54. Ibid., 98.

55. My account of the Beach–Storms mission to Mexico is based on the work of Anna K. Nelson, "The Secret Diplomacy of James K. Polk During the Mexican War, 1846–1847" (Ph.D. diss., George Washington University, 1972), chap. 4. See also Nelson's "Mission to Mexico—Moses Y. Beach, Secret Agent," *New-York Historical Society Quarterly* 59, no. 3 (July 1975): 226–45.

56. James Buchanan to Moses Y. Beach, November 21, 1846, in *U.S. Diplomatic Correspondence*, ed. Manning, 8:196.

57. Nelson, "Mission to Mexico," 236.

58. Nelson, "Secret Diplomacy of Polk," 162.

59. Beach to Buchanan, June 4, 1847, in *U.S. Diplomatic Correspondence*, ed. Manning, 8:906.

60. In her dissertation, historian Anna Nelson is somewhat skeptical of the claims made by Beach and Storms regarding their intrigue with the Catholic Church. She notes the lack of independent corroboration of much of their "overly dramatic" story and dismisses the idea that they ignited the clerical rebellion. She admits that Beach and Storms had "joined and participated" in a movement to foment rebellion, but Nelson believes it was one well under way by the time they arrived on the scene. Nelson's position shifted somewhat in two essays that grew out of her dissertation. Those articles appear to reflect a greater acceptance of the clandestine aspects of the Beach mission and an acknowledgment that Beach "seems to have meddled extensively in the affairs of that city [Mexico City]" ("Secret Agents," 98).

Nelson's thorough account of the Beach mission falters somewhat in its discussion of Polk's intentions in dispatching this mission. I believe that one of the mission's major objectives, perhaps even its primary goal, was the establishment of contacts with the Catholic bishops and other prominent Mexicans to encourage them to pressure the Mexican government to seek peace with the United States on terms favorable to the Americans.

61. Polk, diary entry, April 14, 1847, in *Polk's Diary,* ed. Quaife, 2:476. The reference to Almonte refers to a former Mexican minister to the United States, Juan N. Almonte, an alleged political opponent of Santa Anna and the Mexican war party.

62. Polk, diary entry, May 11, 1847, ibid., 3:22.

63. Wriston, *Executive Agents,* 394–95.

64. Based on circumstantial evidence, several historians have made a case that Polk ordered agents into California for the purpose of covertly inciting hostilities that would have furthered the cause of territorial annexation. See, for instance, Richard Stenberg, "Polk and Fremont, 1845–1846," *Pacific Historical Review* 7, no. 1 (September 1937): 211–27.

65. See Ethan Allen Hitchcock, *Fifty Years in Camp and Field* (New York: Putnam, 1909), and U.S. Congress, Senate, *Final Report of the Select Committee to Study Governmental Operations with Respect to Intelligence Activities: Supplementary Report on Intelligence Activities,* S. Rept. 94–755, 94th Cong., 2d sess., 1976, 21–24. The Dimond spy ring in Vera Cruz is mentioned in Nelson, "Mission to Mexico," 236.

Chapter 7

1. *Totten, Administrator,* v. *United States,* 92 U.S. 105 (1875).

2. Quoted in John Bigelow, *France and the Confederate Navy, 1862–1868* (New York: Harper, 1888), 167. Bulloch was writing to the Confederate secretary of the navy. The author of this book was a key Union agent in Europe during the war.

3. This account of Sanford's activities is based on Harriet Chappell Owsley, "Henry Shelton Sanford and Federal Surveillance Abroad, 1861–1865," *Mississippi Valley Historical Review* 48, no. 2 (September 1961): 211–28, and Joseph A. Fry, *Henry S. Sanford: Diplomacy and Business in Nineteenth-Century America* (Reno: University of Nevada Press, 1982). Seward's instructions to Sanford can be found on 38.

4. Owsley, "Sanford and Surveillance," 212.

5. Ibid., 214.

6. Ibid., 216.

7. Ibid., 219.

8. Ibid., 221.

9. This account of Sanford's campaign of media manipulation is taken from Fry, *Sanford: Diplomacy and Business,* 38–41, and Owsley, "Sanford and Surveillance," 222–23.

10. See Lynn M. Case and Warren F. Spencer, *The United States and France: Civil War Diplomacy* (Philadelphia: University of Pennsylvania Press, 1970), 604.

11. Fry, *Sanford: Diplomacy and Business,* 38, 49; Margaret Clapp, *Forgotten First Citizen: John Bigelow* (Boston: Little, Brown, 1947), 170.

12. Glyndon G. Van Deusen, *Thurlow Weed: Wizard of the Lobby* (Boston: Little, Brown, 1947), 278. Seward originally considered using private funds to finance Weed's mission to Europe and in fact arranged for a private contribution from a wealthy New Yorker before deciding to draw on the Contingency Fund. See John H. Kiger, "Federal Governmental Propaganda in Great Britain During

the American Civil War," *Historical Outlook* 19, no. 5 (May 1928): 204. Seward seems to have been comfortable with the idea of using private sources of funding for special operations.

13. See Victor F. O'Daniel, "Archbishop John Hughes, American Envoy to France (1861)," *Catholic Historical Review* 3, no. 3 (October 1917): 338.

14. See Jay Monaghan, *Diplomat in Carpet Slippers: Abraham Lincoln Deals with Foreign Affairs* (Indianapolis: Bobbs-Merrill, 1945), 176, and Charles P. Cullop, *Confederate Propaganda in Europe, 1861–1865* (Coral Gables, Fla.: University of Miami Press, 1969), 104. See also Glyndon G. Van Deusen, *William Henry Seward* (New York: Oxford University Press, 1967), 307.

15. See O'Daniel, "Archbishop Hughes," 338n.6.

16. See J. G. Randall, "The Blundering Generation," *Mississippi Valley Historical Review* 27, no. 1 (June 1940): 26, and Van Deusen, *Seward*, 307.

17. See Martin P. Claussen, "Peace Factors in Anglo-American Relations, 1861–1865," *Mississippi Valley Historical Review* 26, no. 4 (March 1940): 521n.31.

18. Van Deusen, *Seward*, 306.

19. See Clapp, *Bigelow*, 189.

20. See William Seward to Abraham Lincoln, "Some thoughts for the President's consideration," April 1, 1861, in *The Collected Works of Abraham Lincoln*, ed. Roy P. Basler (New Brunswick, N.J.: Rutgers University Press, 1953), 4:317–18. (Hereafter cited as *Lincoln's Works*)

21. See F. Lauriston Bullard, "Abraham Lincoln and George Ashmun," *New England Quarterly* 19, no. 1 (March 1946): 197–98.

22. Quoted in Robin W. Winks, *Canada and the United States: The Civil War Years* (Baltimore: Johns Hopkins University Press, 1960), 38.

23. Ibid., 39–40. Winks notes that Seward's cancellation of the mission indicates that Ashmun was intended to be a "propagandist . . . for only in this capacity would public knowledge of his appointment have undermined the mission." Winks states that after the failure of the Ashmun mission, Seward made no other attempt to dispatch agents to Canada for purposes of influencing public and official opinion. This appears to be the case, though Winks's credibility on this matter is somewhat diminished in light of his statements that "the North had no propaganda system at work in the provinces or in *England*" (emphasis added) and that Seward "failed to recognize the importance of a friendly public opinion" (ibid., 230, 236).

24. Thurlow Weed, *Autobiography of Thurlow Weed*, ed. Harriet Weed (Boston: Houghton Mifflin, 1883), 615, 617.

25. See Harry J. Carman and Reinhard H. Luthin, *Lincoln and the Patronage* (New York: Columbia University Press, 1943), 122–25, and James L. Crouthamel, *Bennett's "New York Herald" and the Rise of the Popular Press* (Syracuse, N.Y.: Syracuse University Press, 1989), 118.

26. See Lincoln to James G. Bennett, February 20, 1865, *Lincoln's Works*, 8:307–8.

27. Carman and Luthin, *Lincoln and the Patronage*, 125.

28. See George Winston Smith, "Union Propaganda in the American Civil War," *Social Studies* 35, no. 1 (January 1944): 28.

29. See Lincoln to Seward, November 17, 1864, *Lincoln's Works*, 8:114. It is unclear whether this proposal was implemented by the administration.

30. Lincoln to William S. Rosecrans, May 28, 1863, ibid., 6:236.

31. Lincoln to Rosecrans, May 21, 1863, ibid., 6:225, and Lincoln to Robert C. Schenck, July 14, 1863, ibid., 6:329.

32. Although the operation was apparently aimed at domestic interests, it was conducted under the direction of the secretaries of state and war and justified as a national security measure. For this reason and the others previously mentioned, I have chosen to include it in my study.

33. *Lincoln's Works*, 6:112–13. One of the few accounts that I have seen discussing this obscure incident from Lincoln's presidency is found in the Sources and Commentary section of a work of fiction, William Safire's *Freedom: A Novel of Abraham Lincoln and the Civil War* (New York: Avon Books, 1987), 1318–20. Safire remarks the apparent unwillingness of Lincoln scholars to deal with this controversial event from Lincoln's presidency.

34. Lincoln to Thurlow Weed, February 19, 1863, *Lincoln's Works*, 6:112–13. According to Safire, the sum of $15,000 would be worth over $150,000 in 1987 (*Freedom*, 1320).

35. Gideon Welles, *The Diary of Gideon Welles* (Boston: Houghton Mifflin, 1911), 1:235.

36. Quoted in *Lincoln's Works*, 6:113. Basler is responsible for piecing together the correspondence that seems to indicate that the operation was directed at influencing election races in Connecticut and New Hampshire. Safire is not convinced that this was the purpose of the operation. He notes (1) that Secretary Welles was from Connecticut and would have been the more likely candidate to handle such an operation and (2) that money raised in New York to influence the political process in Connecticut and New York need not have traveled back to the president in Washington in order to be disbursed (*Freedom*, 1320).

There is compelling evidence, however, that in the spring of 1863 the administration was deeply concerned about Republican electoral prospects in New England and devoted considerable resources from the federal government to ensure the defeat of "peace" Democrats. See William B. Hesseltine, *Lincoln and the War Governors* (New York: Knopf, 1948), chap. 15, and John Niven, *Connecticut for the Union: The Role of the State in the Civil War* (New Haven, Conn.: Yale University Press, 1965), 305–8.

37. See *Totten, Administrator*, v. *United States*, 92 U.S. 105 (1875).

38. See Jeffrey M. Dorwart, *The Office of Naval Intelligence: The Birth of America's First Intelligence Agency, 1865–1918* (Annapolis, Md.: Naval Institute Press, 1979).

39. Secretary of State Foster was the grandfather of future CIA director Allen Dulles. See Rhodri Jeffreys-Jones, *American Espionage: From Secret Service to CIA* (New York: Free Press, 1977), 27.

40. See Henry B. Cox, *War, Foreign Affairs, and Constitutional Power, 1829–1901* (Cambridge, Mass.: Ballinger, 1984), 258–60, and Julius W. Pratt, *Expansionists of 1898: The Acquisition of Hawaii and the Spanish Islands* (Baltimore: Johns Hopkins University Press, 1936), 69, 69n.83. These two authors had access to material related to both "the open historical aspect" and "matters of personal intrigue."

41. Cox, *War, Foreign Affairs, and Constitutional Power*, 306–8.

42. Pratt, *Expansionists*, 52–53.

43. Ibid., 54–57, 57n.61.

44. Ibid., 60–61.

45. Ibid., 70–72. Pratt notes that a newspaper where John Stevens had formerly been employed was one of the first to publish accounts of British intrigue in the islands (ibid., 70n.86). He also cites a report from a Hawaiian envoy that accused the State and Navy Departments of leaking reports to the press (ibid., 72n.91).

46. Cox, *War, Foreign Affairs, and Constitutional Power*, 306–8. On October 27, 1993, the Senate offered an apology to native Hawaiians on behalf of the United States for the ousting of their monarchy. Senator Daniel Inouye of Hawaii stated that this "illegal act" had overthrown "our Queen." However, opponents to the measure, such as Colorado Senator Hank Brown, protested that the Senate was apologizing for "having replaced a monarchy with a representative democracy." The resolution passed on a 65 to 34 vote. See *Congressional Record*, Senate, 103rd Cong., 1st sess., October 27, 1993, 139, no. 147.

47. Dorwart, *Office of Naval Intelligence*, 23.

48. See Thomas F. Troy, "The Quaintness of the U.S. Intelligence Community: Its Origin, Theory, and Problems," *International Journal of Intelligence and Counterintelligence* 2, no. 2 (Summer 1988): 245–47, and Rhodri Jeffreys-Jones, *The CIA and American Democracy* (New Haven, Conn.: Yale University Press, 1989), 13–14.

49. Jeffreys-Jones, *American Espionage*, chaps. 2, 3, and Fred L. Israel, ed., *U.S. Secret Service* (New York: Chelsea House, 1987).

50. Dorwart, *Office of Naval Intelligence*, 64–65.

51. See Edward F. Sayle, "The Historical Underpinnings of the U.S. Intelligence Community," *International Journal of Intelligence and Counterintelligence* 1, no. 1 (Spring 1986): 20–21.

52. Dorwart, *Office of Naval Intelligence*, chap. 14; Troy, "Quaintness of U.S. Intelligence," 246.

53. Dorwart, *Office of Naval Intelligence*, 102.

54. See U.S. Congress, Senate, *Final Report of the Select Committee to Study Governmental Operations with Respect to Intelligence Activities: Supplementary Report on Intelligence Activities,* S. Rept. 94–755, 94th Cong., 2d sess., 1976, 90, and Dorwart, *Office of Naval Intelligence*, 129–30.

55. See George Creel to Woodrow Wilson, October 24, 1917, and Wilson to Creel, October 24, 1917, in *The Papers of Woodrow Wilson,* ed. Arthur S. Link, 44:434–35 (Princeton, N.J.: Princeton University Press, 1983), and Creel to Edgar Grant Sisson, December 3, 1917, ibid., 45:194.

56. Dorwart, *Office of Naval Intelligence*, 103–4, 130.

57. Ibid., 133.

58. See Josephus Daniels, *The Wilson Era: Years of War and After, 1917–1923* (Chapel Hill: University of North Carolina Press, 1946), 627.

59. Woodrow Wilson to Secretary of State Robert Lansing, August 30, 1917, in *Papers of Woodrow Wilson,* ed. Link, 44:90–91, 91n.1.

60. Frederick Katz, *The Secret War in Mexico: Europe, the United States, and the Mexican Revolution* (Chicago: University of Chicago Press, 1981), 453–59.

61. "Historians: US Plotted to Poison Villa," *Boston Globe,* May 29, 1988, 13.

62. Quoted in Sayle, "Historical Underpinnings," 23.

63. See John Ranelagh, *The Agency: The Rise and Decline of the CIA* (New York: Simon and Schuster, 1986), 27.

64. The American tradition of opening mail for national security reasons has deep historical roots. One of George Washington's earliest directives upon assuming command of the Continental Army was to issue an order for "seizing . . . the mail by the next packet" because of the "inumerable" [*sic*] advantages that would result from such an act. See William Corson, *The Armies of Ignorance: The Rise of the American Intelligence Empire* (New York: Dial Press, 1977), 504.

65. Troy, "Quaintness of U.S. Intelligence," 245–47; Jeffreys-Jones, *CIA and American Democracy,* 13–15.

66. See Jeffreys-Jones, *CIA and American Democracy,* 14–19, and Troy, "Quaintness of U.S. Intelligence," 249–50.

67. The OSS had no jurisdiction in Latin America, which fell under the purview of the FBI. In addition, General Douglas MacArthur would not allow the OSS to operate in the Pacific theater. Interview with Walter L. Pforzheimer, former CIA legislative counsel, May 1991.

68. Ranelagh, *Agency,* chap. 2.

69. Interview with Walter L. Pforzheimer, May 1991.

70. The question arose again in another form in 1953, when it became necessary to obtain statutory authority for a deputy DCI. In the course of passing such legislation, the Senate included provisions for senatorial confirmation for nominees to both these posts and stipulated that only one of the positions could be occupied by a military man at any time. Interview with Walter L. Pforzheimer, May 1991.

71. See Jeffreys-Jones, *CIA and American Democracy,* chap. 2; Ranelagh, *Agency,* chaps. 3, 4; and Anne Karalekas, "History of the Central Intelligence Agency," in *The Central Intelligence Agency: History and Documents,* ed. William M. Leary (Mobile: University of Alabama Press, 1984), 27.

72. See Jeffreys-Jones, *CIA and American Democracy,* chap. 3.

73. The text of the act states that "for objects of a confidential, extraordinary, or emergency nature, such expenditures are to be accounted for solely on the certificate of the Director, and every such certificate shall be deemed a sufficient voucher for the amount therein certified." Thus the accounting is based solely on the director's certificate of expenditure. Interview with Walter L. Pforzheimer, May 1991.

74. Ranelagh, *Agency,* 193–95.

75. Ibid., 260–69; Gregory Treverton, *Covert Action: The Limits of Intervention in the Postwar World* (New York: Basic Books, 1987), chap. 2 and 178.

Chapter 8

1. U.S. Congress, Senate, *Final Report of the Select Committee to Study Governmental Operations with Respect to Intelligence Activities, Foreign and Military Intelligence,* S. Rept. 94–755, 94th Cong., 2d sess., 1976, bk. 1, 152. (Hereafter cited as Church Committee, *Final Report*)

2. Anne Karalekas, "History of the Central Intelligence Agency," in *The

Central Intelligence Agency: History and Documents, ed. William M. Leary (Mobile: University of Alabama Press, 1984), 51.

3. Ibid.

4. Ibid., 67.

5. Ibid., 50–52. According to Walter L. Pforzheimer, the authorization bills were created with the establishment of the Senate Select Committee on Intelligence and the House Permanent Select Committee on Intelligence. Prior to their establishment, the chairmen of the House and Senate Appropriations committees wrote to the director of the Bureau of the Budget (now the Office of Management and Budget) certifying the amounts of the budget that had been approved. Interview with Walter L. Pforzheimer, May 1991.

6. Interview with Walter L. Pforzheimer, May 1991; Karalekas, "History of the CIA," 50–52.

7. Karalekas, "History of the CIA," 50–52.

8. Harry Howe Ransom, *The Intelligence Establishment* (Cambridge, Mass.: Harvard University Press, 1970), 159–60.

9. Quoted in ibid., 163.

10. John Ranelagh, *The Agency: The Rise and Decline of the CIA* (New York: Simon and Schuster, 1986), 281–85; Rhodri Jeffreys-Jones, *The CIA and American Democracy* (New Haven, Conn.: Yale University Press, 1989), 78–80, 178; Ransom, *Intelligence Establishment,* 163–79.

11. Ranelagh, *Agency,* 284–85, 479–82.

12. Ibid., 481.

13. Quoted in Tyrus G. Fain, Katherine C. Plant, and Ross Milloy, eds., *The Intelligence Community: History, Organization, and Issues* (New York: Bowker, 1977), 521.

14. U.S. Congress, Senate, S. Res. 3394, amendment no. 1922, *Congressional Record,* 93rd Cong., 2d sess., October 2, 1974, 33477.

15. Ibid.

16. Ibid.

17. Ibid., 33481.

18. Ibid., 33482.

19. Ranelagh, *Agency,* 572–73.

20. See Thomas Powers, *The Man Who Kept the Secrets: Richard Helms and the CIA* (New York: Pocket Books, 1979), 314–20.

21. William Colby and Peter Forbath, *Honorable Men: My Life in the CIA* (New York: Simon and Schuster, 1978), 314–15.

22. Loch K. Johnson, *A Season of Inquiry: Congress and Intelligence* (Chicago: Dorsey Press, 1988), 11.

23. See Gregory Treverton, *Covert Action: The Limits of Intervention in the Postwar World* (New York: Basic Books, 1987), 237–38.

24. Gerald R. Ford, *A Time to Heal* (New York: Harper & Row, 1979), xxv.

25. Quoted in Gary J. Schmitt and Abram N. Shulsky, "The Theory and Practice of Separation of Powers: The Case of Covert Action," in *The Fettered Presidency: Legal Constraints on the Executive Branch,* ed. L. Gordon Crovitz and Jeremy A. Rabkin (Washington, D.C.: American Enterprise Institute, 1989), 64.

26. Jeffreys-Jones, *CIA and American Democracy,* 144.

27. *Congressional Quarterly Almanac,* 94th Cong., 2d sess., 32:303.

28. U.S. Congress, Senate, *Final Report of the Select Committee to Study Governmental Operations with Respect to Intelligence Activities: Supplementary Report on Intelligence Activities,* S. Rept. 94–755, 94th Cong., 2d sess., 1976, bk. 6.

29. Church Committee, *Final Report,* bk. 1, 6.

30. Ibid., 9–10.

31. Ibid., 34, 34n.19.

32. Henry M. Wriston, *Executive Agents in American Foreign Policy* (Baltimore: Johns Hopkins University Press, 1929).

33. Church Committee, *Final Report,* 35, 35n.25. The report says this process began in 1793, rather than in 1790.

34. Ibid., 34.

35. Ibid., 152.

36. Ibid., 33n.15. See also *Totten, Administrator, v. United States,* 92 U.S. 105 (1875).

37. Church Committee, *Final Report,* 201.

38. Ibid., 203.

39. For a discussion of Hale's mission and his academic "cover," see Edmund R. Thompson, "Nathan Hale's Necessary Service," in *Secret New England: Spies of the American Revolution* (Kennebunk, Maine: Association of Former Intelligence Officers, 1991), chap. 3.

40. Johnson, *Season of Inquiry,* 215.

41. Ibid., 221.

42. Ranelagh, *Agency,* 385.

43. Ibid., 383–90.

44. See Johnson, *Season of Inquiry,* chap. 4, and Ranelagh, *Agency,* 336–45.

45. Johnson, *Season of Inquiry,* 57.

46. Ranelagh, *Agency,* 336.

47. Johnson, *Season of Inquiry,* 46.

48. Ibid., 52; Ranelagh, *Agency,* 596.

49. Johnson, *Season of Inquiry,* 55.

50. Jefferson to Madison, August 28, 1789, *Jefferson's Papers,* 15:367.

51. Burke Davis, *Get Yamamoto* (New York: Random House, 1969), 10. Davis alleges that President Franklin Roosevelt personally approved the plan to kill Yamamoto.

52. See Jefferson to President Monroe, June 11, 1823, *Jefferson's Writings,* 7:288. Dumas Malone notes that Jefferson "had long coveted Cuba for strategic reasons" (*Jefferson and His Time: The Sage of Monticello* [Boston: Little, Brown, 1981], 429).

53. Quoted in *Congressional Quarterly Almanac,* 94th Cong., 2d sess., 1976, 32:308.

54. Quoted in Church Committee, *Final Report,* bk. 1, 9.

55. Quoted in Johnson, *Season of Inquiry,* 137.

56. "Toward Restoring the CIA," *Time,* September 29, 1975, 24.

57. "Church: 'Entering the 1984 Decade,'" *Time,* March 24, 1975, 26.

58. U.S. Congress, Senate, Senator Frank Church speaking on behalf of Senate Resolution 400, *Congressional Record,* 94th Cong., 2d sess., May 13, 1976, S 13981.

59. *Congressional Quarterly Almanac,* 94th Cong., 2d sess., 1976, 32:308.

60. U.S. Congress, Senate, Senator Charles Mathias speaking on behalf of Senate Resolution 400, *Congressional Record,* 94th Cong., 2d sess., May 12, 1976, S 13695.

61. U.S. Congress, Senate, Senator Walter Mondale speaking on behalf of Senate Resolution 400, *Congressional Record,* 94th Cong., 2d sess., May 13, 1976, S 13979 and May 17, 1976, S 14157.

62. U.S. Congress, Senate, Senator Edmund Muskie speaking on behalf of Senate Resolution 400, *Congressional Record,* 94th Cong., 2d sess., May 19, 1976, S 14651.

63. Johnson, *Season of Inquiry,* 102.

64. Ibid., 184.

65. Ibid., 208–9.

66. Quoted in Judith F. Buncher, ed., *The CIA and the Security Debate: 1971–1975,* (New York: Facts on File, 1976), 24.

67. Quoted in Jeffreys-Jones, *CIA and American Democracy,* 83.

68. Ibid., 217.

69. *The Presidential Campaign, 1976, Volume One, Part One, Jimmy Carter* (Washington, D.C.: Government Printing Office, 1978), 306.

70. Ibid., 314.

71. Ibid., 697.

72. Ibid., 111.

73. See Jules Witcover, *Marathon: The Pursuit of the Presidency, 1972–1976* (New York: Viking Press, 1977), 547.

74. Jeffreys-Jones, *CIA and American Democracy,* 217.

75. Powers, *Man Who Kept the Secrets,* 9.

76. "Where Spies Really Matter," *U.S. News & World Report,* September 4, 1989, 24.

77. See Bretton G. Sciaroni, "The Theory and Practice of Executive Branch Intelligence Oversight," *Harvard Journal of Law and Public Policy* 12, no. 2 (Spring 1989): 407–8.

78. See Loch Johnson, "Controlling the CIA: A Critique of Current Safeguards," *Harvard Journal of Law and Public Policy* 12, no. 2 (Spring 1989): 388.

79. Ibid., 386.

80. For an example of this attitude, see Johnson, *Season of Inquiry.* Johnson lauds those senators who engage in vigorous oversight of the intelligence community due to their "dedication to the principle that close supervision of the bureaucracy is necessary for the proper control of government" (264).

81. "CIA Nominee Expected to Win Senate Backing," *New York Times,* February 19, 1987, A-1.

82. "A CIA Insider Looks at the Battle over Intelligence," *Washington Post,* November 29, 1987, L-1.

83. Bob Woodward, *Veil: The Secret Wars of the CIA, 1981–1987* (New York: Pocket Books, 1987), 265–66; "C.I.A. Reported Blocked in Plot on Surinamese," *New York Times,* June 1, 1983, A-1.

84. "Cloak-and-Dagger Relics," *Washington Post,* November 14, 1985, A-23. Helms's opposition was not to covert action per se, but to the potential beneficiaries of such action; he supported the rightist ARENA party rather than Duarte.

85. "Mighty Mouth," *New Republic,* September 1, 1986, 20.

86. See Woodward, *CIA Secret Wars,* 89–91, 166–69.

87. Quoted in Schmitt and Shulsky, "Theory and Practice of Separation of Powers," 79n.53.

88. "How to Reduce Leaks," *Washington Times,* October 12, 1987, D-4.

89. Woodward, *CIA Secret Wars,* 479–82.

90. Donald F. B. Jameson, "The 'Iran Affair,' Presidential Authority and Covert Operations," *Strategic Review* 15, no. 1 (Winter 1987): 29.

91. *Congressional Quarterly Almanac,* 100th Cong., 1st sess., 1987, 158.

92. "Wright Says CIA Fomented Nicaragua Unrest," *Boston Globe,* September 21, 1988, 3; "Wright on Hot Seat over CIA Remarks," *Boston Globe,* September 23, 1988, 6.

93. Quoted in Edward F. Sayle, "The Historical Underpinnings of the U.S. Intelligence Community," *International Journal of Intelligence and Counterintelligence* 1, no. 1 (Spring 1986): 5–6.

94. Powers, *Man Who Kept the Secrets,* 227.

95. See Treverton, *Covert Action,* 253, and Iran-Contra Report, 489.

96. Woodward notes that the public exposure of the mining operation occurred on the Senate floor when a "well-medicated" Senator Goldwater, who was suffering from medical problems, rose to speak "after the cocktail hour" (*CIA Secret Wars,* 361–62). Although the senator's remarks were removed from the *Congressional Record,* a reporter from the *Wall Street Journal* heard about them the next day.

97. "Can Congress Keep a Secret?" *National Review,* August 24, 1984, 46.

98. Woodward, *CIA Secret Wars,* 368.

99. "U.S. Officials Say Senators Balked at Noriega Ouster," *New York Times,* April 24, 1989, A-1.

100. "The Stovepipe Problem," *Time,* November 6, 1989, 35.

101. "White House, Noriega, and Battle in Congress," *New York Times,* October 25, 1989, A-10.

102. "Doubts Aired on CIA Policy," *Boston Globe,* April 7, 1990.

103. "Inside the Invasion," *Newsweek,* June 25, 1990, 28–31.

104. *The MacNeil-Lehrer NewsHour,* PBS, July 3, 1989.

105. See Edward F. Sayle, "The Déjà Vu of American Secret Diplomacy," *International Journal of Intelligence and Counterintelligence* 2, no. 3 (Fall 1988): 400.

106. See James Thomas Flexner, *George Washington and the New Nation, 1783–1793* (Boston: Little, Brown, 1969), 357.

107. See Iran-Contra Report, 489–500.

108. Ibid., 375.

109. See *Taking the Stand: The Testimony of Lieutenant Colonel Oliver L. North* (New York: Pocket Books, 1987), 722–23.

110. Bill Moyers, *The Secret Government: The Constitution in Crisis* (Cabin John, Md.: Seven Locks Press, 1988), 16.

111. "Wright, in Gesture to Bush, Shelves Bill on Covert Acts," *New York Times,* February 1, 1989, A-12.

112. "Bush Agrees to Notify Congress on Covert Actions," *New York Times,* October 27, 1989, A-9.

113. "The CIA Gets a New Watchdog," *Newsweek,* December 11, 1989, 46.

114. "Senate Debates Independent CIA Inspector," *New York Times*, November 8, 1989, A-22; U.S. Congress, Senate, Senator Ernest Hollings speaking for an amendment that would strike out provisions relating to the inspector general, S 1324, *Congressional Record*, 101st Cong., 1st sess., November 7, 1989, S 15114.

115. Ibid.

116. In April 1986, President Reagan ordered a military strike against Libya using units of the air force and navy. Qaddafi's operatives had been linked to the bombing of a Berlin disco in which an American serviceman was killed and fifty other servicemen were injured. In the view of some observers, the primary purpose of the strike was to assassinate Qaddafi. See Seymour M. Hersh, "Target Qaddafi," *New York Times Magazine*, February 22, 1987, 17. Woodward notes that prior to the raid, the French turned down American requests for assistance out of a belief that the United States would not design a plan that would "finish him off" (*CIA Secret Wars*, 510).

117. According to Hersh, there was some concern among the House Select Committee on Intelligence that one CIA plan aimed at Qaddafi might lead to his assassination; this prompted the administration to send Secretary of State George Shultz to appear before the committee to prevent a veto of the operation ("Target Qaddafi," 48).

118. David Newman and Tyll Van Geel, "Executive Order 12, 333: The Risks of a Clear Declaration of Intent," *Harvard Journal of Law and Public Policy* 12, no. 2 (Spring 1989): 433–47.

119. "Building a Better Coup," *Newsweek*, October 30, 1989, 55.

120. This is the conclusion put forth in Newman and Van Geel, "Executive Order," 447.

121. "CIA Is Said to Get Leeway in Policy on Assassination," *Boston Globe*, April 3, 1990, 1; "CIA Seeks Looser Rules on Killings During Coups," *New York Times*, October 17, 1989, A-1.

122. "Assassinations: Can't We Learn?" *New York Times*, October 20, 1989, A-35.

123. See Iran-Contra Report, 583–85.

124. "Safety in the Skies," *Boston Globe*, May 17, 1990, 14.

125. Edward Jay Epstein, *Deception: The Invisible War Between the KGB and the CIA* (New York: Simon and Schuster, 1989).

126. See Charles Ameringer, *U.S. Foreign Intelligence: The Secret Side of American History* (Lexington, Mass.: Lexington Books, 1990), 244. Ameringer has compiled a list, based on public documents, of CIA covert operations since 1948. By no means exhaustive, the list nonetheless indicates that the bulk of the CIA's targets were Soviet client states or nations perceived to be targets of Soviet-sponsored insurgencies.

127. See Fred F. Manget, "Presidential War Powers," in *Extracts from Studies in Intelligence: A Commemoration of the Bicentennial of the U.S. Constitution* (Washington, D.C.: Central Intelligence Agency, 1987), 103.

128. *Public Papers of the Presidents of the United States: John F. Kennedy, January 20 to December 31, 1961* (Washington, D.C.: Government Printing Office, 1962), 753.

Bibliography

Books and Articles

Adams, Henry. *History of the United States During the Administrations of James Madison*. New York: Library of America, 1986.

———. *History of the United States During the Administrations of Thomas Jefferson*. New York: Library of America, 1986.

Adams, John Quincy. *Memoirs of John Quincy Adams: Comprising Portions of His Diary from 1795 to 1848*. Edited by Charles Francis Adams. 12 vols. Philadelphia: Lippincott, 1874–1877.

Ameringer, Charles D. *U.S. Foreign Intelligence: The Secret Side of American History*. Lexington, Mass.: Lexington Books, 1990.

Ammon, Harry. *James Monroe: The Quest for National Identity*. New York: McGraw-Hill, 1971.

Andrew, Christopher. *For the President's Eyes Only: Secret Intelligence and the American Presidency from Washington to Bush*. New York: Harper-Collins, 1995.

Auger, Helen. *The Secret War of Independence*. New York: Duell, Sloan, and Pearce, 1955.

Bakeless, John. "General Washington's Spy System." *Manuscripts* 12, no. 2 (Spring 1960).

———. *Lewis and Clark: Partners in Discovery*. New York: Morrow, 1947.

———. *Turncoats, Traitors, and Heroes*. Philadelphia: Lippincott, 1959.

Barker, Eugene. "President Jackson and the Texas Revolution." *American Historical Review* 12, no. 4 (July 1907).

Baxter, Maurice. *One and Inseparable: Daniel Webster and the Union*. Cambridge, Mass.: Belknap Press, 1984.

Bemis, Samuel Flagg. *John Quincy Adams and the Foundations of American Foreign Policy*. Westport, Conn.: Greenwood Press, 1949.

———, ed. *The American Secretaries of State and Their Diplomacy*. 17 vols. New York: Knopf, 1927–1967.

Bergeron, Paul. *The Presidency of James K. Polk*. Lawrence: University Press of Kansas, 1987.

Bidwell, Bruce. *History of the Military Intelligence Division, Department of the Army General Staff: 1775–1941*. Frederick, Md.: University Publications of America, 1986.

Bigelow, John. *France and the Confederate Navy, 1862–1868*. New York: Harper, 1888.

Biographical Directory of the American Congress, 1774–1927. Washington, D.C.: Government Printing Office, 1928.

Boyd, George. *Elias Boudinot: Patriot and Statesman, 1740–1821*. Princeton, N.J.: Princeton University Press, 1952.

Brant, Irving. *James Madison*. 6 vols. Indianapolis: Bobbs-Merrill, 1941–1961.

Bullard, F. Lauriston. "Abraham Lincoln and George Ashmun." *New England Quarterly* 19, no. 1 (March 1946).

Buncher, Judith F., ed. *The CIA and the Security Debate: 1971–1975*. New York: Facts on File, 1976.

Burnett, Edmund C., ed. *Letters of Members of the Continental Congress*. 8 vols. Washington, D.C.: Carnegie Institution, 1921.

Butterfield, Lyman. "Psychological Warfare in 1776: The Jefferson–Franklin Plan to Cause Hessian Desertions." *Proceedings of the American Philosophical Society* 94, no. 3 (June 1950).

Carman, Harry, and Reinhard Luthin. *Lincoln and the Patronage*. New York: Columbia University Press, 1943.

Case, Lynn, and Warren Spencer. *The United States and France: Civil War Diplomacy*. Philadelphia: University of Pennsylvania Press, 1970.

Casey, William J. *Where and How the War Was Fought: An Armchair Tour of the American Revolution*. New York: Morrow, 1976.

Cecil, Robert. "The Thinking Behind Intelligence." *Times Literary Supplement*, November 10–16, 1989.

Central Intelligence Agency. *Intelligence in the War of Independence*. Washington, D.C.: CIA, 1976.

Cifelli, Edward. *David Humphreys*. Boston: Twayne, 1982.

Clapp, Margaret. *Forgotten First Citizen: John Bigelow*. Boston: Little, Brown, 1947.

Clark, William. *Ben Franklin's Privateers: A Naval Epic of the American Revolution*. Baton Rouge: Louisiana State University Press, 1956.

———. "John the Painter." *Pennsylvania Magazine of History and Biography* 63, no. 1 (January 1939).

Claussen, Martin. "Peace Factors in Anglo-American Relations." *Mississippi Valley Historical Review* 27, no. 1 (June 1940).

Clay, Henry. *The Papers of Henry Clay*. Edited by James F. Hopkins. 10 vols. and supplemental vol. Lexington: University Press of Kentucky, 1959–1992.

Cohen, William S. "Congressional Oversight of Covert Actions: The Public's Stake in the Forty-Eight Hour Rule." *Harvard Journal of Law and Public Policy* 12, no. 2 (Spring 1989).

Colby, William, and Peter Forbath. *Honorable Men: My Life in the CIA*. New York: Simon and Schuster, 1978.

Commager, Henry S. "'Intelligence': The Constitution Betrayed." *New York Review of Books*, September 30, 1976.

Constantinides, George. *Intelligence and Espionage: An Analytical Bibliography*. Boulder, Colo.: Westview Press, 1983.

Corson, William. *The Armies of Ignorance: The Rise of the American Intelligence Empire*. New York: Dial Press, 1977.

Corwin, Edward. *The President's Control of Foreign Relations.* Princeton, N.J.: Princeton University Press, 1917.

Cox, Henry. "Reasons for Joel Poinsett's Refusal of a Second Mission to South America." *Hispanic American Historical Review* 43, no. 3 (August 1963).

———. *War, Foreign Affairs, and Constitutional Power, 1829–1901.* Cambridge, Mass.: Ballinger, 1984.

Cox, Isaac J. "The American Intervention in West Florida." *American Historical Review* 17, no. 2 (January 1912).

———. "The Border Missions of General George Mathews." *Mississippi Valley Historical Review* 12, no. 3 (December 1925).

———. "The New Invasion of the Goths and the Vandals." *Proceedings of the Mississippi Valley Historical Review of the Year 1914–15* 3 (1916).

———. *The West Florida Controversy, 1798–1813: A Study in American Diplomacy.* Baltimore: Johns Hopkins University Press, 1918.

Cronin, Thomas, ed. *Inventing the American Presidency.* Lawrence: University Press of Kansas, 1989.

Crouthamel, James. *Bennett's "New York Herald" and the Rise of the Popular Press.* Syracuse, N.Y.: Syracuse University Press, 1989.

Crovitz, L. Gordon, and Jeremy A. Rabkin, eds. *The Fettered Presidency: Legal Constraints on the Executive Branch.* Washington, D.C.: American Enterprise Institute, 1989.

Cullop, Charles. *Confederate Propaganda in Europe, 1861–1865.* Coral Gables, Fla.: University of Miami Press, 1969.

Current, Richard. "Webster's Propaganda and the Ashburton Treaty." *Mississippi Valley Historical Review* 34, no. 2 (September 1947).

Daniels, Josephus. *The Wilson Era: Years of War and After, 1917–1923.* Chapel Hill: University of North Carolina Press, 1946.

Davis, Burke. *Get Yamamoto.* New York: Random House, 1969.

Dearmont, Nelson. "Federalist Attitudes Toward Governmental Secrecy in the Age of Jefferson." *Historian* 37, no. 2 (February 1975).

DeConde, Alexander. *A History of American Foreign Policy.* New York: Scribner's, 1971.

Diamond, Martin, Winston Mills Fisk, and Herbert Garfinkel. *The Democratic Republic: An Introduction to American National Government.* Chicago: Rand McNally, 1970.

Dorwart, Jeffrey. *The Office of Naval Intelligence: The Birth of America's First Intelligence Agency, 1865–1918.* Annapolis, Md.: Naval Institute Press, 1979.

Edwards, Samuel. *Barbary General: The Life of William H. Eaton.* Englewood Cliffs, N.J.: Prentice-Hall, 1968.

Epstein, Edward J. *Deception: The Invisible War Between the KGB and the CIA.* New York: Simon and Schuster, 1988.

Fain, Tyrus G., Katherine Plant, and Ross Milloy. *The Intelligence Community: History, Organization, and Issues.* New York: Bowker, 1977.

Flexner, James T. *George Washington and the New Nation, 1783–1793.* Boston: Little, Brown, 1969.

———. *George Washington in the American Revolution, 1775–1783.* Boston: Little, Brown, 1967.

Flick, Alexander. *Loyalism in New York During the American Revolution.* New York: Columbia University Press, 1901.

Ford, Corey. *A Peculiar Service: A Narrative of Espionage in and Around New York During the American Revolution.* Boston: Little, Brown, 1965.

Ford, Gerald R. *A Time to Heal.* New York: Harper & Row, 1979.

Ford, Worthington, ed. *Journals of the Continental Congress, 1774–1789.* 34 vols. Washington, D.C.: Government Printing Office, 1904–1937.

Franklin, Benjamin. *The Writings of Benjamin Franklin.* Edited by Albert Smyth. 10 vols. London: Macmillan, 1905–1907.

French, Allen. *General Gage's Informers.* Ann Arbor: University of Michigan Press, 1932.

Fry, Joseph. *Henry S. Sanford: Diplomacy and Business in Nineteenth Century America.* Reno: University of Nevada Press, 1982.

Gales, Joseph, comp. *Annals of Congress, 1789–1824.* 42 vols. Washington, D.C.: Gales and Seaton, 1834–1856.

Goldsmith, William. *The Growth of Presidential Power: A Documented History.* 3 vols. New York: Chelsea House, 1974.

Guilday, Peter. *The Life and Times of John Carroll, Archbishop of Baltimore, 1735–1815.* Westminster, Md.: Newman Press, 1954.

Hall, Charles S. *Benjamin Tallmadge: Revolutionary Soldier and American Businessman.* New York: Columbia University Press, 1943.

Hamilton, Alexander. *The Papers of Alexander Hamilton.* Edited by Harold Syrett. 27 vols. New York: Columbia University Press, 1961–1975.

Hamilton, Alexander, James Madison, and John Jay. *The Federalist.* Edited by Jacob Cooke. Middletown, Conn.: Wesleyan University Press, 1961.

Hargreaves, Mary. *The Presidency of John Quincy Adams.* Lawrence: University Press of Kansas, 1985.

Hazard, Blanche. *Beaumarchais and the American Revolution.* Boston: Slocomb, 1910.

Henderson, H. James. *Party Politics in the Continental Congress.* New York: McGraw-Hill, 1974.

Hesseltine, William. *Lincoln and the War Governors.* New York: Knopf, 1948.

Hitchcock, Ethan Allen. *Fifty Years in Camp and Field.* New York: Putnam, 1909.

Horsman, Reginald. "American Indian Policy in the Old Northwest, 1783–1812." *William and Mary Quarterly* 18, no. 1 (January 1961).

———. *Expansion and American Indian Policy, 1783–1812.* East Lansing: Michigan State University Press, 1967.

Ind, Allison. *A Short History of Espionage.* New York: McKay, 1963.

Israel, Fred L. *U.S. Secret Service.* New York: Chelsea House, 1987.

Jackson, Andrew. *Correspondence of Andrew Jackson.* Edited by John Spencer Bassett. 7 vols. Washington, D.C.: Carnegie Institution, 1926–1935.

Jameson, Donald F. B. "The 'Iran Affair': Presidential Authority and Covert Operations." *Strategic Review* 15, no. 1 (Winter 1987).

Jay, John. *The Correspondence and Public Papers of John Jay, 1763–1826.* Edited by Henry Johnston. New York: Da Capo Press, 1971.

———. *John Jay: The Making of a Revolutionary—Unpublished Papers, 1745–1780.* Edited by Richard Morris. New York: Harper & Row, 1975.

Jay, William. *The Life of John Jay with Selections from his Correspondence and Miscellaneous Papers.* New York: Harper, 1833.

Jefferson, Thomas. *The Life and Selected Writings of Thomas Jefferson.* Edited by Adrienne Koch and William Peden. New York: Modern Library, 1944.

———. *The Papers of Thomas Jefferson.* Edited by Julian Boyd. 28 vols. Princeton, N.J.: Princeton University Press, 1950–.

———. *The Works of Thomas Jefferson.* Edited by Paul Ford. 12 vols. New York: Knickerbocker Press, 1905.

———. *The Writings of Thomas Jefferson.* Edited by H. A. Washington. 9 vols. Washington, D.C.: Taylor and Maury, 1853.

Jeffreys-Jones, Rhodri. *American Espionage: From Secret Service to CIA.* New York: Free Press, 1977.

———. *The CIA and American Democracy.* New Haven, Conn.: Yale University Press, 1989.

Johnson, Loch. *America's Secret Power: The CIA in a Democratic Society.* New York: Oxford University Press, 1989.

———. "Controlling the CIA: A Critique of Current Safeguards." *Harvard Journal of Law and Public Policy* 12, no. 2 (Spring 1989).

———. *A Season of Inquiry: Congress and Intelligence.* Chicago: Dorsey Press, 1988.

Journals of the Continental Congress. Washington, D.C.: Government Printing Office, 1906.

Kahn, David. *The Codebreakers: The Story of Secret Writing.* New York: Macmillan, 1967.

Kaplan, Lawrence. *Colonies into Nation: American Diplomacy, 1763–1801.* New York: Macmillan, 1972.

Katz, Frederick. *The Secret War in Mexico: Europe, the United States, and the Mexican Revolution.* Chicago: University of Chicago Press, 1981.

Kiger, John. "Federal Governmental Propaganda in Great Britain During the American Civil War." *Historical Outlook* 19, no. 5 (May 1928).

Kruse, Paul. "A Secret Agent in East Florida: General George Mathews and the Patriot War." *Journal of Southern History* 18, no. 2 (May 1952).

Lanctot, Gustave. *Canada and the American Revolution, 1774–1783.* Cambridge, Mass.: Harvard University Press, 1967.

Laurens, Henry. *The Papers of Henry Laurens.* Edited by David Chesnutt. 11 vols. Columbia: University of South Carolina Press, 1968–1988.

Lavender, David. *The American Heritage History of the Great West.* New York: American Heritage, 1965.

Leary, William M., ed. *The Central Intelligence Agency: History and Documents.* Mobile: University of Alabama Press, 1984.

Lee, Richard Henry. *Life of Arthur Lee, L.L.D., Joint Commissioner of the United States to the Court of France, and Sole Commissioner to the Court of Spain and Prussia, During the Revolutionary War.* Boston: Wells and Lilly, 1829.

Lincoln, Abraham. *The Collected Works of Abraham Lincoln.* Edited by Roy Basler. 9 vols. New Brunswick, N.J.: Rutgers University Press, 1953–1955.

Maclay, William. *The Journal of William Maclay, United States Senator from Pennsylvania, 1789–1791.* New York: Boni, 1927.

Madison, James. *Letters and Other Writings of James Madison, Fourth President of the United States.* Published by order of Congress. Philadelphia: Lippincott, 1865.

———. *Notes of Debates in the Federal Convention of 1787.* New York: Norton, 1987.

———. *The Writings of James Madison.* Edited by Gaillard Hunt. 9 vols. New York: Putnam, 1900–1910.

Malone, Dumas. *Jefferson and His Time.* 6 vols. Boston: Little, Brown, 1948–1981.

Manget, Fred F. "Presidential War Powers." In *Extracts from Studies in Intelligence: A Commemoration of the Bicentennial of the U.S. Constitution.* Washington, D.C.: Central Intelligence Agency, 1987.

Mann, Thomas, ed. *A Question of Balance: The President, the Congress, and Foreign Policy.* Washington, D.C.: Brookings Institution, 1990.

Manning, William, ed. *Diplomatic Correspondence of the United States: Inter-American Affairs, 1831–1860.* 12 vols. Washington, D.C.: Carnegie Endowment, 1932–1939.

———. *Diplomatic Correspondence of the United States Concerning the Independence of the Latin American Nations.* 3 vols. New York: Oxford University Press, 1925.

Marston, Jerrilyn. *King and Congress: The Transfer of Political Legitimacy, 1774–1776.* Princeton, N.J.: Princeton University Press, 1987.

Mason, Bernard. *The Road to Independence: The Revolutionary Movement in New York, 1773–1777.* Lexington: University of Kentucky Press, 1966.

McDonald, Forrest. *E Pluribus Unum: The Formation of the American Republic, 1776–1790.* Indianapolis: Liberty Press, 1979.

Melville, Annabelle. *John Carroll of Baltimore: Founder of the American Catholic Hierarchy.* New York: Scribner's, 1955.

Merk, Frederick. *Fruits of Propaganda in the Tyler Administration.* Cambridge, Mass.: Harvard University Press, 1971.

Meyers, Marvin. *The Mind of the Founder: Sources of the Political Thought of James Madison.* Hanover, N.H.: University Press of New England, 1981.

Middlekauff, Robert. *The Glorious Cause: The American Revolution, 1763–1789.* New York: Oxford University Press, 1982.

Miller, David. *Secret Statutes of the United States.* Washington, D.C.: Government Printing Office, 1918.

Miller, Nathan. *Spying for America: The Hidden History of U.S. Intelligence.* New York: Paragon House, 1989.

Mitchell, Broadus. *Alexander Hamilton: Youth to Maturity, 1755–1788.* New York: Macmillan, 1957.

Monaghan, Frank. *John Jay.* New York: Bobbs-Merrill, 1935.

Monaghan, Jay. *Diplomat in Carpet Slippers: Abraham Lincoln Deals with Foreign Affairs.* Indianapolis: Bobbs-Merrill, 1945.

Monroe, James. *The Writings of James Monroe.* Edited by Stanislaus Hamilton. 7 vols. New York: Putnam, 1898–1903.

Morris, Richard. *The Peacemakers: The Great Powers and American Independence.* New York: Harper & Row, 1965.

———, ed. *Alexander Hamilton and the Founding of the Nation.* New York: Dial Press, 1957.

Morison, Samuel Eliot. *By Land and by Sea*. New York: Knopf, 1953.

Moyers, Bill. *The Secret Government: The Constitution in Crisis*. Cabin John, Md.: Seven Locks Press, 1988.

Naval Documents Related to the United States Wars with the Barbary Powers, 1785–1807. 7 vols. Washington, D.C.: Government Printing Office, 1939–1944.

Nelson, Anna K. "Mission to Mexico—Moses Y. Beach, Secret Agent." *New-York Historical Society Quarterly* 59, no. 3 (July 1975).

———. "Secret Agents and Security Leaks: President Polk and the Mexican War." *Journalism Quarterly* 52 (Spring 1975).

———. "The Secret Diplomacy of James K. Polk During the Mexican War, 1846–1847." Ph.D. diss., George Washington University, 1972.

Neumann, William L. "United States Aid to the Chilean Wars of Independence." *Hispanic American Historical Review* 27, no. 2 (May 1947).

Newman, David, and Tyll Van Geel. "Executive Order 12,333: The Risks of a Clear Declaration of Intent." *Harvard Journal of Law and Public Policy* 12, no. 2 (Spring 1989).

Niven, John. *Connecticut for the Union: The Role of the State in the Civil War*. New Haven, Conn.: Yale University Press, 1965.

O'Brien, Michael. *Hercules Mulligan: Confidential Correspondent of General Washington*. New York: Kennedy, 1937.

O'Daniel, Victor. "Archbishop John Hughes, American Envoy to France (1861)." *Catholic Historical Review* 3, no. 3 (October 1917).

Owsley, Harriet C. "Henry Shelton Sanford and Federal Surveillance Abroad, 1861–1865." *Mississippi Valley Historical Review* 48, no. 2 (September 1961).

Parton, Dorothy. "The Diplomatic Career of Joel Roberts Poinsett." Ph.D. diss., Catholic University, 1934.

Patrick, Rembert. *Florida Fiasco: Rampant Rebels on the Georgia–Florida Border, 1810–1815*. Athens: University of Georgia Press, 1954.

Pennypacker, Morton. *General Washington's Spies on Long Island and in New York*. Brooklyn, N.Y.: Long Island Historical Society, 1939.

———. *The Two Spies: Nathan Hale and Robert Townsend*. Boston: Houghton Mifflin, 1930.

Perkins, Bradford. *Prologue to War: England and the United States, 1805–1812*. Berkeley: University of California Press, 1963.

Peterson, Norma L. *The Presidencies of William Henry Harrison and John Tyler*. Lawrence: University Press of Kansas, 1989.

Pletcher, David. *The Diplomacy of Annexation: Texas, Oregon, and the Mexican War*. Columbia: University of Missouri Press, 1973.

Polk, James. *The Diary of James K. Polk During His Presidency, 1845–1849*. Edited by Milo Quaife. 4 vols. Chicago: McClurg, 1910.

Porter, Kenneth. "Negroes and the East Florida Annexation Plot, 1811–1813." *Journal of Negro History* 30, no. 1 (January 1945).

Powers, Thomas. *The Man Who Kept the Secrets: Richard Helms and the CIA*. New York: Pocket Books, 1979.

———. "Panama: Our Dangerous Liaison." *New York Times Book Review*, February 18, 1990.

Prados, John. *Presidents' Secret Wars: CIA and Pentagon Covert Operations from World War II Through Iranscam.* New York: Morrow, 1986.

Pratt, Julius W. *Expansionists of 1898: The Acquisition of Hawaii and the Spanish Islands.* Baltimore: Johns Hopkins University Press, 1936.

———. *Expansionists of 1812.* Gloucester, Mass.: Smith, 1957.

The Presidential Campaign, 1976, Volume One, Part One, Jimmy Carter. Washington, D.C.: Government Printing Office, 1978.

Price, Glenn. *Origins of the War with Mexico: The Polk–Stockton Intrigue.* Austin: University of Texas Press, 1967.

Prucha, Francis. *The United States Army on the Frontier: 1783–1846.* Lincoln: University of Nebraska, 1969.

Public Papers of the Presidents of the United States: John F. Kennedy, January 20 to December 31, 1961. Washington, D.C.: Government Printing Office, 1962.

Quirk, John P. *The Central Intelligence Agency: A Photographic History.* Guilford, Conn.: Foreign Intelligence Press, 1986.

Randall, J. G. "The Blundering Generation." *Mississippi Valley Historical Review* 27, no. 1 (June 1940).

Ranelagh, John. *The Agency: The Rise and Decline of the CIA.* New York: Simon and Schuster, 1986.

Ransom, Harry H. *The Intelligence Establishment.* Cambridge, Mass.: Harvard University Press, 1970.

Records of the Department of State: Communications from Special Agents, 1794–1906.

Register of Debates in Congress.

Remini, Robert. *Andrew Jackson.* 3 vols. New York: Harper & Row, 1977–1984.

Richardson, James, ed. *A Compilation of the Messages and Papers of the Presidents, 1798–1908.* Washington, D.C.: Bureau of National Literature and Art, 1908.

Rippy, J. Fred. "Britain's Role in the Early Relations of the United States and Mexico." *Hispanic American Historical Review* 7, no. 1 (February 1927).

———. *Joel R. Poinsett: Versatile American.* Durham, N.C.: Duke University Press, 1935.

Rowan, Richard. *The Story of Secret Service.* New York: Literary Guild of America, 1938.

Safire, William. *Freedom: A Novel of Abraham Lincoln and the Civil War.* New York: Avon Books, 1987.

Sayle, Edward F. "The Déjà Vu of American Secret Diplomacy." *International Journal of Intelligence and Counterintelligence* 2, no. 3 (Fall 1988).

———. "The Historical Underpinnings of the U.S. Intelligence Community." *International Journal of Intelligence and Counterintelligence* 1, no. 1 (Spring 1986).

Schlesinger, Arthur, Jr. *The Imperial Presidency.* Boston: Houghton Mifflin, 1973.

Schultz, Richard. "Covert Action and Executive–Legislative Relations: The Iran-Contra Affair and Its Aftermath." *Harvard Journal of Law and Public Policy* 12, no. 2 (Spring 1989).

Sciaroni, Bretton G. "The Theory and Practice of Executive Branch Intelligence

Oversight." *Harvard Journal of Law and Public Policy* 12, no. 2 (Spring 1989).

Secret Journals of the Acts and Proceedings of Congress. Boston: Wait, 1821.

Smith, Donald. *John Jay: Founder of a State and Nation.* New York: Teachers College Press, 1968.

Smith, George. "Union Propaganda in the American Civil War." *Social Studies* 35, no. 1 (January 1944).

Smith, Paul H., ed. *Letters of Delegates to Congress, 1774–1789.* 19 vols. Washington, D.C.: Library of Congress, 1976–.

Sofaer, Abraham D. *War, Foreign Affairs, and Constitutional Power: The Origins.* Cambridge, Mass.: Ballinger, 1976.

State Department Territorial Papers, Florida Series.

Stenberg, Richard. "The Failure of Polk's Mexican War Intrigue of 1845." *Pacific Historical Review* 4, no. 1 (March 1935).

———. "Polk and Fremont, 1845–1846." *Pacific Historical Review* 7, no. 1 (September 1937).

———. "President Jackson and Anthony Butler." *Southwest Review* 22 (July 1937).

———. "President Polk and California: Additional Documents." *Pacific Historical Review* 10, no. 2 (June 1941).

Taking the Stand: The Testimony of Lieutenant Colonel Oliver L. North. New York: Pocket Books, 1987.

Tallmadge, Benjamin. *Memoir of Colonel Benjamin Tallmadge.* New York: Society of Sons of the Revolution in the State of New York, 1904.

Tebeau, Charlton. *A History of Florida.* Coral Gables, Fla.: University of Miami Press, 1971.

Thompson, Edmund R. "Intelligence at Yorktown." *Defense/81,* October 1981.

———, ed. *Secret New England: Spies of the American Revolution.* Kennebunk, Maine: Association of Former Intelligence Officers, 1991.

Thwaites, R. G., ed. *Early Western Travels.* Cleveland: Clark, 1904.

Totten, Administrator, v. *United States,* 92 U.S. 105 (1875).

Treverton, Gregory. *Covert Action: The Limits of Intervention in the Postwar World.* New York: Basic Books, 1987.

Troy, Thomas. "The Quaintness of the U.S. Intelligence Community: Its Origin, Theory, and Problems." *International Journal of Intelligence and Counterintelligence* 2, no. 2 (Summer 1988).

Tucker, Glenn. *Dawn Like Thunder: The Barbary Wars and the Birth of the U.S. Navy.* Indianapolis: Bobbs-Merrill, 1963.

Turner, Frederick J. "Genet's Attack on Louisiana and Florida." *American Historical Review,* 3 (1898).

U.S. Congress. *Report of the Congressional Committees Investigating the Iran-Contra Affair with Supplemental, Minority and Additional Views.* H. Rept. 100–433 and S. Rept. 100–216, 100th Cong., 1st sess. 1987.

U.S. Congress, Senate. *Final Report of the Select Committee to Study Governmental Operations with Respect to Intelligence Activities* (Church Committee Report), S. Rept. 94–755, 94th Cong., 2nd sess. 1976. Books 1–6.

Van Alstyne, R. W. *The Rising American Empire.* New York: Oxford University Press, 1960.

Van Deusen, Glyndon. *Thurlow Weed: Wizard of the Lobby.* Boston: Little, Brown, 1947.

————. *William Henry Seward.* New York: Oxford University Press, 1967.

Van Doren, Carl. *Secret History of the American Revolution.* New York: Viking Press, 1941.

Walther, Daniel. *Gouverneur Morris: Witness of Two Revolutions.* New York: Funk and Wagnalls, 1934.

Washington, George. *The Diaries of George Washington, 1748–1799.* Edited by John Fitzpatrick. 4 vols. Boston: Houghton Mifflin, 1925.

————. *The Writings of George Washington from the Original Manuscript Sources, 1745–1799.* Edited by John Fitzpatrick. 39 vols. Washington, D.C.: Government Printing Office, 1931–1944.

Weber, Ralph. "As Others Saw Us." In *Extracts from Studies in Intelligence: A Commemoration of the Bicentennial of the U.S. Constitution.* Washington, D.C.: Central Intelligence Agency, 1987.

Webster, Daniel. *The Papers of Daniel Webster: Correspondence.* Edited by Charles Wiltse. 7 vols. Hanover, N.H.: University Press of New England, 1974–1986.

————. *The Papers of Daniel Webster: Diplomatic Papers.* Edited by Kenneth Shewmaker. 2 vols. Hanover, N.H.: University Press of New England, 1983–1987.

Weed, Thurlow. *Autobiography of Thurlow Weed.* Edited by Harriet Weed. Boston: Houghton Mifflin, 1883.

Weil, Thomas E., Jan Knippers Black, Kenneth W. Martindale, David S. McMorris, Frederick P. Munson, and Kathryn E. Parachini. *Area Handbook for Chile.* Washington, D.C.: Government Printing Office, 1969.

Welles, Gideon. *The Diary of Gideon Welles.* 3 vols. Boston: Houghton Mifflin, 1911.

Wharton, Francis, ed. *The Revolutionary Diplomatic Correspondence of the United States.* 6 vols. Washington, D.C.: Government Printing Office, 1889.

Wilson, Woodrow. *The Papers of Woodrow Wilson.* Edited by Arthur S. Link. 69 vols. Princeton, N.J.: Princeton University Press, 1966–1993.

Winks, Robin. *Canada and the United States: The Civil War Years.* Baltimore: Johns Hopkins University Press, 1960.

Witcover, Jules. *Marathon: The Pursuit of the Presidency, 1972–1976.* New York: Viking Press, 1977.

Woodward, Bob. *Veil: The Secret Wars of the CIA, 1981–1987.* New York: Pocket Books, 1987.

Wright, Louis, and Julia Macleod. *The First Americans in North Africa: William Eaton's Struggle for a Vigorous Policy Against the Barbary Pirates, 1799–1805.* Princeton, N.J.: Princeton University Press, 1945.

Wriston, Henry M. *Executive Agents in American Foreign Relations.* Baltimore: Johns Hopkins University Press, 1929.

Wyllys, Rufus. "The East Florida Revolution of 1812–1814." *Hispanic American Historical Review* 9, no. 4 (November 1929).

Ziegler, Philip. *King William IV.* London: Collins, 1971.

Newspapers and Periodicals

Boston Globe
National Review
Newsweek
New York Times

Time
U.S. News & World Report
Washington Post
Washington Times

Index

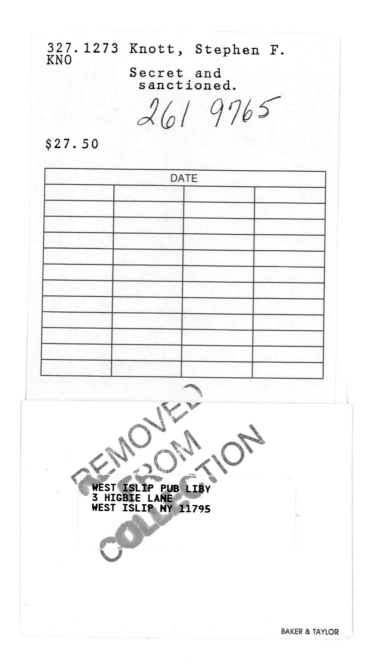

9/16